VOICES FROM THE DUST
Volume 2

Robert Kay

EDITION NOTE

CONTENTS

DEDICATION

This book is dedicated to
The House of Israel
the associated First Nations of America
and Jews
for whom it was written and preserved
and to those Gentiles by whom it came

1- DELIVERING UP THE RECORD

4 And now I Mur'mon being about to deliver up the record
5 which I have been making into the hands of my son M'runi

7 Behold I have witnessed almost all the destruction
8 of my people the Nephiy
9 and it is many hundred years
10 after the coming of Mashiach
11 that I deliver these records into the hands of my son

13 And it supposes me
14 that he will witness the entire destruction of my people
15 but may Elohiym grant
16 that he may survive them
17 that he may write somewhat concerning them
18 and somewhat concerning Mashiach
19 that perhaps someday it may profit them

21 And now I speak somewhat concerning
22 that which I have written
23 for after that I had made an abridgment
24 from the plates of Nephi down
25 to the reign of this King Binyamin of which Amaleki spoke
26 I searched among the records
27 which had been delivered into my hands

29 And I found these plates
30 which contained this small account of the prophets
31 from Yacov down to the reign of this King Binyamin
32 and also many of the words of Nephi
33 and the things which are upon these plates please me
34 because of the prophecies of the coming of Mashiach

1   and my fathers knowing
2   that many of them have been fulfilled
3   Yes and I also know
4   that as many things as have been prophesied
5   concerning us down to this day have been fulfilled
6   and as many as go beyond this day must surely come to pass
7
8   Therefore I chose these things
9   to finish my record upon them
10 which remainder of my record I shall take
11 from the plates of Nephi
12 and I cannot write a hundredth part
13 of the things of my people
14
15 But behold I shall take these plates
16 which contain these prophecies and revelations
17 and put them with the remainder of my record
18
19 For they are choice unto me
20 and I know they will be choice unto my brothers
21 and I do this for a wise purpose
22 for thus it whispers me
23 according to the workings of the Ruach of YHVH
24 which is in me
25 and now I do not know all things
26 but YHVH knows all things which are to come
27 therefore he works in me to do according to His will
28 and my prayer to Elohiym is concerning my brothers
29 that they may once again come to the knowledge of Elohiym
30 Yes the redemption of Mashiach
31 that they may once again be an observant people
32
33 And now I Mur'mon proceed to finish out my record

1 which I take from the plates of Nephi
2 and I make it according to the knowledge and the understanding
3 which Elohiym has given me
4
5 Therefore it came to pass
6 that after Amaleki had delivered up these plates
7 into the hands of King Binyamin
8 he took them and put them
9 with the other plates which contained records
10 which had been handed down by the kings
11 from generation to generation
12 until the days of King Binyamin
13
14 And they were handed down from King Binyamin
15 from generation to generation
16 until they have fallen into my hands
17
18 And I Mur'mon pray to Elohiym
19 that they may be preserved from this time forward
20 and I know that they will be preserved
21 for there are great things written upon them out
22 of which my people and their brothers shall be judged
23 at the great and last day
24 according to the word of Elohiym which is written
25
26
27
28
29
30
31
32
33
34

1
2
3   ## 2-KING BINYAMIN

3 And now concerning this King Binyamin he had
4 somewhat contentions among his own people
5
6 And it came to pass also
7 that the armies of the Lamaniy came down out
8 of the Land of Nephi
9 to battle against his people
10 but behold King Binyamin gathered together his armies
11 and he did stand against them
12 and he did fight with the strength of his own arm
13 with the sword of Laban
14 and in the strength of YHVH
15 they did contend against their enemies
16 until they had killed many thousands of the Lamaniy
17
18 And it came to pass
19 that they did contend against the Lamaniy
20 until they had driven them out
21 of all the lands of their inheritance
22
23 And it came to pass
24 that after there had been false mashiachim
25 and their mouths had been shut
26 and they punished according to their crimes
27 and after there had been false prophets
28 and false preachers and morim
29 among the people
30 and all these having been punished
31 according to their crimes
32 and after there having been much contentions
33 and many dissensions away

1   unto the Lamaniy

2

3   Behold it came to pass

4   that King Binyamin with the assistance of the holy prophets

5   which were among his people

6   for behold King Binyamin was a holy man

7   and he did reign over his people in righteousness

8   and there were many holy men in the land

9   and they did speak the word of Elohiym

10 with power and with authority

11 and they did use much sharpness

12 because of the stubbornness of the people

13 therefore with the help of these King Binyamin

14 by laboring with all the might of his body

15 and the faculty of his whole soul and also the prophets

16 therefore they did once more establish peace in the land

17

18 And now there was no more contention

19 in all the Land of Zarahemla

20 among all the people

21 which belonged to King Binyamin

22 so that King Binyamin had continual peace

23 all the remainder of his days

24

25 And it came to pass

26 that he had three sons

27 and he called their names Mosheyahu and Helorum and Helaman

28 and he caused that they should be taught

29 in all the language of his fathers

30 that thereby they might become men of understanding

31 and that they might know concerning the prophecies

32 which had been spoken by the mouths of their fathers

33 which were delivered them by the hand of YHVH

1

2 And he also taught them concerning the records

3 which were engraved on the plates of brass saying

4

5 "My sons I would that you should remember

6 that were it not for these plates

7 which contain these records

8 and these mitzvot we must have suffered in ignorance

9 even at this present time not knowing the mysteries of Elohiym

10

11 For it were not possible

12 that our father Lechi could have remembered

13 all these things to have taught them to his children

14 except it were for the help of these plates

15

16 For he having been taught in the language of the Egyptians

17 therefore he could read these engravings

18 and teach them to his children

19 that thereby they could teach them to their children

20 and so fulfilling the mitzvot of Elohiym

21 even down to this present time

22

23 I say unto you my sons were it not for these things

24 which have been kept and preserved by the hand of Elohiym

25 that we might read and understand of his mysteries

26 and have his mitzvot always before our eyes

27 that even our fathers would have fallen away in unbelief

28 and we should have been like unto our brothers the Lamaniy

29 which know nothing concerning these things

30 or even do not believe them when they are taught them

31 because of the traditions of their fathers

32 which are not correct

33

1 O my sons I would that you should remember

2 that these sayings are true

3 and also that these records are true

4

5 And behold also the plates of Nephi

6 which contain the records and the sayings of our fathers

7 from the time they left Yerushalayim until now

8 and they are true

9 and we can know of their surety because

10 we have them before our eyes

11

12 And now my sons I would that you should remember

13 to search them diligently

14 that you may profit thereby

15 and I would that you should keep the mitzvot of Elohiym

16 that you may prosper in the land

17 according to the promises

18 which YHVH made unto our fathers"

19

20 And many more things did King Binyamin teach his sons

21 which are not written in this book

22

23 And it came to pass

24 that after King Binyamin had made an end of teaching his sons

25 that he waxed old

26 and he saw that he must very soon go the way of all the earth

27 therefore he thought it expedient

28 that he should confer the kingdom upon one of his sons

29 therefore he had Mosheyahu brought before him

30 and these are the words

31 which he spoke unto him saying

32

33 "My son I would that you should make a proclamation

1 throughout all this land among all this people
2 or the people of Zarahemla
3 and the people of Mosheyahu
4 which dwell in this land
5 that thereby they may be gathered together
6
7 For on the next day I shall proclaim
8 unto this my people out of my own mouth
9 that you are a king and a ruler over this people
10 which YHVH our Elohiym has given us
11
12 And furthermore I shall give this people a name
13 that thereby they may be distinguished
14 above all the people
15 which YHVH Elohiym has brought
16 out of the Land of Yerushalayim
17 and this I do
18 because they have been a diligent people
19 in keeping the mitzvot of YHVH
20 and I give unto them a name
21 that never shall be blotted out
22 except it be through rebellion
23 yes and furthermore I say unto you
24 that if this highly favored people of YHVH
25 should fall into rebellion
26 and become a wicked and an adulterous people
27 that YHVH will deliver them up
28 that thereby they become weak like unto their brothers
29 and he will no more preserve them
30 by his matchless and marvelous power
31 as he has previously preserved our fathers
32
33 For I say unto you

1   that if he had not extended his arm

2   in the preservation of our fathers

3   they must have fallen

4   into the hands of the Lamaniy

5   and become victims to their hatred"

6

7   And it came to pass

8   that after King Binyamin had made an end

9   of these sayings to his son

10   that he gave him charge

11   concerning all the affairs of the kingdom

12   and furthermore he also gave him charge

13   concerning the records

14   which were engraved on the plates of brass

15   and also the plates of Nephi

16   and also the sword of Laban

17   and the ball or director

18   which led our fathers through the wilderness

19   which was prepared by the hand of YHVH

20   that thereby they might be led everyone

21   according to the heed and diligence

22   which they gave unto him

23   therefore as they were unfaithful

24   they did not prosper nor progress in their journey

25   but were driven back

26   and incurred the displeasure of Elohiym upon them

27   and therefore they were smitten

28   with famine and sore afflictions

29   to stir them up in remembrance of their duty

30

31   And Now it came to pass

32   that Mosheyahu went and did

33   as his father had commanded him

1   and proclaimed unto all the people
2   which were in the Land of Zarahemla
3   that thereby they might gather themselves together
4   to go up to the temple to hear the words
5   which his father should speak unto them
6
7   And it came to pass
8   that after Mosheyahu had done
9   as his father had commanded him
10 and had made a proclamation
11 throughout all the land
12 that the people gathered themselves together
13 throughout all the land
14 that they might go up to the temple
15 to hear the words
16 which King Binyamin should speak unto them
17 and there were a great number
18 even so many that they did not number them
19 for they had multiplied exceedingly
20 and waxed great in the land
21
22 And they also took of the firstlings of their flocks
23 that they might offer sacrifice and burnt offerings
24 according to the Torah of Moshe
25 and also that they might give thanks to YHVH their Elohiym
26 who had brought them out of the Land of Yerushalayim
27 and who had delivered them out of the hands of their enemies
28 and had appointed just men to be their morim
29 and also a just man to be their king
30 who had established peace in the Land of Zarahemla
31 and who had taught them to keep the mitzvot of Elohiym
32 that thereby they might rejoice
33 and be filled with love toward Elohiym

1   and all men

2

3   And it came to pass

4   that when they came up to the temple

5   they pitched their tents round about

6   every man according to his family consisting of his wife

7   and his sons and his daughters

8   and their sons and their daughters

9   from the eldest down to the youngest

10   every family being separate one from another

11   and they pitched their tents round about the temple

12   every man having his tent with the door thereof

13   toward the temple

14   that thereby they might remain in their tents

15   and hear the words which King Binyamin should speak unto them

16   for the multitude being so great

17   that King Binyamin could not teach them all within the walls

18   of the temple

19   therefore he caused a tower to be erected

20   that thereby his people might hear the words

21   which he should speak unto them

22

23   And it came to pass

24   that he began to speak to his people from the tower

25   and they could not all hear his words

26   because of the greatness of the multitude

27   therefore he caused that the words which he spoke

28   should be written and sent forth among those

29   that were not under the sound of his voice

30   that they might also receive his words

31   and these are the words which he spoke

32   and caused to be written saying

33

1   "My brothers all you

2   that have assembled yourselves together you

3   that can hear my words

4   which I shall speak unto you this day

5

6   For I have not commanded you to come up here

7   to trifle with the words which I shall speak

8   but that you should listen unto me

9   and open your ears that you may hear

10   and your hearts that you may understand

11   and your minds that the mysteries of Elohiym

12   may be unfolded to your view

13

14   I have not commanded you to come up here

15   that you should fear me or that you should think

16   that I of myself am more than a mortal man

17   but I am like as yourselves subject to all manner

18   of infirmities in body and mind

19

20   Yet as I have been chosen by this people

21   and was consecrated by my father

22   and was allowed by the hand of YHVH

23   that I should be a ruler and a king over this people

24   and have been kept and preserved by his matchless power

25   to serve you with all the might mind and strength

26   which YHVH has granted unto me

27

28   I say unto you

29   that as I have been allowed

30   to spend my days in your service

31   even up to this time

32   and have not sought gold nor silver

33   nor no manner of riches of you

1   neither have I allowed
2   that you should be confined in dungeons
3   nor that you should make slaves one of another
4   or that you should murder
5   or plunder
6   or steal
7   or commit adultery
8   or even I have not allowed
9   that you should commit any manner of wickedness
10
11   And have taught you
12   that you should keep the mitzvot of YHVH
13   in all things which he has commanded you
14   and even I myself have labored with mine own hands
15   that I might serve you
16   and that you should not be laden with taxes
17   and that there should nothing come upon you
18   which was grievous to be borne
19   and of all these things
20   which I have spoken you yourselves are witnesses this day
21
22   Yet my brothers I have not done these things
23   that I might boast
24   neither do I tell these things
25   that thereby I might accuse you
26   but I tell you these things
27   that you may know that I can answer a clear conscience
28   before Elohiym this day
29
30   Behold I say unto you that because I said unto you
31   that I had spent my days in your service I do not desire to boast
32   for I have only been in the service of Elohiym
33   and behold I tell you these things

1   that you may learn wisdom
2   that you may learn
3   that when you are in the service
4   of your fellow beings
5   you are only in the service of your Elohiym
6
7   Behold you have called me your king
8   and if I whom you call your king do labor to serve you
9   then had not you ought to labor to serve one another
10
11   And behold also if I whom you call your king
12   who has spent his days in your service
13   and yet has been in the service of Elohiym do merit
14   any thanks from you
15   O how had you ought
16   to thank your heavenly King
17
18   I say unto you my brothers
19   that if you should render all the thanks and praise
20   which your whole souls have power to possess
21   to that Elohiym who has created you
22   and has kept and preserved you
23   and has caused that you should rejoice
24   and has granted that you should live in peace one with another
25
26   I say unto you that if you should serve him
27   who has created you from the beginning
28   and is preserving you from day to day
29   by lending you breath
30   that you may live and move and do
31   according to your own will
32   and even supporting you from one moment to another
33   I say if you should serve him with all your whole soul

1 and yet you would be unprofitable servants

2

3 And behold all that he requires of you is

4 to keep his mitzvot

5 and he has promised you

6 that if you would keep his mitzvot you

7 should prosper in the land

8 and he never does vary

9 from that which he has said

10 therefore if you do keep his mitzvot

11 he does bless you and prosper you

12

13 And now in the first place he has created you

14 and granted unto you your lives

15 for which you are indebted unto him

16

17 And secondly he does require that you should do

18 as he has commanded you

19 for which if you do he does immediately bless you

20 and therefore he has paid you

21 and you are still indebted unto him

22 and are and will be forever and ever

23 therefore of what have you to boast

24

25 And now I ask can you say anything of yourselves

26 I answer you No

27 you cannot say that you are even as much as the dust of the earth

28 yet you were created of the dust of the earth

29 but behold it belongs to him who created you

30 and I even I whom you call your king am no better

31 than you yourselves are for I am also of the dust

32

33 And you behold that I am old

1 and am about to yield up this mortal frame
2 to its mother earth
3 therefore as I said unto you
4 that I had served you walking with a clear conscience before Elohiym
5 even so I at this time have caused
6 that you should assemble yourselves together
7 that I might be found blameless
8
9 And that your blood should not come upon me
10 when I shall stand to be judged of Elohiym
11 of the things whereof he has commanded me concerning you
12 I say unto you
13 that I have caused that you should assemble yourselves together
14 that I might rid my garments of your blood
15 at this period of time
16 when I am about to go down to my grave
17 that I might go down in peace
18 and my soul may join the choirs above
19 in singing the praises of a just Elohiym
20
21 And furthermore I say unto you
22 that I have caused that you should assemble yourselves together
23 that I might declare unto you
24 that I can no longer be your moreh
25 nor your king
26 for even at this time
27 my whole frame does tremble exceedingly
28 while attempting to speak unto you
29 but YHVH Elohiym does support me
30 and has put upon me that I should speak unto you
31 and has commanded me
32 that I should declare unto you this day
33 that my son Mosheyahu is a king and a ruler over you

1
2 And now my brothers I would that you should do
3 as you has previously done
4 as you have kept my mitzvot
5 and also the mitzvot of my father
6 and have prospered
7 and have been kept from falling
8 into the hands of your enemies
9 even so if you shall keep the mitzvot of my son
10 or the mitzvot of Elohiym
11 which shall be delivered unto you by him
12 you shall prosper in the land
13 and your enemies shall have no power over you
14 but O my people beware
15 for fear that there shall arise contentions among you
16 and you list to obey the evil one
17 which was spoken of by my father Mosheyahu
18
19 For behold
20 there is an OY pronounced upon him
21 that enlists to obey that ruach
22 for if he enlists to obey him
23 and remains and dies in his sins
24 the same drinks condemnation to his own soul
25 for he receives for his wages
26 an everlasting punishment
27 having transgressed the Torah of Elohiym
28 contrary to his own knowledge
29 I say unto you
30 that there are not any among you
31 except it be your little children
32 that have not been taught
33 concerning these things but that know

1   that you are eternally indebted
2   to your heavenly Father
3   to render to him
4   all that you have and are
5   and also have been taught
6   concerning the records
7   which contain the prophecies
8   which have been spoken
9   by the holy prophets
10   even down to the time
11   our father Lechi left Yerushalayim
12   and also all that has been spoken
13   by our fathers until now
14   and behold also they spoke
15   that which was commanded them of YHVH
16   therefore they are just and true
17   and now I say unto you my brothers
18   that after you have known
19   and have been taught all these things
20   if you should rebel
21   and go contrary to that which has been spoken
22   that you do withdraw yourselves from the Ruach Elohiym
23   that it may have no place in you
24   to guide you in wisdom's paths
25   that you may be blessed prospered and preserved
26
27   I say unto you
28   that the man that does this the same comes out
29   in open rebellion against Elohiym
30   therefore he enlists to obey the evil ruach
31   and becomes an enemy to all righteousness
32   therefore YHVH has no place in him
33   for he dwells not in unholy temples

1 therefore if that man repents not
2 and remains and dies an enemy to Elohiym
3 the demands of divine justice
4 do awaken his soul
5 to a lively sense of his own guilt
6 which does cause him to shrink
7 from the presence of YHVH
8 and does fill his breast with guilt
9 and pain and anguish
10 which is like an unquenchable fire
11 whose flame ascends up forever and ever
12 and now I say unto you
13 that mercy has no claim on that man
14 therefore his final condemnation is
15 to endure an endless purification
16
17 O all you old men
18 and also you young men
19 and you little children
20 who can understand my words
21 for I have spoken plainly unto you
22 that you might understand
23 I pray that you should awake
24 to a remembrance of the awful situation
25 of those that have fallen into rebellion
26 and furthermore I would desire
27 that you should consider
28 on the blessed and happy state of those
29 that keep the mitzvot of Elohiym
30
31 For behold
32 they are blessed in all things
33 both temporal and spiritual

1   and if they hold out faithful to the end
2   they are received into heaven
3   that thereby they may dwell with Elohiym
4   in a state of never ending happiness
5   O remember remember
6   that these things are true
7   for YHVH Elohiym has spoken it
8
9   And again my brothers I would call your attention
10 for I have somewhat more to speak unto you
11 for behold I have things to tell you
12 concerning that which is to come
13 and the things which I shall tell you are made known
14 unto me by an angel from Elohiym
15 and he said unto me
16
17 "Awake"
18
19 And I awoke
20 and behold he stood before me
21 and he said unto me
22
23 "Awake
24 and hear the words
25 which I shall tell you
26 for behold I am come
27 to declare unto you
28 the glad tidings of great joy
29 for YHVH has heard your prayers
30 and has judged of your righteousness
31 and has sent me to declare unto you
32 that you may rejoice
33 and that you may declare unto your people

1   that they may also be filled with joy

2   for behold the time comes

3   and is not far distant

4   that with power YHVH El Shaddai

5   who reigns

6   who was and is

7   from all eternity to all eternity s

8   shall come down from heaven

9   among the children of men

10 and shall dwell in a tabernacle of clay

11 and shall go forth among men working mighty miracles

12 such as healing the sick

13 raising the dead

14 causing the lame to walk

15 the blind to receive their sight

16 and the deaf to hear

17 and curing all manner of diseases

18 and he shall cast out demons

19 or the evil spirits

20 which dwell in the hearts of the children of men

21

22 And behold he shall suffer temptations

23 and pain of body hunger thirst

24 and fatigue even more than man can suffer

25 except it be unto death

26 for behold blood comes from every pore

27 so great shall be his anguish

28 for the wickedness

29 and the abominations of his people

30 and he shall be called Yehoshua Mashiach

31 the Chosen Son of Elohiym

32 the Father of heaven and earth

33 the Creator of all things

1 from the beginning
2 and his mother shall be called Miryam
3
4 And behold he comes unto his own
5 that salvation might come
6 unto the children of men
7 even through faith on his name
8 and even after all this
9 they shall consider him a man
10 and say that he has a devil
11 and shall beat him
12 and shall crucify him
13 and he shall rise the third day from the dead
14 and behold he stands to judge the world
15 and behold all these things are done
16 that a righteous judgment might come
17 upon the children of men
18
19 For behold
20 and also his blood atones for the sins
21 of those who have fallen
22 by the rebellion of Adam
23 who have died not knowing the will
24 of Elohiym concerning them
25 or who have ignorantly sinned
26
27 But OY OY unto him
28 who knows that he rebels against Elohiym
29 For salvation comes to none such
30 except it be through repentance
31 and faith on Adon Yehoshua Mashiach
32 and YHVH Elohiym has sent his holy prophets
33 among all the children of men

1   to declare these things
2   to every tribe nation and language
3   that thereby whoever should believe
4   that Mashiach should come the same
5   might receive remission of their sins
6   and rejoice with exceedingly great joy
7   even as though he had already come among them
8
9   Yet YHVH Elohiym saw
10 that his people were a stubborn people
11 and he appointed unto them Torah
12 even the Torah of Moshe
13 and many signs and wonders
14 and types and shadows showed he unto them
15 concerning his coming
16 and also holy prophets spoke unto them
17 concerning his coming
18 and yet they hardened their hearts
19 and understood not
20 that the Torah of Moshe avails nothing
21 except it were through the atonement of his blood
22
23 And even if it were possible
24 that little children could sin
25 they could not be saved
26 but I say unto you they are blessed
27 for behold as in Adam
28 or by nature they fall
29 even so the blood of Mashiach atones for their sins
30 and furthermore I say unto you
31 that there shall be no other name given
32 nor any other way nor means
33 whereby salvation can come

1   unto the children of men

2   only in and through the name

3   of Mashiach

4   YHVH El Shaddai

5

6   For behold he judges

7   and his judgment is just

8   and the infant perishes not

9   that dies in his infancy

10   but men drink condemnation

11   to their own souls

12   except they humble themselves

13   and become as little children

14   and believe that salvation was

15   and is

16   and is to come in

17   and through the atoning blood

18   of Mashiach

19   YHVH El Shaddai

20

21   For the natural man is an enemy to Elohiym

22   and has been from the fall of Adam

23   and will be forever and ever

24   unless he yields to the enticing of the Ruach Elohiym

25   and puts off the natural man

26   and becomes a set apart one

27   through the atonement of Mashiach

28   and becomes as a child

29   submissive

30   meek

31   humble

32   patient

33   full of love

1 willing to submit to all things
2 which YHVH sees fit to inflict upon him
3 even as a child does submit to his father
4
5 And furthermore I say unto you
6 that the time shall come
7 when the knowledge of a Savior
8 shall spread throughout
9 every nation tribe language and people
10 and behold when that time comes
11 none shall be found blameless before Elohiym
12 except it be little children
13 only through repentance and faith
14 on the name of YHVH Elohiym
15 El Shaddai
16
17 And even at this time
18 when you shall have taught your people the things
19 which YHVH your Elohiym has commanded you
20 even then are they found
21 no more blameless in the sight of Elohiym
22 only according to the words
23 which I have spoken unto you
24 and now I have spoken the words
25 which YHVH Elohiym has commanded me
26 and thus says YHVH
27
28 "They shall stand
29 as a bright testimony against this people
30 at the judgment day
31 where they shall be judged
32 every man according to his works
33 whether they be good

1   or whether they be evil
2   and if they be evil
3   they are delivered to an awful view
4   of their own guilt and abominations
5   which does cause them to shrink
6   from the presence of YHVH
7   into a state of misery and endless purification
8   from where they can no more return
9   therefore they have drunk condemnation
10 to their own souls
11 therefore they have drunk
12 out of the cup of the anger of Elohiym
13 which justice could no more deny unto them
14 than it could deny that Adam should fall
15 because of his partaking of the fruit
16 of the Tree of Knowledge good and evil
17 therefore mercy could have claim on them
18 no more forever
19 and their purification is as a lake of fire and brimstone
20 whose flames are unquenchable
21 and whose smoke ascends up
22 forever and ever"
23 thus has YHVH commanded me
24 Amein"
25
26 And Now it came to pass
27 that when king Benyamin had made an end
28 of speaking the words
29 which had been delivered unto him
30 by the angel of YHVH
31 that he cast his eyes round about on the multitude
32 and behold they had fallen to the earth
33 for the wisdom of YHVH had come upon them

1 and they had viewed themselves
2 in their own carnal state
3 even less than the dust of the earth
4 and they all cried aloud
5 with one voice saying
6
7 "O have mercy
8 and apply the atoning blood of Mashiach
9 that we may receive forgiveness of our sins
10 and our hearts may be purified
11 for we believe in Yehoshua Mashiach
12 the Chosen Son of Elohiym
13 who created heaven and earth and all things
14 who shall come down
15 among the children of men"
16
17 And it came to pass
18 that after they had spoken these words
19 the Ruach Elohiym came upon them
20 and they were filled with joy
21 having received a remission of their sins
22 and having peace of conscience
23 because of the exceeding faith
24 which they had in Yehoshua Mashiach
25 who should come
26 according to the words
27 which king Benyamin had spoken unto them
28 and king Benyamin again opened his mouth
29 and began to speak unto them saying
30
31 "my friends and my brothers
32 my family and my people
33 I would again call your attention

1 that you may hear
2 and understand the remainder of my words
3 which I shall speak unto you
4
5 For behold
6 if the knowledge
7 of the goodness of Elohiym
8 at this time has awakened you
9 to a sense of your nothingness
10 and your worthless and fallen state
11 I say unto you
12 if you have come to a knowledge
13 of the goodness of Elohiym
14 and his matchless power and his wisdom
15 and his patience and his long-suffering
16 towards the children of men
17 and also the atonement
18 which has been prepared
19 from the creation of the world
20 that thereby salvation might come to him
21 that should put his trust in YHVH
22 and should be diligent in keeping his mitzvot
23 and continue in the faith
24   even unto the end of his life
25 I mean the life of the mortal body
26
27 I say that this is the man
28 who receives salvation
29 through the atonement
30 which was prepared
31 from the creation of the world
32 for all mankind who ever were
33 since the fall of Adam

1   or who are or who ever shall be

2   even unto the end of the world

3

4   And this is the means

5   by which salvation comes

6   and there is no other salvation

7   except this that has been spoken of

8   neither are there any conditions

9   by which man can be saved

10   except the conditions

11   which I have told you

12   believe in Elohiym

13   believe that he is

14   and that he created all things

15   both in heaven and in earth believe

16   that he has all wisdom and all power

17   both in heaven and in earth believe

18   that man does not comprehend

19   all the things

20   which YHVH can comprehend

21   and again believe

22   that you must repent of your sins

23   and forsake them

24   and humble yourselves before Elohiym

25   and ask in sincerity of heart

26   that he would forgive you

27   and now if you believe all these things see

28   that you do them

29

30   And again I say unto you

31   as I have said before

32   that as you have come to the knowledge

33   of the glory of Elohiym

1 or if you have known of his goodness

2 and have tasted of his love

3 and have received a remission of your sins

4 which causes such exceedingly great joy in your souls

5 even so I would that you should remember

6 and always retain in remembrance the greatness of Elohiym

7 and your own nothingness

8 and his goodness and long-suffering

9 towards you unworthy creatures

10 and humble yourselves

11 even in the depths of humility calling

12 on the name of YHVH daily

13 and standing firm in the faith

14 of that which is to come

15 which was spoken

16 by the mouth of the angel

17

18 and behold I say unto you

19 that if you do this you shall always rejoice

20 and be filled with the love of Elohiym

21 and always retain a remission of your sins

22 and you shall grow in the knowledge

23 of the glory of him that created you

24 or in the knowledge of that

25 which is just and true

26 and you will not have a mind

27 to injure one another

28 but to live peaceably

29 and to render to every man

30 according to that which is his due

31

32 And you will not allow your children

33 that they go hungry or naked

1   neither will you allow
2   that they rebel against the mitzvot of Elohiym
3   and fight and quarrel one with another
4   and serve the evil one
5   who is the master of sin
6   or who is the evil one
7   which has been spoken of
8   by our fathers he being
9   an enemy to all righteousness
10   but you will teach them to walk
11   in the ways of truth and observance
12   you will teach them to love one another
13   and to serve one another
14
15   And also you yourselves will help those
16   that stand in need of your help
17   you will administer of your substance
18   unto him that stands in need
19   and you will not allow
20   that the beggar puts up his petition
21   to you in vain
22   and turn him out to perish
23   perhaps you shall say
24
25   'The man has brought upon himself his misery
26   therefore I will stay my hand
27   and will not give unto him
28   of my food nor impart unto him
29   of my substance
30   that he may not suffer
31   for his punishment is just'
32
33   But I say unto you O man

1 whoever does this
2 the same has great cause to repent
3 and except he repents
4 of that which he has done he perishes forever
5 and has no interest
6 in the kingdom of Elohiym
7
8 For behold are we not all beggars
9 Do we not all depend upon the same being
10 even Elohiym
11 for all the substance
12 which we have
13 for both food and clothing
14 and for gold and for silver
15 and for all the riches
16 which we have
17 of every kind
18
19 And behold
20 even at this time you have been calling on his name
21 and begging for a remission of your sins
22 and has he allowed that you have begged in vain
23 No he has poured out his Ruach upon you
24 and has caused that your hearts should be filled with joy
25 and has caused that your mouths should be stopped
26 that you could not find utterance
27 so exceedingly great was your joy
28 and now if Elohiym
29 who has created you
30 on whom you are dependent for your lives
31 and for all that you have and are
32 does grant unto you
33 whatever you ask that is right

1 in faith believing

2 that you shall receive

3 O then how you ought

4 to impart of the substance

5 that you have one to another

6

7 And if you judge the man

8 who puts up his petition to you

9 for your substance

10 that he perish not and condemn him

11 how much more just will be your condemnation

12 for withholding your substance

13 which does not belong to you

14 but to Elohiym

15 to whom also your life belongs

16 and yet you put up no petition

17 nor repent of the thing

18 which you have done

19

20 I say unto you

21 OY be unto that man

22 for his substance shall perish with him

23 and now I say these things

24 unto those who are rich

25 as pertaining to the things of this world

26 and again I say unto the poor you

27 who have not

28 and yet have sufficient

29 that you live from day to day

30 I mean all you who deny the beggar

31 because you have not

32   I would that you say in your hearts that

33

1   'I give not
2   because I have not
3   but if I had I would give'
4
5   And now
6   if you say this
7   in your hearts you remain guiltless
8   otherwise you are condemned
9   and your condemnation is just
10   for you covet that
11   which you have not received
12
13   And now
14   for the sake of these things
15   which I have spoken unto you
16   that is for the sake of retaining a remission of your sins
17   from day to day
18   that you may walk guiltless before Elohiym
19   I would that you should impart
20   of your substance to the poor every man
21   according to that which he has
22   such as feeding the hungry
23   clothing the naked
24   visiting the sick
25   and administering to their relief
26   both spiritually and temporally
27   according to their wants
28   and see that all these things are done
29   in wisdom and order
30   for it is not requisite
31   that a man should run faster
32   than he has strength
33   and again it is necessary

1   that he should be diligent

2   that thereby he might win the prize

3   therefore all things must be done

4   in order

5

6   And I would that you should remember

7   that whoever among you borrows from his neighbor

8   should return the thing that he borrows

9   according as he does agree

10 or else you shall commit sin

11 and perhaps you shall cause your neighbor

12 to commit sin also

13

14 And finally I cannot tell you all the things

15 by which you may commit sin

16 for there are various ways and means

17 even so many

18 that I cannot number them

19 but this much I can tell you

20 that if you do not watch yourselves

21 and your thoughts and your words

22 and your deeds and observe the mitzvot of Elohiym

23 and continue in the faith

24 of what you have heard

25 concerning the coming of Adonai

26 even unto the end of your lives you must perish

27 and now O man remember and perish not

28 And Now it came to pass

29 that when king Benyamin had thus spoken

30 to his people he sent among them desiring

31 to know of his people

32 if they believed the words

33 which he had spoken unto them

1 and they all cried

2 with one voice saying

3

4 "Yes we believe all the words

5 which you hast spoken unto us

6 and also we know of their certainty and truth

7 because of the Ruach Elohoym

8 even of EL Shaddai

9 which has worked a mighty change in us

10 or in our hearts

11 that we have no more disposition

12 to do evil

13 but to do good continually

14 and we ourselves also

15 through the infinite goodness of Elohiym

16 and the manifestations of his Ruach have great views

17 of that which is to come

18 and were it necessary we could prophesy

19 of all things

20 and it is the faith which we have had

21 on the things which our king has spoken unto us

22 that has brought us

23 to this great knowledge

24 by which we do rejoice

25 with such exceedingly great joy

26 and we are willing to enter into a covenant

27 with our Elohiym

28 to do his will

29 and to be obedient to his mitzvot

30 in all things

31 that he shall command us

32 all the remainder of our days

33 that we may not bring

1 upon ourselves a never ending torment
2 as has been spoken by the angel
3 that we may not drink out of the cup
4 of the anger of Elohiym"
5
6 And now these are the words
7 which king Benyamin desired of them
8 and therefore he said unto them
9
10 "You have spoken the words
11 that I desired
12 and the covenant
13 which you have made is a righteous covenant
14 and now
15 because of the covenant
16 which you have made
17 you shall be called the children of Mashiach
18 his sons and his daughters
19 for behold
20 this day he has spiritually begotten you
21 for you say that your hearts are changed
22 through faith on his name
23 therefore you are born of him
24 and have become his sons and his daughters
25 and under this head
26 you are made free
27 and there is no other head
28 by which you can be made free
29 there is no other name given
30 by which salvation comes
31 therefore I would
32 that you should take upon you the name of Mashiach
33 all you that have entered into the covenant with Elohiym

1 that you should be obedient
2 unto the end of your lives
3
4 And it shall come to pass
5 that whoever does this
6 shall be found at the right hand of Elohiym
7 for he shall know the name
8 by which he is called
9 for he shall be called by the name of Mashiach
10
11 And now it shall come to pass
12 that whoever shall not take
13 upon him the name of Mashiach
14 must be called by some other name
15 therefore he finds himself
16 on the left hand of Elohiym
17 and I would
18 that you should remember also
19 that this is the name
20 that I said I should give unto you
21 that never should be blotted out
22 except it be through rebellion
23 therefore take heed
24 that you do not rebel
25 that the name be not blotted out
26 of your hearts
27
28 I say unto you I would
29 that you should remember
30 to retain the name written
31 always in your hearts
32 that you are not found
33 on the left hand of Elohiym

1 but that you hear and know the voice
2 by which you shall be called
3 and also the name
4 by which he shall call you
5 For how knows a man the master
6 whom he has not served
7 and who is a stranger unto him
8 and is far from the thoughts
9 and intents of his heart
10 and again does a man take an ass
11 which belongs to his neighbor
12 and keep him
13 I say unto you
14 No he will not even allow
15 that he shall feed among his flocks
16 but will drive him away
17 and cast him out
18 I say unto you
19 that even so shall it be among you
20 if you know not the name
21 by which you are called
22 therefore I would
23 that you should be unwavering and immovable
24 always abounding in good works
25 that Mashiach
26 YHVH Elohiym
27 El Shaddai may seal you his
28 that you may be brought to heaven
29 that you may have everlasting salvation
30 and eternal life
31 through the wisdom and power
32 and justice and mercy of him
33 who created all things

1 in heaven and in earth

2 who is Elohiym above all

3 Amein"

4 and now king Benyamin thought it was necessary

5 after having finished speaking to the people

6 that he should take the names

7 of all those who had entered

8 into a covenant with Elohiym

9 to keep his mitzvot

10

11 And it came to pass

12 that there was not one person

13 except it were little children

14 but who had entered into the covenant

15 and had taken upon them the name of Mashiach

16

17 And again it came to pass

18 that when king Benyamin had made an end

19 of all these things

20 and had consecrated his son Mosheyahu

21 to be a ruler and a king over his people

22 and had given him all the charges

23 concerning the kingdom

24 and also had appointed kohanim

25 to teach the people

26 that thereby they might hear

27 and know the mitzvot of Elohiym

28 and to stir them up in remembrance

29 of the oath

30 which they had made

31 he dismissed the multitude

32 and they returned every one

33 according to their families

1 to their own houses
2 and Mosheyahu began to rule in his father's place
3 and he began to rule
4 in the thirtieth year of his age making
5 in the whole about four hundred and seventy-six years
6 from the time that Lechi left Yerushalayim
7 and king Benyamin lived three years
8 and he died
9
10 And it came to pass
11 that king Mosheyahu did walk in the ways of YHVH
12 and did observe his mishpatim and his chukkim
13 and did keep his mitzvot in all things
14 whatever he commanded him
15 and king Mosheyahu did instruct his people
16 that they should till the earth
17 and he also himself did till the earth
18 that thereby he might not
19 become burdensome to his people
20 that he might do according to that
21 which his father had done in all things
22 and there was no contention
23 among all his people
24 for the space of three years
25
26 And Now it came to pass
27 that after king Mosheyahu had had continual peace
28 for the space of three years he was desired
29 to know concerning the people
30 who went up to dwell
31 in the land of Lechi Nephi
32 or in the city of Lechi Nephi
33 for his people had heard nothing from them

1 from the time they left the land of Zarahemla
2 therefore they wearied him with their inquiry
3
4 And it came to pass
5 that king Mosheyahu granted
6 that sixteen of their strong men
7 might go up to the land of Lechi Nephi to inquire
8 concerning their brothers
9
10 And it came to pass
11 that on the next day
12 they started to go up having with them
13 one Ammon he being a strong and mighty man
14 and a descendant of Zarahemla
15 and he was also their leader
16 and now they knew not the course
17 they should travel in the wilderness
18 to go up to the land of Lechi Nephi
19 therefore they wandered many days
20 in the wilderness
21 even forty days did they wander
22 and when they had wandered forty days
23 they came to a hill
24 which is north of the land of Shilom
25 and there they pitched their tents
26 and Ammon took three of his brothers
27 and their names were
28 Amaleki
29 Chelem
30 and Chem
31 and they went down into the land of Nephi
32 and behold they met the king of the people
33 who were in the land of Nephi

1 and in the land of Shilom

2 and they were surrounded by the king's guard

3 and were taken and were bound

4 and were committed to prison

5

6 And it came to pass

7 when they had been in prison two days

8 they were again brought before the king

9 and their bands were loosed

10 and they stood before the king

11 and were permitted

12 or rather commanded

13 that they should answer the questions

14 which he should ask them

15 and he said unto them

16

17 "behold I am Lemhi the son of Noach

18 who was the son of Zeniff

19 who came up out of the land of Zarahemla

20 to inherit this land

21 which was the land of their fathers

22 who was made a king

23 by the voice of the people

24 and now I desire to know the reason

25 that you were so bold

26 as to come near the walls of the city

27 when I myself was with my guards

28 outside the gate

29 and now for this reason have I allowed

30 that you should be preserved

31 that I might inquire of you

32 or else I should have caused that my guards

33 should have put you to death

1 You are permitted to speak"

2

3 And now when Ammon saw

4 that he was permitted to speak he went forth

5 and bowed himself before the king

6 and rising again he said

7

8 "O king I am very thankful

9 before Elohiym this day

10 that I am yet alive

11 and am permitted to speak

12 and I will endeavor to speak

13 with boldness

14 for I am sure

15 that if you had known me

16 you would not have allowed

17 that I should have worn these bands

18 for I am Ammon

19 and am a descendant of Zarahemla

20 and have come up out

21 of the land of Zarahemla

22 to inquire concerning our brothers

23 whom Zeniff brought up out of that land"

24

25 And Now it came to pass

26 that after Lemhi had heard

27 the words of Ammon

28 he was exceedingly glad and said

29

30 "Now I know of a certainty

31 that my brothers

32 who were in the land of Zarahemla

33 are yet alive

1   and now I will rejoice
2   and on the next day I will cause
3   that my people shall rejoice also
4   for behold we are in bondage to the Lamaniy
5   and are taxed with a tax
6   which is hard to be borne
7   and now behold our brothers will deliver us
8   out of our bondage
9   or out of the hands of the Lamaniy
10   and we will be their slaves
11   for it is better that we be slaves to the Nephiy
12   than to pay tribute to the king of the Lamaniy"
13   and now king Lemhi commanded his guards
14   that they should no more bind Ammon
15   nor his brothers but caused
16   that they should go to the hill
17   which was north of Shilom
18   and bring their brothers into the city
19   that thereby they might eat and drink
20   and rest themselves
21   from the labors of their journey
22   for they had suffered many things
23   they had suffered hunger thirst and fatigue
24

25   And Now it came to pass
26   on the next day
27   that king Lemhi sent a proclamation
28   among all his people that thereby
29   they might gather themselves together
30   to the temple
31   to hear the words
32   which he should speak unto them
33

1 And it came to pass
2 that when they had gathered themselves together
3 that he spoke unto them
4 in this manner saying
5
6 "O you my people lift up your heads
7 and be comforted
8 for behold the time is at hand
9 or is not far distant
10 when we shall no longer be in subjection
11 to our enemies
12 notwithstanding our many struggles
13 which have been in vain
14 yet I trust there remains
15 a veracious struggle to be made
16 therefore lift up your heads and rejoice
17 and put your trust in Elohiym
18 in that Elohiym
19 who was the Eloah of Avraham
20 and Yitzchak
21 and Yacov
22 and also that Elohiym
23 who brought the children of Israel out
24 of the land of Egypt
25 and caused that they should walk
26 through the Red Sea on dry ground
27 and fed them with manna
28 that they might not perish in the wilderness
29 and many more things did he do for them
30 and again
31 that same Elohiym has brought our fathers out
32 of the land of Yerushalayim
33 and has kept and preserved his people

1 even until now
2 and behold it is because
3 of our lawlessness and abominations
4 that he has brought us into bondage
5 and you all are witnesses this day
6 that Zeniff
7 who was made king over this people
8 he being overzealous to inherit the land of his fathers
9 therefore being deceived
10 by the cunning and craftiness of king Laman
11 who having entered into a treaty with king Zeniff
12 and having yielded up
13 into his hands the possessions
14 of a part of the land
15 or even the city of Lechi Nephi
16 and the city of Shilom
17 and the land roundabout
18 and all this he did
19 for the sole purpose of bringing this people
20 into subjection or into bondage
21 and behold we
22 at this time do pay tribute
23 to the king of the Lamaniy
24 to the amount of one half
25 of our corn and our barley
26 and even all our grain of every kind
27 and one half of the increase
28 of our flocks and our herds
29 and even one half
30 of all we have or possess
31 the king of the Lamaniy does exact
32 of us or our lives
33 and now is not this hard to be borne

1   and is not this our affliction great
2   now behold
3   how great reason we have to mourn
4   yes I say unto you great are the reasons
5   which we have to mourn
6   for behold how many
7   of our brothers have been killed
8   and their blood has been spilt in vain
9   and all because of lawlessness
10 for if this people had not fallen
11 into rebellion YHVH would not have allowed
12 that this great evil should come upon them
13 but behold they would not listen to and obey his words
14 but there arose contentions among them
15 even so much that they did shed blood
16 among themselves
17 and a prophet of YHVH have they killed
18 yes a chosen man of Elohiym
19 who told them of their wickedness and abominations
20 and prophesied of many things
21 which are to come
22 yes even the coming of Mashiach
23 and because he said unto them
24 that Mashiach was Elohiym
25 the Father of all things
26 and said that he should take upon him the image of man
27 and it should be the image
28 after which man was created in the beginning
29 or in other words he said
30 that man was created after the image of Elohiym
31 and that Elohiym should come down
32 among the children of men
33 and take upon him flesh and blood

1 and go forth upon the face of the earth
2 and now because he said this
3 they did put him to death
4 and many more things did they do
5 which brought down the wrath of Elohiym upon them
6 therefore who is astonished
7 that they are in bondage
8 and that they are struck
9 with sore afflictions
10 for behold YHVH has said
11
12 'I will not help my people
13 in the day of their rebellion
14 but I will obstruct their way
15 that they prosper not
16 and their doings shall be
17 as a stumbling block before them'
18
19 And again he says
20
21 'If my people shall sow filthiness
22 they shall reap the refuse thereof
23 in the whirlwind
24 and the effect thereof is poison'
25
26 And again he says
27
28 'If my people shall sow filthiness
29 they shall reap the east wind
30 which brings immediate destruction'
31
32 And now behold the promise of YHVH is fulfilled
33 and you are struck and afflicted

1   but if you will turn to YHVH
2   with full purpose of heart
3   and put your trust in him
4   and serve him
5   with all diligence of mind
6   if you do this he will
7   according to his own will and pleasure
8   deliver you out of bondage"
9
10   And it came to pass
11   that after king Lemhi had made
12   an end of speaking to his people
13   for he spoke many things unto them
14   and only a few of them have I written
15   in this book
16   he told his people all the things
17   concerning their brothers
18   who were in the land of Zarahemla
19   and he caused
20   that Ammon should stand up
21   before the multitude and rehearse unto them
22   all that had happened unto their brothers
23   from the time that Zeniff went up out
24   of the land
25   even until the time
26   that he himself came up out
27   of the land
28   and he also rehearsed
29   unto them the last words
30   which king Benyamin had taught them
31   and explained them to the people of king Lemhi
32   so that they might understand
33   all the words which he spoke

1
2 And it came to pass
3 that after he had done all this
4 that king Lemhi dismissed the multitude
5 and caused that they should return
6 every one unto his own house
7
8 And it came to pass
9 that he caused that the plates
10 which contained the record of his people
11 from the time that they left the land of Zarahemla
12 should be brought before Ammon
13 that he might read them
14 now as soon as Ammon had read the record
15 the king inquired of him
16 to know if he could interpret languages
17 and Ammon told him
18 that he could not
19 and the king said unto him
20
21 "Being sorrowful for the afflictions
22 of my people I caused
23 that forty and three of my people
24 should take a journey into the wilderness
25 that thereby they might find the land of Zarahemla
26 that we might appeal
27 unto our brothers
28 to deliver us out of bondage
29 and they were lost in the wilderness
30 for the space of many days
31 yet they were diligent
32 and found not the land of Zarahemla
33 but returned to this land having traveled

1   in a land among many waters
2   having discovered a land
3   which was covered
4   with bones of men and of beasts
5   and was also covered
6   with ruins of buildings
7   of every kind
8   having discovered a land
9   which had been peopled
10   with a people
11   who were as numerous
12   as the numbers of Israel
13   and for a testimony
14   that the things that they had said are true
15   they have brought twenty four plates
16   which are filled with engravings
17   and they are of pure gold
18
19   And behold also
20   they have brought breastplates
21   which are large
22   and they are of brass and of copper
23   and are perfectly sound
24   and again
25   they have brought swords the hilts
26   thereof have perished
27   and the blades thereof
28   were corrupted with rust
29   and there is no one in the land
30   that is able to interpret the language
31   or the engravings
32   that are on the plates
33   therefore I said unto you

1
2   'Can you translate'
3
4   and I say unto you again
5
6   "Know you of any one
7   that can translate
8   for I desire that these records
9   should be translated into our language
10 for perhaps they will give us a knowledge
11 of a remnant of the people
12 who have been destroyed
13 from where these records came
14 or perhaps they will give us a knowledge
15 of this very people
16 who have been destroyed
17 and I desire to know the cause
18 of their destruction"
19
20 now Ammon said unto him
21
22 "I can certainly tell you O king
23 of a man that can translate the records
24 for he has that by which he can look
25 and translate all records
26 that are of ancient date
27 and it is a gift from Elohiym
28 and the things are called interpreters
29 and no man can look in them
30 except he be commanded
31 for fear that he should look
32 for that which he ought not
33 and he should perish

1 and whoever is commanded
2 to look in them
3 the same is called seer
4 and behold the king of the people
5 who are in the land of Zarahemla is the man
6 that is commanded to do these things
7 and who has this high gift from Elohiym"
8
9 And the king said that
10
11 "a seer is greater than a prophet"
12
13 And Ammon said that
14
15 "a seer is a revelator
16 and a prophet also
17 and a gift which is greater can no man have
18 except he should possess the power of Elohiym
19 which no man can
20 yet a man may have great power given him from Elohiym
21 but a seer can know of things
22 which are past
23 and also of things
24 which are to come
25 and by them shall all things be revealed
26 or rather shall secret things be made manifest
27 and hidden things shall come to light
28 and things which are not known
29 shall be made known by them
30 and also things shall be made known by them
31 which otherwise could not be known
32 thus Elohiym has provided a means
33 that man through faith

1   might work mighty miracles

2   therefore he becomes a great benefit

3   to his fellow beings"

4

5   And now when Ammon had made an end

6   of speaking these words the king rejoiced exceedingly

7   and gave thanks to Elohiym saying

8

9   "Doubtless a great mystery is contained

10 within these plates

11 and these interpreters were doubtless prepared

12 for the purpose of unfolding

13 all such mysteries

14 to the children of men

15 O how marvelous are the works of YHVH

16 and how long does he bear with his people

17 yes and how blind

18 and impenetrable are the understandings

19 of the children of men

20 for they will not seek wisdom

21 neither do they desire

22 that she should rule over them

23 yes they are as a wild flock

24 which flees from the shepherd

25 and are scattered and are driven

26 and are devoured

27 by the beasts of the forest"

28

29

30

31

32

33 **The Record of Zeniff**

1 **an account of his people**
2 **from the time they left the land of Zarahemla**
3 **until the time that they were delivered out**
4 **of the hands of the Lamaniy**
5
6 I Zeniff having been taught
7 in all the language of the Nephiy
8 and having had a knowledge of the land of Nephi
9 or of the land of our fathers' first inheritance
10 and having been sent as a spy among the Lamaniy
11 that I might spy out their forces
12 that our army might come upon them
13 and destroy them
14 but when I saw that which was good
15 among them I was desired
16 that they should not be destroyed
17 therefore I contended
18 with my brothers in the wilderness
19 for I would that our ruler
20 should make a treaty with them
21 but he being an harsh and a blood-thirsty man commanded
22 that I should be killed
23 but I was rescued
24 by the shedding of much blood
25 for father fought against father
26 and brother against brother
27 until the greater number
28 of our army was destroyed in the wilderness
29 and we returned
30 those of us that were spared
31 to the land of Zarahemla
32 to relate that tale
33 to their wives and their children

1 and yet I being overzealous

2 to inherit the land of our fathers collected

3 as many as desired to go up

4 to possess the land

5 and started again on our journey

6 into the wilderness

7 to go up to the land

8 but we were struck

9 with famine and sore afflictions

10 for we were slow

11 to remember YHVH our Elohiym

12 nevertheless after many days' wandering

13 in the wilderness we pitched our tents

14 in the place where our brothers were killed

15 which was near to the land of our fathers

16

17 And it came to pass

18 that I went again with four of my men

19 into the city

20 in unto the king

21 that I might know of the disposition

22 of the king

23 and that I might know

24 if I might go in with my people

25 and possess the land in peace

26 and I went in unto the king

27 and he covenanted with me

28 that I might possess the land of Lechi Nephi

29 and the land of Shilom

30 and he also commanded

31 that his people

32 should depart out of the land

33 and I and my people went

1 into the land
2 that we might possess it
3 and we began to build buildings
4 and to repair the walls of the city
5 yes even the walls of the city of Lechi Nephi
6 and the city of Shilom
7 and we began to till the ground
8 yes even with all manner of seeds
9 with seeds of corn and of wheat
10 and of barley and with neas
11 and with sheum and with seeds
12 of all manner of fruits
13 and we did begin to multiply
14 and prosper in the land
15 now it was the cunning
16 and the craftiness of king Laman
17 to bring my people into bondage
18 that he yielded up the land
19 that we might possess it
20
21 Therefore it came to pass
22 that after we had dwelt in the land
23 for the space of twelve years
24 that king Laman began to grow uneasy
25 for fear that by any means my people
26 should wax strong in the land
27 and that they could not overpower them
28 and bring them into bondage
29 now they were a lazy
30 and an idolatrous people
31 therefore they desired
32 to bring us into bondage
33 that they might glut themselves

1 with the labors of our hands

2 yes that they might feast themselves

3 upon the flocks of our fields

4

5 Therefore it came to pass

6 that king Laman

7 began to stir up his people

8 that they should contend with my people

9 therefore there began to be wars

10 and contentions in the land

11 For in the thirteenth year of my reign

12 in the land of Nephi

13 away on the south of the land of Shilom

14 when my people were watering

15 and feeding their flocks

16 and tilling their lands a numerous host

17 of Lamaniy came upon them

18 and began to kill them

19 and to take off their flocks

20 and the corn of their fields

21

22 Yes And it came to pass

23 that they fled

24 all that were not overtaken

25 even into the city of Nephi

26 and did call upon me for protection

27

28 And it came to pass

29 that I did arm them

30 with bows and with arrows

31 with swords and with cimeters

32 and with clubs and with slings

33 and with all manner of weapons

1   which we could invent
2   and I and my people did go forth
3   against the Lamaniy to battle
4   yes in the strength of YHVH did we go forth
5   to battle against the Lamaniy for I
6   and my people did cry mightily to YHVH
7   that he would deliver us out
8   of the hands of our enemies
9   for we were awakened
10   to a remembrance
11   of the deliverance
12   of our fathers
13   and Elohiym did hear our cries
14   and did answer our prayers
15   and we did go forth in his might
16   yes we did go forth
17   against the Lamaniy
18   and in one day and a night
19   we did kill three thousand and forty-three
20   we did kill them
21   even until we had driven them
22   out of our land
23   and I myself
24   with my own hands did help
25   to bury their dead
26   and behold to our great sorrow
27   and lamentation two hundred and seventy-nine
28   of our brothers were killed
29
30   And it came to pass
31   that we again began to establish the kingdom
32   and we again began to possess the land in peace
33   and I caused that there should be weapons

1 of war made of every kind
2 that thereby I might have weapons
3 for my people
4 against the time the Lamaniy
5 should come up again
6 to war against my people
7 and I set guards round about the land
8 that the Lamaniy might not come
9 upon us again unawares
10 and destroy us
11 and thus I did guard my people
12 and my flocks
13 and keep them from falling
14 into the hands of our enemies
15
16 And it came to pass
17 that we did inherit the land
18 of our fathers for many years
19 yes for the space of twenty and two years
20 and I did cause
21 that the men should till the ground
22 and raise all manner of grain
23 and all manner of fruit of every kind
24 and I did cause
25 that the women
26 should spin and toil and work
27 and work all manner of fine linen
28 yes and cloth of every kind
29 that we might clothe our nakedness
30 and thus we did prosper in the land
31 thus we did have continual peace in the land
32 for the space of twenty and two years
33

1 And it came to pass
2 that king Laman died
3 and his son began to reign in his place
4 and he began to stir his people up in rebellion
5 against my people
6 therefore they began to prepare for war
7 and to come up to battle
8 against my people
9 but I had sent my spies out
10 round about the land of Shemlon
11 that I might discover their preparations
12 that I might guard against them
13 that they might not come upon my people
14 and destroy them
15
16 And it came to pass
17 that they came up upon the north
18 of the land of Shilom
19 with their numerous armies of men armed
20 with bows and with arrows
21 and with swords and with cimeters
22 and with stones and with slings
23 and they had their heads shaved
24 that they were naked
25 and they were girded
26 with a leathern girdle
27 about their loins
28
29 And it came to pass
30 that I caused
31 that the women and children of my people
32 should be hid in the wilderness
33 and I also caused

1   that all my old men
2   that could bear arms
3   and also all my young men
4   that were able to bear arms
5   should gather themselves together
6   to go to battle against the Lamaniy
7   and I did place them in their ranks
8   every man according to his age
9
10 And it came to pass
11 that we did go up
12 to battle against the Lamaniy
13 and I even I in my old age did go up
14 to battle against the Lamaniy
15
16 And it came to pass
17 that we did go up
18 in the strength of YHVH to battle
19 now the Lamaniy knew nothing
20 concerning YHVH
21 nor the strength of YHVH
22 therefore they depended
23 upon their own strength
24 yet they were a strong people
25 as to the strength of men
26 they were a wild and ferocious
27 and a bloodthirsty people believing
28 in the tradition of their fathers
29 which is this believing
30 that they were driven out
31 of the land of Yerushalayim
32 because of the lawlessness of their fathers
33 and that they were wronged

1   in the wilderness
2   by their brothers
3   and they were also wronged
4   while crossing the sea
5   and again
6   that they were wronged
7   while in the land of their first inheritance
8   after they had crossed the sea
9   and all this because
10 that Nephi was more faithful
11 in keeping the mitzvot of YHVH
12 therefore he was favored of YHVH
13 for YHVH heard his prayers
14 and answered them
15 and he took the lead of their journey
16 in the wilderness
17 and his brothers were angry with him
18 because they understood not the dealings of YHVH
19 they were also angry with him
20 upon the waters
21 because they hardened their hearts
22 against YHVH
23 and again they were angry with him
24 when they had arrived in the promised land
25 because they said
26 that he had taken the ruling of the people
27 out of their hands
28 and they sought to kill him
29 and again they were angry with him
30 because he departed into the wilderness
31 as YHVH had commanded him
32 and took the records
33 which were engraved on the plates of brass

1   for they said that he robbed them
2   and thus they have taught their children
3   that they should hate them
4   and that they should murder them
5   and that they should rob and plunder them
6   and do all they could to destroy them
7   therefore they have an eternal hatred
8   towards the children of Nephi
9   for this very reason has king Laman
10 by his cunning and lying craftiness
11 and his fair promises deceived me
12 that I have brought this my people
13 up into this land
14 that they may destroy them
15 yes and we have suffered
16 these many years in the land
17 and now I Zeniff
18 after having told all these things
19 unto my people
20 concerning the Lamaniy I did stimulate them
21 to go to battle with their might
22 putting their trust in YHVH
23 therefore we did contend
24 with them face to face
25
26 And it came to pass
27 that we did drive them again
28 out of our land
29 and we killed them with a great slaughter
30 even so many that we did not number them
31
32 And it came to pass
33 that we returned again

1 to our own land

2 and my people again began

3 to tend their flocks

4 and to till their ground

5 and now I being old did confer the kingdom

6 upon one of my sons

7 therefore I say no more

8 and may YHVH bless my people

9 Amein

10

11 And Now it came to pass

12 that Zeniff conferred the kingdom

13 upon Noach one of his sons

14 therefore Noach began to reign in his place

15 and he did not walk

16 in the ways of his father

17 For behold he did not keep the mitzvot of Elohiym

18 but he did walk

19 after the desires of his own heart

20 and he had many wives and concubines

21 and he did cause his people to commit sin

22 and do that which was abominable in the sight of YHVH

23 yes and they did commit whoredoms

24 and all manner of wickedness

25 and he laid a tax of one fifth part

26 of all they possessed a fifth part of their gold

27 and of their silver

28 and a fifth part of their ziff

29 and of their copper

30 and of their brass

31 and their iron

32 and a fifth part of their fatlings

33 and also a fifth part of all their grain

1 and all this did he take

2 to support himself

3 and his wives and his concubines

4 and also his kohanim

5 and their wives and their concubines

6 thus he had changed the affairs of the kingdom

7 for he put down all the kohanim

8 that had been consecrated by his father

9 and consecrated new ones in their place

10 such as were lifted up

11 in the pride of their hearts

12 yes and thus they were supported

13 in their laziness

14 and in their idolatry

15 and in their whoredoms

16 by the taxes

17 which king Noach had put upon his people

18 thus did the people labor exceedingly

19 to support lawlessness

20 yes and they also became idolatrous

21 because they were deceived

22 by the vain and flattering words

23 of the king and kohanim

24 for they did speak flattering things unto them

25

26 And it came to pass

27 that king Noach built

28 many elegant and spacious buildings

29 and he ornamented them

30 with fine work of wood

31 and of all manner of precious things

32 of gold and of silver

33 and of iron and of brass

1 and of ziff and of copper
2 and he also built him a spacious palace
3 and a throne in the midst thereof
4 all of which was of fine wood
5 and was ornamented with gold and silver
6 and with precious things
7 and he also caused that his workmen
8 should work all manner of fine work
9 within the walls of the temple
10 of fine wood and of copper and of brass
11 and the seats
12 which were set apart for the high kohanim
13 which were above all the other seats
14 he did ornament with pure gold
15 and he caused a breastwork
16 to be built before them
17 that they might rest
18 their bodies and their arms upon
19 while they should speak lying
20 and vain words to his people
21
22 And it came to pass
23 that he built a tower near the temple
24 yes a very high tower
25 even so high
26 that he could stand upon the top thereof
27 and overlook the land of Shilom
28 and also the land of Shemlon
29 which was possessed by the Lamaniy
30 and he could even look over
31 all the land round about
32
33 And it came to pass

1   that he caused many buildings to be built
2   in the land Shilom
3   and he caused a great tower to be built
4   on the hill north of the land Shilom
5   which had been a place of escape
6   for the children of Nephi
7   at the time they fled out of the land
8   and thus he did do with the riches
9   which he obtained
10 by the taxation of his people
11
12 And it came to pass
13 that he placed his heart
14 upon his riches
15 and he spent his time
16 in riotous living
17 with his wives and his concubines
18 and so did also his kohanim spend their time
19 with harlots
20
21 And it came to pass
22 that he planted vineyards
23 round about in the land
24 and he built wine-presses
25 and made wine in abundance
26 and therefore he became a wine bibber
27 and also his people
28
29 And it came to pass
30 that the Lamaniy began to come in
31 upon his people
32 upon small numbers
33 and to kill them in their fields

1 and while they were tending their flocks

2 and king Noach sent guards

3 round about the land

4 to keep them off

5 but he did not send a sufficient number

6 and the Lamaniy came upon them

7 and killed them

8 and drove many of their flocks

9 out of the land

10 thus the Lamaniy began to destroy them

11 and to exercise their hatred upon them

12

13 And it came to pass

14 that king Noach sent his armies against them

15 and they were driven back

16 or they drove them back for a time

17 therefore they returned rejoicing in their spoil

18 and now because of this great victory

19 they were lifted up

20 in the pride of their hearts

21 they did boast in their own strength saying

22 that their fifty could stand against thousands

23 of the Lamaniy

24 and thus they did boast

25 and did delight in blood

26 and the shedding of the blood

27 of their brothers

28 and this because of the wickedness

29 of their king and kohanim

30

31 And it came to pass

32 that there was a man among them

33 whose name was Abinadi

1 and he went forth among them

2 and began to prophesy saying

3

4 "Behold thus says YHVH

5 and thus has he commanded me saying

6 'Go forth and say unto this people

7 thus says YHVH

8 'OY be unto this people

9 for I have seen their abominations

10 and their wickedness

11 and their whoredoms

12 and except they repent

13 I will visit them in my anger

14 and except they repent

15 and turn to YHVH their Elohiym

16 behold I will deliver them

17 into the hands of their enemies

18 yes and they shall be brought into bondage

19 and they shall be afflicted

20 by the hand of their enemies

21

22 And it shall come to pass

23 that they shall know

24 that I am YHVH their Elohiym

25 and am a jealous Elohiym visiting

26 the lawlessness of my people

27 And it shall come to pass

28 that except this people repent

29 and turn unto YHVH their Elohiym

30 they shall be brought into bondage

31 and none shall deliver them

32 except it be YVHV El Shaddai

33

1 Yes And it shall come to pass

2 that when they shall cry unto me

3 I will be slow to hear their cries

4 yes and I will suffer them

5 that they be struck by their enemies

6 and except they repent

7 in sackcloth and ashes

8 and cry mightily to YHVH their Elohiym

9 I will not hear their prayers

10 neither will I deliver them out

11 of their afflictions'

12 and thus says YHVH

13 and thus has he commanded me"

14

15 Now it came to pass

16 that when Abinadi had spoken

17 these words unto them

18 they were angry with him

19 and sought to take away his life

20 but YHVH delivered him out of their hands

21 now when king Noach had heard

22 of the words which Abinadi had spoken

23 unto the people he was also angry

24 and he said

25

26 "Who is Abinadi

27 that I and my people

28 should be judged of him

29 or who is YHVH

30 that shall bring upon my people

31 such great affliction

32 I command you to bring Abinadi here

33 that I may kill him

1   for he has said these things
2   that he might stir up my people
3   to anger one with another
4   and to raise contentions
5   among my people
6   therefore I will kill him"
7
8   Now the eyes of the people were blinded
9   therefore they hardened their hearts
10 against the words of Abinadi
11 and they sought
12 from that time forward
13 to take him
14 and king Noach hardened his heart
15 against the word of YHVH
16 and he did not repent
17 of his evil doings
18
19 And it came to pass
20 that after the space of two years
21 that Abinadi came among them in disguise
22 that they knew him not
23 and began to prophesy
24 among them saying
25
26 "thus has YHVH commanded me saying
27
28 'Abinadi go and prophesy
29 unto this my people
30 for they have hardened their hearts
31 against my words
32 they have repented not
33 of their evil doings

1 therefore I will visit them in my anger

2 yes in my fierce anger will I visit them

3 in their lawlessness and abominations

4 yes OY be unto this generation'

5

6 And YHVH said unto me

7

8 'Stretch forth your hand

9 and prophesy saying

10 thus says YHVH

11 it shall come to pass

12 that this generation

13 because of their lawlessness

14 shall be brought into bondage

15 and shall be struck on the cheek

16 yes and shall be driven by men

17 and shall be killed

18 and the vultures of the air

19 and the dogs

20 yes and the wild beasts

21 shall devour their flesh

22

23 And it shall come to pass

24 that the life of king Noach shall be valued

25 even as a garment in a hot furnace

26 for he shall know

27 that I am YHVH

28

29 And it shall come to pass

30 that I will strike this my people

31 with sore afflictions

32 yes with famine and with pestilence

33 and I will cause

1 that they shall howl

2 all the day long

3 yes and I will cause

4 that they shall have burdens lashed

5 upon their backs

6 and they shall be driven

7 before like a dumb ass

8

9 And it shall come to pass

10 that I will send forth hail among them

11 and it shall strike them

12 and they shall also be struck

13 with the east wind

14 and insects shall pester their land also

15 and devour their grain

16 and they shall be struck

17 with a great pestilence

18 and all this will I do

19 because of their lawlessness and abominations

20

21 And it shall come to pass

22 that except they repent

23 I will utterly destroy them

24 from off the face of the earth

25 yet they shall leave a record behind them

26 and I will preserve them for other nations

27 which shall possess the land

28 yes even this will I do

29 that I may discover the abominations

30 of this people to other nations"

31

32 and many things did Abinadi prophesy

33 against this people

1
2 And it came to pass
3 that they were angry with him
4 and they took him
5 and carried him bound
6 before the king
7 and said unto the king
8
9 "Behold we have brought a man before you
10 who has prophesied evil
11 concerning your people
12 and says that Elohiym will destroy them
13 and he also prophesies evil
14 concerning your life
15 and says that your life
16 shall be as a garment
17 in a furnace of fire
18 and again he says
19 that you shall be as a stalk
20 even as a dry stalk of the field
21 which is run over by the beasts
22 and trodden under foot
23 and again he says you
24 shall be as the blossoms of a thistle
25 which when it is fully ripe
26 if the wind blows it is driven forth
27 upon the face of the land
28 and he pretends YHVH has spoken it
29 and he says
30 all this shall come upon you
31 except you repent
32 and this because of your lawlessness
33

1   And now O king
2   what great evil have you done
3   or what great sins have your people committed
4   that we should be condemned of Elohiym
5   or judged of this man
6   and now O king
7   behold we are guiltless
8   and you O king have not sinned
9   therefore this man has lied
10 concerning you
11 and he has prophesied in vain
12
13 And behold we are strong
14 we shall not come into bondage
15 or be taken captive by our enemies
16 yes and you have prospered in the land
17 and you shall also prosper
18 behold here is the man
19 we deliver him into your hands
20 you may do with him as seems you good"
21
22 And it came to pass
23 that king Noach caused
24 that Abinadi should be cast into prison
25 and he commanded that the kohanim
26 should gather themselves together
27 that he might hold a council with them
28 what he should do with him
29
30 And it came to pass
31 that they said unto the king
32
33 "Bring him here that we may question him"

1
2 And the king commanded
3 that he should be brought
4 before them
5
6 And they began to question him
7 that they might cross him
8 that thereby they might have with which
9 to accuse him
10 but he answered them boldly
11 and withstood all their questions
12 yes to their astonishment
13 for he did withstand them
14 in all their questions
15 and did confound them
16 in all their words
17
18 And it came to pass
19 that one of them said unto him
20
21 "What means the words
22 which are written
23 and which have been taught
24 by our fathers saying
25
26 'How beautiful upon the mountains are the feet
27 of him that brings good tidings
28 that publishes peace
29 that bringes good tidings of good
30 that publishes salvation
31 that says unto Zion
32 Your Elohiym reigns
33 Your watchmen shall lift up the voice

1   with the voice together

2   shall they sing

3   for they shall see eye to eye

4   when YHVH shall bring again Zion

5   Break forth into joy

6   sing together you waste places

7   of Yerushalayim

8   for YHVH has comforted his people

9   he has redeemed Yerushalayim

10   YHVH has made bare his holy arm

11   in the eyes of all the nations

12   and all the ends of the earth

13   shall see the salvation of our Elohiym'"

14

15   And now Abinadi said unto them

16

17   "Are you kohanim

18   and pretend to teach this people

19   and to understand the ruach of prophesying

20   and yet desire to know of me

21   what these things mean

22   I say unto you

23   OY be unto you

24   for perverting the ways of YHVH

25   for if you understand these things

26   you have not taught them

27   therefore you have perverted

28   the ways of YHVH

29   You have not applied your hearts

30   to understanding

31   therefore you have not been wise

32   therefore what teach you this people"

33

1 And they said

2

3 "We teach the Torah of Moshe"

4

5 And again he said unto them

6

7 "If you teach the Torah of Moshe

8 why do you not keep it

9 Why do you set your hearts upon riches

10 Why do you commit whoredoms

11 and spend your strength with harlots

12 yes and cause this people to commit sin

13 that YHVH has cause to send me

14 to prophesy against this people

15 yes even a great evil against this people

16 Know you not that I speak the truth

17 yes you know that I speak the truth

18 and you ought to tremble before Elohiym

19

20 And it shall come to pass

21 that you shall be struck down

22 for your lawlessness

23 for you have said

24 that you teach the Torah of Moshe

25 and what know you

26 concerning the Torah of Moshe

27 Does salvation come by the Torah of Moshe

28 What say you"

29

30 And they answered

31 and said that salvation did come

32 by the Torah of Moshe

33

1   But now Abinadi said unto them

2

3   "I know

4   if you keep the mitzvot of Elohiym you

5   shall be saved

6   yes if you keep the mitzvot

7   which YHVH delivered unto Moshe

8   in the mount of Sinai saying

9

10   'I am YHVH your Elohiym

11   who has brought you

12   out of the land of Egypt

13   out of the house of bondage

14   You shall have no other Elohiym before me

15   You shall not make unto you

16   any graven image

17   or any likeness of anything

18   in heaven above

19   or things which are in the earth beneath'

20

21   Now Abinadi said unto them

22

23   "Have you done all this

24   I say unto you

25   No you have not

26   and have you taught this people

27   that they should do all these things

28   I say unto you

29   No you have not"

30

31   And now when the king had heard

32   these words he said unto his kohanim

33

1   "Away with this fellow

2   and kill him

3   for what have we to do with him

4   for he is mad"

5

6   And they stood forth

7   and attempted to lay their hands on him

8   but he withstood them

9   and said unto them

10

11   "Touch me not

12   for Elohiym shall strike you down

13   if you lay your hands upon me

14   for I have not delivered the message

15   which YHVH sent me to deliver

16   neither have I told you

17   that which you requested

18   that I should tell

19   therefore Elohiym will not allow

20   that I shall be destroyed at this time

21   but I must fulfil the mitzvot

22   with which Elohiym has commanded me

23   and because I have told you the truth

24   you are angry with me

25   and again

26   because I have spoken the word

27   of Elohiym you have judged me

28   that I am mad"

29

30   Now it came to pass

31   after Abinadi had spoken these words

32   that the people of king Noach did not lay their hands on him

33   for the Ruach YHVH was upon him

1 and his face shone with exceeding luster
2 even as Moshe did
3 while in the mount of Sinai
4 while speaking with YHVH
5 and he spoke with power and authority
6 from Elohiym
7 and he continued his words saying
8
9 "You see that you have not power to kill me
10 therefore I finish my message
11 yes and I perceive that it cuts you
12 to your hearts
13 because I tell you the truth
14 concerning your lawlessness
15 yes and my words fill you
16 with wonder and amazement
17 and with anger
18 but I finish my message
19 and then it matters not where I go
20 if it so be that I am saved
21 but this much I tell you
22 what you do with me after this
23 shall be as a type and a shadow of things
24 which are to come
25
26 And now I read unto you the remainder
27 of the mitzvot of Elohiym
28 for I perceive
29 that they are not written in your hearts
30 I perceive that you have studied
31 and taught lawlessness the most part of your lives
32 and now you remember
33 that I said unto you

1
2   "You shall not make unto you
3   any graven image or any likeness of things
4   which are in heaven above
5   or which are in the earth beneath
6   or which are in the water under the earth
7
8   And again
9   You shall not bow down yourself unto them
10 nor serve them for I YHVH your Elohiym
11 am a jealous Elohiym visiting the lawlessness
12 of the fathers
13 upon the children
14 unto the third and fourth generations
15 of them that hate me
16 and showing mercy unto thousands
17 of them that love me
18 and keep my mitzvot
19
20 You shall not take the name
21 of YHVH your Elohiym in vain
22 for YHVH will not hold him guiltless
23 that taketh his name in vain
24
25 Remember the Shabbat day
26 to keep it holy
27 Six days shall you labor
28 and do all your work
29 but the seventh day
30 the Shabbat of YHVH your Elohiym
31 you shall not do any work
32 you nor your son
33 nor your daughter

1 your man-servant

2 nor your maid-servant

3 nor your cattle

4 nor your stranger

5 that is within your gates

6 for in six days YHVH made heaven and earth

7 and the sea and all that in them is

8 therefore YHVH blessed the Shabbat day

9 and made it holy

10

11 Honor your father and your mother

12 that your days

13 may be long upon the land

14 which YHVH your Elohiym gives you

15

16 You shall not Murder

17

18 You shall not commit adultery

19

20 You shall not steal

21

22 You shall not bear false witness

23 against your neighbor

24

25 You shall not covet your neighbor's house

26 you shall not covet your neighbor's wife

27 nor his man-servant nor his maid-servant

28 nor his ox nor his ass

29 nor anything that is your neighbor's"

30

31 And it came to pass

32 that after Abinadi had made

33 an end of these sayings

1 that he said unto them

2

3 "Have you taught this people

4 that they should observe to do

5 all these things for to keep these mitzvot

6 I say unto you No

7 for if you had YHVH would not have caused me

8 to come forth

9 and to prophesy evil

10 concerning this people

11

12 And now you have said

13 that salvation comes

14 by the Torah of Moshe

15 I say unto you

16 that it is necessary

17 that you should keep the Torah of Moshe as yet

18 but I say unto you that the time shall come

19 when it shall no more be necessary

20 to keep the ma'asim and takanot

21 of the Torah of Moshe

22

23 and furthermore I say unto you

24 that salvation does not come by the Torah alone

25 and were it not for the atonement

26 which Elohiym himself shall make

27 for the sins and lawlessness of his people

28 that they must unavoidably perish

29 despite the Torah of Moshe

30 and now I say unto you

31 that it was necessary

32 that there should be a Torah given

33 to the children of Israel

1 yes even a very strict Torah
2 for they were a stubborn people
3 quick to do lawlessness
4 and slow to remember YHVH their Elohiym
5 therefore there was a Torah given them
6 yes a Torah of ma'asim and of Takanot
7 a Torah which they were to observe strictly
8 from day to day
9 to keep them in remembrance of Elohiym
10 and their duty towards him
11
12 But behold I say unto you
13 that all these things were types
14 of things to come
15 and now did they understand the Torah
16 I say unto you No
17 they did not all understand the Torah
18 and this because of the hardness of their hearts
19 for they understood not
20 that there could not any man be saved
21 except it were through the redemption of Elohiym
22
23 For behold did not Moshe prophesy unto them
24 concerning the coming of the Mashiach
25 and that Elohiym should redeem his people
26 yes and even all the prophets
27 who have prophesied
28 ever since the world began
29 have they not spoken more or less
30 concerning these things
31 Have they not said that Elohiym himself
32 should come down
33 among the children of men

1 and take upon him the form of man
2 and go forth in mighty power
3 upon the face of the earth
4 yes and have they not said also
5 that he should bring to pass
6 the resurrection of the dead
7 and that he himself
8 should be oppressed and afflicted
9 yes even does not Yeshayahu say[1]
10
11 "Who has believed our report
12 and to whom is the arm of YHVH revealed
13 For he shall grow up before him
14 as a tender plant
15 and as a root out of dry ground
16 he has no form nor majesty
17 and when we shall see him
18 there is no beauty
19 that we should desire him
20 he is despised and rejected of men
21 a man of sorrows
22 and acquainted with grief
23 and we hid our faces from him
24 he was despised and we esteemed him not
25 Surely he has borne our griefs
26 and carried our sorrows
27 yet we did esteem him stricken
28 struck down by Elohiym and afflicted
29 but he was wounded for our rebellion
30 he was bruised for our lawlessness
31 upon him was the punishment that brought peace
32 and with his wounds we are healed

---

[1] Yeshayahu (Isaiah) 53

1   all we like sheep have gone astray

2   we have turned every one to his own way

3   and YHVH has laid on him the lawlessness of us all

4   he was oppressed and he was afflicted

5   yet he opened not his mouth

6   he is brought as a lamb to the slaughter

7   and as a sheep before her shearers is dumb

8   so he opened not his mouth

9   he was taken from prison and from judgment

10   and who shall declare his generation

11   for he was cut off out of the land of the living

12   for the transgressions of my people was he stricken

13   and he made his grave with the wicked

14   and with the rich in his death

15   because he had done no evil

16   neither was any deceit in his mouth

17   yet it pleased YHVH to bruise him

18   he has put him to grief

19   when you shall make his nephesh an offering for sin

20   he shall see his seed

21   he shall prolong his days

22   and the pleasure of YHVH

23   shall prosper in his hand

24   he shall see the travail of his nephesh

25   and shall be satisfied

26   by his knowledge

27   shall my righteous servant justify many

28   for he shall bear their lawlessness

29   therefore will I divide him a portion with the great

30   and he shall divide the spoil with the strong

31   because he has poured out his soul unto death

32   and he was numbered with the transgressors

33   and he bore the sins of many

1   and made intercession for the transgressors"

2

3   and now Abinadi said unto them

4

5   "I would that you should understand

6   that Elohiym himself shall come down

7   among the children of men

8   and shall redeem his people

9   and because he dwells in flesh

10 he shall be called the Chosen Son of Elohiym

11 and having subjected the flesh

12 to the will of the Father

13 being the Father and the Son

14 the Father

15 because he was conceived by the power of Elohiym

16 and the Son

17 because of the flesh

18 thus becoming the Father and Son

19 and they are one Elohiym

20 yes the very Eternal Father

21 of heaven and of earth

22 and thus the flesh

23 becoming subject to the Ruach

24 or the Son to the Father

25 being one Elohiym

26 suffering temptation

27 and yielding not to the temptation

28 but allows himself

29 to be mocked and scourged

30 and cast out and disowned by his people

31

32 And after all this

33 after working many mighty miracles

1   among the children of men he shall be led
2   yes even as Yeshayahu said
3   'as a sheep before the shearer is dumb
4   so he opened not his mouth'
5   yes even so he
6   shall be led crucified and killed
7   the flesh becoming subject even unto death
8   the will of the Son being swallowed up
9   in the will of the Father
10 and thus Elohiym breaks the bands of death
11 having gained the victory over death
12 giving the Son power
13 to make intercession
14 for the children of men
15 having ascended into heaven
16 having the bowels of mercy
17 being filled with compassion
18 towards the children of men
19 standing between them and justice
20 having broken the bands of death
21 taken upon himself their lawlessness
22 and their transgressions
23 having redeemed them
24 and satisfied the demands of justice
25
26 And now I say unto you
27 who shall declare his generation
28 behold I say unto you
29 that when his soul has been made
30 an offering for sin
31 he shall see his seed
32 and now what say you
33 and who shall be his seed

1
2 behold I say unto you
3 that whoever has heard the words of the prophets
4 yes all the holy prophets who have prophesied
5 concerning the coming of YHVH
6 I say unto you
7 that all those
8 who have listened to and obeyed their words
9 and believed that YHVH would redeem his people
10 and have looked forward to that day
11 for a remission of their sins
12 I say unto you
13 that these are his seed
14 or they are the heirs
15 of the kingdom of Elohiym
16 for these are they
17 whose sins he has borne
18 these are they
19 for whom he has died
20 to redeem them
21 from their rebellion
22 and now are they not his seed
23 yes and are not the prophets
24 every one that has opened his mouth to prophesy
25 that has not fallen into rebellion
26 I mean all the holy prophets
27 ever since the world began
28 I say unto you
29 that they are his seed
30 and these are they
31 who have published peace
32 who have brought good tidings of good
33 who have published salvation

1   and said unto Zion

2

3   "Your Elohiym reigns"

4   and O how beautiful

5   upon the mountains were their feet

6   and again

7   how beautiful upon the mountains are the feet

8   of those that are still publishing peace

9   and again

10   how beautiful upon the mountains are the feet of those

11   who shall hereafter publish peace

12   yes from this time forward and forever

13

14   and behold I say unto you

15   this is not all

16   for O how beautiful upon the mountains are the feet of him

17   that brings good tidings

18   that is the founder of peace

19   yes even YHVH

20   who has redeemed his people

21   yes him who has granted salvation

22   unto his people

23   for were it not for the redemption

24   which he has made for his people

25   which was prepared

26   from the foundation of the world

27   I say unto you

28   were it not for this

29   all mankind must have perished

30   but behold the bands of death shall be broken

31   and the Son reigns

32   and has power over the dead

33   therefore he brings to pass the resurrection of the dead

1 and there comes a resurrection

2 even a first resurrection

3 yes even a resurrection of those

4 that have been

5 and who are

6 and who shall be

7 even until the resurrection of Mashiach

8 for so shall he be called

9

10 And now the resurrection

11 of all the prophets

12 and all those

13 that have believed in their words

14 or all those

15 that have kept the mitzvot of Elohiym

16 shall come forth in the first resurrection

17 therefore they are the first resurrection

18 they are raised to dwell with Elohiym

19 who has redeemed them

20 thus they have eternal life through Mashiach

21 who has broken the bands of death

22 and these are those

23 who have part in the first resurrection

24 and these are they

25 that have died before Mashiach came

26 in their ignorance

27 not having salvation declared unto them

28 and thus YHVH brings about the restoration of these

29 and they have a part in the first resurrection

30 or have eternal life being redeemed by YHVH

31 and little children also have eternal life

32

33 But behold

1 and fear and tremble

2 before Elohiym

3 for you ought to tremble

4 for YHVH redeems none such

5 that rebel against him

6 and die in their sins

7 yes even all those

8 that have perished in their sins

9 ever since the world began

10 that have willfully rebelled

11 against Elohiym

12 that have known the mitzvot of Elohiym

13 and would not keep them

14 these are they

15 that have no part

16 in the first resurrection

17 therefore ought you not to tremble

18 for salvation comes to none such

19 for YHVH has redeemed none such

20 yes neither can YHVH redeem such

21 for he cannot deny himself

22 for he cannot deny justice

23 when it has its claim

24

25 And now I say unto you

26 that the time shall come

27 that the salvation of YHVH

28 shall be declared

29 to every nation tribe language and people

30 yes Adonai

31 your watchmen shall lift up their voice

32 with the voice together shall they sing

33 for they shall see eye to eye

1   when YHVH shall bring again Zion

2   break forth into joy

3   sing together you waste places of Yerushalayim

4   for YHVH has comforted his people

5   he has redeemed Yerushalayim

6   YHVH has made bare his holy arm

7   in the eyes of all the nations

8   and all the ends of the earth

9   shall see the salvation of our Elohiym"

10 And Now it came to pass

11 that after Abinadi had spoken these words

12 he stretched forth his hand and said

13

14 "The time shall come

15 when all shall see the salvation of YHVH

16 when every nation tribe language and people

17 shall see eye to eye

18 and shall confess before Elohiym

19 that his judgments are just

20 and then shall the wicked be cast out

21 and they shall have cause

22 to howl and weep

23 and wail and gnash their teeth

24 and this because they would not

25 listen to or obey the voice of YHVH

26 therefore YHVH redeems them not

27 for they are carnal and governed by the evil one

28 and the evil one has power over them

29 yes even that old serpent

30 that did deceive our first parents

31 who was the cause of their fall

32 who was the cause of all mankind

33 becoming carnal sensual evil

1   knowing evil from good
2   subjecting themselves to the evil one
3   thus all mankind were lost
4   and behold
5   they would have been endlessly lost were it not
6   that Elohiym redeemed his people
7   from their lost and fallen state
8   but remember
9   that he that persists in his own carnal nature
10   and goes on
11   in the ways of sin and rebellion
12   against Elohiym remains
13   in his fallen state
14   and the evil one has all power over him
15   therefore he is as though
16   there was no redemption made
17   being an enemy to Elohiym
18   and also is the evil one an enemy to Elohiym
19
20   And now
21   if Mashiach had not come into the world
22   speaking of things to come
23   as though they had already come
24   there could have been no redemption
25   and if Mashiach had not risen from the dead
26   or have broken the bands of death
27   that the grave should have no victory
28   and that death should have no sting
29   there could have been no resurrection
30   but there is a resurrection
31   therefore the grave has no victory
32   and the sting of death is swallowed up in Mashiach
33   he is the light and the life of the world

1 yes a light that is endless
2 that can never be darkened
3 yes and also a life which is endless
4 that there can be no more death
5 even this mortal
6 shall put on immortality
7 and this corruption
8 shall put on incorruption
9 and shall be brought to stand
10 before the porch of Elohiym
11 to be judged of him
12 according to their works
13 whether they be good
14 or whether they be evil
15 if they be good
16 to the resurrection
17 of endless life and happiness
18 and if they be evil
19 to the resurrection of endless condemnation
20 being delivered up to the evil one
21 who has subjected them
22 which is condemnation
23 having gone according
24 to their own carnal wills and desires
25 having never called upon YHVH
26 while the arms of mercy were extended towards them
27 for the arms of mercy were extended towards them
28 and they would not
29 they being warned of their lawlessness
30 and yet they would not depart from them
31 and they were commanded to repent
32 and yet they would not repent
33

1   And now

2   ought you not to tremble

3   and repent of your sins

4   and remember that only in

5   and through Mashiach you can be saved

6   therefore if you teach the Torah of Moshe

7   also teach

8   that it is a shadow of those things

9   which are to come

10   teach them

11   that redemption comes through Mashiach Adonai

12   who is the very Eternal Father

13   Amein"

14

15   And now it came to pass

16   that when Abinadi had finished these sayings

17   that the king commanded

18   that the kohanim should take him

19   and cause that he should be put to death

20   but there was one among them

21   whose name was Almah he

22   also being a descendant of Nephi

23   and he was a young man

24   and he believed the words

25   which Abinadi had spoken

26   for he knew concerning the lawlessness

27   which Abinadi had testified against them

28   therefore he began to plead with the king

29   that he would not be angry with Abinadi

30   but allow that he might depart in peace

31   but the king was more angry

32   and caused that Almah should be cast out

33   from among them

1 and sent his servants after him

2 that they might kill him

3 but he fled from before them

4 and hid himself

5 that they found him not

6 and he being concealed

7 for many days did write

8 all the words

9 which Abinadi had spoken

10

11 And it came to pass

12 that the king caused

13 that his guards should surround Abinadi

14 and take him

15 and they bound him

16 and cast him into prison

17 and after three days

18 having counseled with his kohanim

19 he caused that he should again be brought before him

20 and he said unto him

21

22 "Abinadi we have found

23 an accusation against you

24 and you are worthy of death

25 for you hast said

26 that Elohiym himself should come down

27 among the children of men

28 and now for this reason you

29 shall be put to death

30 unless you will recall all the words

31 which you have spoken evil

32 concerning me and my people"

33

1   now Abinadi said unto him

2

3   "I say unto you

4   I will not recall the words

5   which I have spoken unto you

6   concerning this people

7   for they are true

8   and that you may know of their certainty

9   I have allowed myself

10 that I have fallen into your hands

11 yes and I will suffer even until death

12 and I will not recall my words

13 and they shall stand as a testimony against you

14 and if you kill me you will shed innocent blood

15 and this shall also stand as a testimony against you

16 at the last day"

17

18 and now king Noach was about to release him

19 for he feared his word

20 for he feared

21 that the judgments of Elohiym

22 would come upon him

23 but the kohanim lifted up their voices against him

24 and began to accuse him saying

25

26 "he has reviled the king"

27

28 Therefore the king was stirred up

29 in anger against him

30 and he delivered him up

31 that he might be killed

32

33 And it came to pass

1   that they took him and bound him

2   and burnt his skin with torches

3   yes even unto death

4   and now when the flames began to scorch

5   him he cried unto them saying

6

7   " Behold even as you have done unto me

8   so shall it come to pass

9   that your seed shall cause

10   that many shall suffer the pains

11   that I do suffer

12   even the pains of death by fire

13   and this because they believe

14   in the salvation of YHVH their Elohiym

15

16   And it will come to pass

17   that you shall be afflicted

18   with all manner of diseases

19   because of your lawlessness

20   yes and you shall be struck down on every hand

21   and shall be driven and scattered to and fro

22   even as a wild flock is driven

23   by wild and ferocious beasts

24   and in that day you shall be hunted

25   and you shall be taken

26   by the hand of your enemies

27   and then you shall suffer

28   as I suffer the pains of death by fire

29   thus Elohiym executes judgement

30   upon those that destroy his people

31   O Elohiym receive my soul"

32

33   And now when Abinadi had said these words

1   he fell having suffered death by fire

2   yes having been put to death

3   because he would not deny the mitzvot of Elohiym

4   having sealed the truth of his words by his death

5

6   And now it came to pass

7   that Almah who had fled

8   from the servants of king Noach repented

9   of his sins and lawlessness

10   and went about privately among the people

11   and began to teach the words of Abinadi

12   yes concerning that which was to come

13   and also concerning the resurrection of the dead

14   and the redemption of the people

15   which was to be brought to pass

16   through the power and sufferings

17   and death of Mashiach

18   and his resurrection

19   and ascension into heaven

20   and as many as would hear his word

21   he did teach

22   and he taught them privately

23   that it might not come

24   to the knowledge of the king

25   and many did believe his words

26

27   And it came to pass

28   that as many as did believe him did go forth

29   to a place

30   which was called Mur'mon

31   having received its name from the king

32   being in the borders of the land

33   having been infested

1   by times or at seasons by wild beasts

2   now there was in Mur'mon a fountain of pure water

3   and Almah resorted there

4   there being near the water a thicket of small trees

5   where he did hide himself in the daytime

6   from the searches of the king

7

8   And it came to pass

9   that as many as believed him went there

10   to hear his words

11

12   And it came to pass

13   after many days

14   there were a good number gathered together

15   at the place of Mur'mon

16   to hear the words of Almah

17   yes all were gathered together

18   that believed on his word to hear him

19   and he did teach them

20   and did preach unto them repentance

21   and redemption and faith on YHVH

22

23   And it came to pass

24   that he said unto them

25

26   "behold here are the waters of Mur'mon

27   for thus were they called

28   and now as you desire

29   to come into the fold of Elohiym

30   and to be called his people

31   and are willing to bear one another's burdens

32   that they may be light

33   yes and are willing to mourn

1   with those that mourn

2   yes and comfort those

3   that stand in need of comfort

4   and to stand as witnesses of Elohiym

5   at all times and in all things

6   and in all places

7   that you may be in

8   even until death

9   that you may be redeemed of Elohiym

10   and be numbered with those of the first resurrection

11   that you may have eternal life

12   now I say unto you

13   if this be the desire of your hearts

14   what have you against being immersed

15   in the name of YHVH

16   as a witness before him

17   that you have entered into a covenant with him

18   that you will serve him

19   and keep his mitzvot

20   that he may pour out his Ruach

21   more abundantly upon you"

22

23   And now

24   when the people had heard these words

25   they clapped their hands for joy

26   and exclaimed

27

28   "This is the desire of our hearts"

29

30   And now it came to pass

31   that Almah took Helam

32   he being one of the first

33   and went and stood forth in the water

1   and cried saying

2

3   "O YHVH pour out your Ruach

4   upon your servant

5   that he may do this work

6   with holiness of heart"

7

8   And when he had said these words

9   the Ruach Elohiym was upon him

10 and he said

11

12 "Helam I immerse you

13 having authority from the El Shaddai

14 as a testimony that you have entered

15 into a covenant to serve him

16 until you are dead

17 as to the mortal body

18 and may the Ruach Elohoym

19 be poured out upon you

20 and may he grant unto you eternal life

21 through the redemption of Mashiach

22 whom he has prepared

23 from the creation of the world"

24

25 And after Almah had said these words

26 both Almah and Helam were buried in the water

27 and they arose and came forth out

28 of the water rejoicing

29 being filled with the Ruach

30 and again Almah took another

31 and went forth a second time

32 into the water

33 and immersed him

1 according to the first
2 only he did not bury himself again in the water
3 and after this manner he did immerse
4 every one that went forth
5 to the place of Mur'mon
6 and they were in number
7 about two hundred and four souls
8 yes and they were immersed
9 in the waters of Mur'mon
10 and were filledwith the grace of Elohiym
11 and they were called the assembly of Elohiym
12 or the assembly of Mashiach
13 from that time forward
14
15 And it came to pass
16 that whoever was immersed
17 by the power and authority of Elohiym
18 was added to his assembly
19
20 And it came to pass
21 that Almah having authority
22 from Elohiym decreed kohanim
23 even one kohen to every fifty
24 of their number did he decree
25 to preach unto them
26 and to teach them
27 concerning the things
28 pertaining to the kingdom
29 of Elohiym
30 and he commanded them
31 that they should teach nothing
32 except it were the things
33 which he had taught

1 and which had been spoken
2 by the mouth of the holy prophets
3 yes even he commanded them
4 that they should preach nothing
5 except it were repentance and faith
6 on YHVH
7 who had redeemed his people
8 and he commanded them
9 that there should be
10 no contention one with another
11 but that they should look forward
12 with one eye having one faith
13 and one immersion having
14 their hearts knit together
15 in unity and in love
16 one towards another
17 and thus he commanded them to preach
18 and thus they became the children of Elohiym
19 and he commanded them
20 that they should observe the Shabbat day
21 and keep it holy
22 and also every day
23 they should give thanks
24 to YHVH their Elohiym
25 and he also commanded them
26 that the kohanim
27 whom he had ordained
28 should labor with their own hands
29 for their support
30 and there was one day
31 in every week
32 that was set apart
33 that they should gather themselves together

1   to teach the people
2   and to worship YHVH their Elohiym
3   and also as often as it was in their power
4   to assemble themselves together
5   and the kohanim were not to depend
6   upon the people
7   for their support
8   but for their labor
9   they were to receive the grace of Elohiym
10   that they might grow strong
11   in the Ruach having the knowledge of Elohiym
12   that they might teach
13   with power and authority from Elohiym
14   and again Almah commanded
15   that the people of the assembly
16   should impart of their substance
17   every one according
18   to that which he had
19   if he have more abundantly he
20   should impart more abundantly
21   and of him that had but little
22   but little should be required
23   and to him that had not
24   should be given
25   and thus they should impart of their substance
26   of their own free will
27   and good desires towards Elohiym
28   and to those kohanim
29   that stood in need
30   yes and to every needy naked person
31   and this he said unto them
32   having been commanded of Elohiym
33   and they did walk uprightly before Elohiym imparting

1 to one another

2 both temporally and spiritually

3 according to their needs

4 and their wants

5

6 And now it came to pass

7 that all this was done in Mur'mon

8 yes by the waters of Mur'mon

9 in the forest

10 that was near the waters of Mur'mon

11 yes the place of Mur'mon

12 the waters of Mur'mon

13 the forest of Mur'mon

14 how beautiful are they

15 to the eyes of them

16 who there came to the knowledge

17 of their Redeemer

18 yes and how blessed are they

19 for they shall sing to his praise forever

20 and these things were done

21 in the borders of the land

22 that they might not come

23 to the knowledge of the king

24

25 But behold it came to pass

26 that the king having discovered a movement

27 among the people sent his servants

28 to watch them

29 therefore on the day

30 that they were assembling themselves together

31 to hear the word of YHVH

32 they were discovered unto the king

33 and now the king said

1   that Almah was stirring up the people

2   to rebellion against him

3   therefore he sent his army

4   to destroy them

5   And it came to pass

6   that Almah

7   and the people of YHVH were apprised

8   of the coming of the king's army

9   therefore they took their tents

10   and their families

11   and departed into the wilderness

12   and they were in number

13   about four hundred and fifty souls

14

15   And it came to pass

16   that the army of the king returned

17   having searched in vain

18   for the people of YHVH

19   and now behold

20   the forces of the king were small

21   having been reduced

22   and there began to be a division

23   among the remainder

24   of the people

25   and the lesser part began

26   to breathe out threats against the king

27   and there began to be a great contention among them

28   and now there was a man among them

29   whose name was Gid`on

30   and he being a strong man

31   and an enemy to the king

32   therefore he drew his sword

33   and swore in his anger

1   that he would kill the king

2

3   And it came to pass

4   that he fought with the king

5   and when the king saw

6   that he was about to overpower him he fled

7   and ran and got upon the tower

8   which was near the temple

9   and Gid`on pursued after him

10   and was about to get upon the tower

11   to kill the king

12   and the king cast his eyes round about

13   towards the land of Shemlon

14   and behold the army of the Lamaniy were

15   within the borders of the land

16   and now the king cried out

17   in the anguish of his soul saying

18

19   "Gid`on spare me

20   for the Lamaniy are upon us

21   and they will destroy us

22   yes they will destroy my people"

23

24   And now the king was not so much

25   concerned about his people

26   as he was about his own life

27   nevertheless Gid`on did spare his life

28   and the king commanded the people

29   that they should flee before the Lamaniy

30   and he himself did go before them

31   and they did flee into the wilderness

32   with their women and their children

33

1   And it came to pass
2   that the Lamaniy did pursue them
3   and did overtake them
4   and began to kill them
5
6   Now it came to pass
7   that the king commanded them
8   that all the men should leave
9   their wives and their children
10 and flee before the Lamaniy
11 now there were many
12 that would not leave them
13 but had rather stay and perish with them
14 and the rest left
15 their wives and their children
16 and fled
17
18 And it came to pass
19 that those who stayed
20 with their wives and their children caused
21 that their fair daughters should stand forth
22 and plead with the Lamaniy
23 that they would not kill them
24
25 And it came to pass
26 that the Lamaniy had compassion on them
27 for they were charmed
28 with the beauty of their women
29 therefore the Lamaniy did spare their lives
30 and took them captives
31 and carried them back
32 to the land of Nephi
33 and granted unto them

1   that they might possess the land
2   under the conditions
3   that they would deliver up king Noach
4   into the hands of the Lamaniy
5   and deliver up their property
6   even one half
7   of all they possessed
8   one half of their gold and their silver
9   and all their precious things
10 and thus they should pay tribute
11 to the king of the Lamaniy
12 from year to year
13 and now
14 there was one of the sons of the king
15 among those that were taken captive
16 whose name was Lemhi
17 and now Lemhi desired
18 that his father should not be destroyed
19 nevertheless Lemhi was not ignorant
20 of the lawlessness of his father he himself
21 being a just man
22
23 And it came to pass
24 that Gid`on sent men
25 into the wilderness secretly
26 to search for the king
27 and those that were with him
28
29 And it came to pass
30 that they met the people in the wilderness
31 all save the king and his kohanim
32 now they had sworn in their hearts
33 that they would return to the land of Nephi

1   and if their wives and their children were killed
2   and also those that had stayed with them
3   that they would seek revenge
4   and also perish with them
5   and the king commanded them
6   that they should not return
7   and they were angry with the king
8   and caused that he should suffer
9   even unto death by fire
10 and they were about to take the kohanim also
11 and put them to death
12 and they fled before them
13 And it came to pass
14 that they were about to return
15 to the land of Nephi
16 and they met the men of Gid`on
17 and the men of Gid`on told them
18 of all that had happened to their wives
19 and their children
20 and that the Lamaniy had granted unto them
21 that they might possess the land
22 by paying a tribute to the Lamaniy
23 of one half of all they possessed
24 and the people told the men of Gid`on
25 that they had killed the king
26 and his kohanim had fled from them
27 farther into the wilderness
28
29 And it came to pass
30 that after they had ended the ceremony
31 that they returned
32 to the land of Nephi rejoicing
33 because their wives

1 and their children were not killed
2 and they told Gid`on
3 what they had done to the king
4
5 And it came to pass
6 that the king of the Lamaniy made an oath unto them
7 that his people should not kill them
8 and also Lemhi
9 being the son of the king
10 having the kingdom conferred upon him
11 by the people made oath
12 unto the king of the Lamaniy
13 that his people should pay tribute unto him
14 even one half of all they possessed
15 And it came to pass
16 that Lemhi began to establish the kingdom
17 and to establish peace among his people
18 and the king of the Lamaniy
19 set guards round about the land
20 that he might keep the people of Lemhi in the land
21 that they might not depart into the wilderness
22 and he did support his guards
23 out of the tribute
24 which he did receive from the Nephiy
25 and now king Lemhi did have
26 continual peace in his kingdom
27 for the space of two years
28 that the Lamaniy did not molest them
29 nor seek to destroy them
30 now there was a place in Shemlon
31 where the daughters of the Lamaniy
32 did gather themselves together
33 to sing and to dance

1 and to make themselves merry

2

3 And it came to pass

4 that there was one day

5 a small number of them gathered together

6 to sing and to dance

7 and now the kohanim of king Noach being ashamed

8 to return to the city of Nephi

9 yes and also fearing

10 that the people would kill them

11 therefore they did not return

12 to their wives and their children

13 and having stayed in the wilderness

14 and having discovered the daughters of the Lamaniy

15 they laid and watched them

16 and when there were but few

17 of them gathered together to dance

18 they came forth out of their secret places

19 and took them and carried them

20 into the wilderness

21 yes twenty and four of the daughters

22 of the Lamaniy

23 they carried into the wilderness

24

25 And it came to pass

26 that when the Lamaniy found

27 that their daughters had been missing

28 they were angry

29 with the people of Lemhi

30 for they thought it was the people of Lemhi

31 therefore they sent their armies forth

32 yes even the king himself went before his people

33 and they went up to the land of Nephi

1 to destroy the people of Lemhi
2 and now Lemhi had discovered them
3 from the tower
4 even all their preparations for war did he discover
5 therefore he gathered his people together
6 and laid wait for them
7 in the fields and in the forests
8
9 And it came to pass
10 that when the Lamaniy had come up
11 that the people of Lemhi
12 began to fall upon them
13 from their waiting places
14 and began to kill them
15
16 And it came to pass
17 that the battle became exceedingly sore
18 for they fought like lions
19 for their prey
20
21 And it came to pass
22 that the people of Lemhi began
23 to drive the Lamaniy before them
24 yet they were not half so numerous as the Lamaniy
25 but they fought for their lives
26 and for their wives and for their children
27 therefore they exerted themselves
28 and like dragons did they fight
29
30 And it came to pass
31 that they found the king of the Lamaniy
32 among the number of their dead
33 yet he was not dead having been wounded

1 and left upon the ground
2 so speedy was the flight of his people
3 and they took him
4 and bound up his wounds
5 and brought him before Lemhi and said
6
7 "Behold here is the king of the Lamaniy
8 he having received a wound has fallen
9 among their dead
10 and they have left him
11 and behold we have brought him before you
12 and now let us kill him"
13
14 but Lemhi said unto them
15
16 "You shall not kill him
17 but bring him here that I may see him"
18
19 and they brought him
20 and Lemhi said unto him
21 "What reason have you
22 to come up to war against my people
23 behold my people have not broken the oath
24 that I made unto you
25 therefore why should you break the oath
26 which you made unto my people"
27
28 and now the king said
29
30 "I have broken the oath
31 because your people did carry away
32 the daughters of my people
33 therefore in my anger I did cause

1 my people to come up

2 to war against your people"

3

4 and now Lemhi had heard nothing

5 concerning this matter

6 therefore he said

7

8 "I will search among my people

9 and whoever has done this thing shall perish"

10

11 Therefore he caused a search to be made

12 among his people

13 now when Gid`on had heard these things

14 he being the king's captain

15 he went forth

16 and said unto the king

17

18 "I pray you forbear

19 and do not search this people

20 and lay not this thing to their charge

21 for do you not remember the kohanim of your father

22 whom this people sought to destroy

23 and are they not in the wilderness

24 and are not they the ones

25 who have stolen the daughters

26 of the Lamaniy

27

28 And now behold

29 and tell the king of these things

30 that he may tell his people

31 that they may be pacified towards us

32 for behold

33 they are already preparing to come against us

1 and behold also there are but few of us

2 and behold

3 they come with their numerous armies

4 and except the king does pacify them

5 towards us we must perish

6 for are not the words of Abinadi fulfilled

7 which he prophesied against us

8 and all this because we would not listen to

9 and obey the words of YHVH

10 and turn from our lawlessness

11 and now let us pacify the king

12 and we fulfil the oath

13 which we have made unto him

14 for it is better that we should be in bondage

15 than that we should lose our lives

16 therefore let us put a stop

17 to the shedding of so much blood"

18

19 and now Lemhi told the king

20 all the things concerning his father

21 and the kohanim

22 that had fled into the wilderness

23 and attributed the carrying away

24 of their daughters to them

25 And it came to pass

26 that the king was pacified towards his people

27 and he said unto them

28

29 "Let us go forth

30 to meet my people without arms

31 and I swear unto you with an oath

32 that my people shall not kill your people"

33

1 And it came to pass
2 that they followed the king
3 and went forth without arms
4 to meet the Lamaniy
5
6 And it came to pass
7 that they did meet the Lamaniy
8 and the king of the Lamaniy
9 did bow himself down before them
10 and did plead in behalf of the people of Lemhi
11 and when the Lamaniy saw the people of Lemhi
12 that they were without arms
13 they had compassion on them
14 and were pacified towards them
15 and returned with their king in peace
16 to their own land
17
18 And it came to pass
19 that Lemhi and his people returned
20 to the city of Nephi
21 and began to dwell
22 in the land again in peace
23
24 And it came to pass
25 that after many days the Lamaniy began again
26 to be stirred up in anger against the Nephiy
27 and they began to come
28 into the borders of the land round about
29 now they did not kill them
30 because of the oath
31 which their king had made unto Lemhi
32 but they would strike them on their cheeks
33 and exercise authority over them

1   and began to put heavy burdens upon their backs

2   and drive them as they would a dumb ass

3   yes all this was done

4   that the word of YHVH might be fulfilled

5   and now the afflictions of the Nephiy were great

6   and there was no way

7   that they could deliver themselves out

8   of their hands

9   for the Lamaniy had surrounded them

10 on every side

11

12 And it came to pass

13 that the people began to complain with the king

14 because of their afflictions

15 and they began to desire

16 to go against them to battle

17 and they did afflict the king sorely

18 with their complaints

19 therefore he granted unto them

20 that they should do according to their desires

21 and they gathered themselves together again

22 and put on their armor

23 and went forth against the Lamaniy

24 to drive them out of their land

25

26 And it came to pass

27 that the Lamaniy did beat them

28 and drove them back

29 and killed many of them

30 and now

31 there was a great mourning and lamentation

32 among the people of Lemhi

33 the widow mourning for her husband

1   the son and the daughter mourning

2   for their father

3   and the brothers for their brothers

4   now there were a great many widows in the land

5   and they did cry mightily

6   from day to day

7   for a great fear of the Lamaniy had come

8   upon them

9

10 And it came to pass

11 that their continual cries did stir up the remainder

12 of the people of Lemhi

13 to anger against the Lamaniy

14 and they went again to battle

15 but they were driven back again

16 suffering much loss

17 yes they went again

18 even the third time

19 and suffered in the like manner

20 and those that were not killed returned again

21 to the city of Nephi

22 and they did humble themselves

23 even to the dust subjecting themselves

24 to the yoke of bondage submitting themselves

25 to be struck

26 and to be driven forward and backwards

27 and burdened

28 according to the desires of their enemies

29 and they did humble themselves

30 even in the depths of humility

31 and they did cry mightily to Elohiym

32 yes even all the day long did they cry unto their Elohiym

33 that he would deliver them out of their afflictions

1 and now YHVH was slow to hear their cry
2 because of their lawlessness
3 nevertheless YHVH did hear their cries
4 and began to soften the hearts of the Lamaniy
5 that they began to ease their burdens
6 yet YHVH did not see fit to deliver them
7 out of bondage
8
9 And it came to pass
10 that they began to prosper
11 by degrees in the land
12 and began to raise grain more abundantly
13 and flocks and herds
14 that they did not suffer with hunger
15 now there was a great number of women
16 more than there was of men
17 therefore king Lemhi commanded
18 that every man should impart
19 to the support of the widows and their children that
20 they might not perish with hunger
21 and this they did
22 because of the greatness of their number
23 that had been killed
24 now the people of Lemhi kept together in a body
25 as much as it was possible
26 and secured their grain and their flocks
27 and the king himself did not trust his person
28 outside the walls of the city
29 unless he took his guards with him fearing
30 that he might by some means fall
31 into the hands of the Lamaniy
32 and he caused that his people
33 should watch the land round about

1   that by some means

2   they might take those kohanim

3   that fled into the wilderness

4   who had stolen the daughters of the Lamaniy

5   and that had caused such a great destruction

6   to come upon them

7   for they desired to take them

8   that they might punish them

9   for they had come into the land of Nephi by night

10   and carried off their grain

11   and many of their precious things

12   therefore they laid wait for them

13

14   And it came to pass

15   that there was no more disturbance

16   between the Lamaniy

17   and the people of Lemhi

18   even until the time that Ammon

19   and his brothers came into the land

20   and the king having been

21   outside the gates of the city

22   with his guard discovered Ammon

23   and his brothers

24   and supposing them to be kohanim of Noach

25   therefore he caused

26   that they should be taken and bound

27   and cast into prison

28   and had they been the kohanim of Noach

29   he would have caused

30   that they should be put to death

31   but when he found that they were not

32   but that they were his brothers

33   and had come from the land of Zarahemla he was filled

1 with exceedingly great joy
2 now king Lemhi had sent
3 previous to the coming of Ammon a small number of men
4 to search for the land of Zarahemla
5 but they could not find it
6 and they were lost in the wilderness
7 nevertheless they did find a land
8 which had been peopled
9 yes a land which was covered with dry bones
10 yes a land which had been peopled
11 and which had been destroyed
12 and they having supposed it
13 to be the land of Zarahemla returned
14 to the land of Nephi having arrived
15 in the borders of the land
16 not many days
17 before the coming of Ammon
18 and they brought a record with them
19 even a record of the people
20 whose bones they had found
21 and it was engraved on plates of ore
22 and now Lemhi was again filled with joy
23 on learning from the mouth of Ammon
24 that king Mosheyahu had a gift from Elohiym
25 by which he could interpret such engravings
26 yes and Ammon also did rejoice
27 Yet Ammon and his brothers were filled with sorrow
28 because so many of their brothers had been killed
29 and also that king Noach
30 and his kohanim had caused the people
31 to commit so many sins and lawlessness against Elohiym
32 and they also did mourn for the death of Abinadi
33 and also for the departure of Almah

1 and the people that went with him

2 who had formed an assembly of Elohiym

3 through the strength and power of Elohiym

4 and faith on the words

5 which had been spoken by Abinadi

6 yes they did mourn for their departure

7 for they knew not where they had fled

8 now they would have gladly joined with them

9 for they themselves had entered into a covenant with Elohiym

10 to serve him and keep his mitzvot

11 and now since the coming of Ammon

12 king Lemhi had also entered into a covenant with Elohiym

13 and also many of his people

14 to serve him and keep his mitzvot

15

16 And it came to pass

17 that king Lemhi

18 and many of his people desired to be immersed

19 but there was none in the land

20 that had authority from Elohiym

21 and Ammon declined doing this thing

22 considering himself an unworthy servant

23 therefore they did not at that time

24 form themselves into an assembly waiting

25 upon the Ruach Elohiym

26 now they desired to become

27 even as Almah and his brothers

28 who had fled into the wilderness

29 They desired to be immersed

30 as a witness and a testimony

31 that they were willing to serve Elohiym

32 with all their hearts

33 nevertheless they did prolong the time

1 and an account of their immersion
2 shall be given hereafter
3 and now all the study
4 of Ammon and his people
5 and king Lemhi and his people was
6 to deliver themselves out
7 of the hands of the Lamaniy
8 and from bondage
9
10 And now it came to pass
11 that Ammon and king Lemhi began
12 to consult with the people
13 how they should deliver themselves out of bondage
14 and even they did cause that all the people
15 should gather themselves together
16 and this they did
17 that they might have the voice of the people
18 concerning the matter
19
20 And it came to pass
21 that they could find no way
22 to deliver themselves out of bondage
23 except it were to take their women and children
24 and their flocks and their herds
25 and their tents and depart into the wilderness
26 for the Lamaniy being so numerous it was impossible
27 for the people of Lemhi to contend with them thinking
28 to deliver themselves out of bondage
29 by the sword
30
31 Now it came to pass
32 that Gid`on went forth
33 and stood before the king

1 and said unto him

2

3 "now O king you have yet listened to

4 and obeyed my words many times

5 when we have been contending

6 with our brothers the Lamaniy

7 and now O king

8 if you have not found me

9 to be an unprofitable servant

10 or if you have to this time listened to my words

11 in any degree

12 and they have been of service to you

13 even so I desire

14 that you wouldst listen to my words

15 at this time

16 and I will be your servant

17 and deliver this people

18 out of bondage"

19

20 And the king granted unto him

21 that he might speak

22 and Gid`on said unto him

23

24 "Behold the back pass

25 through the back wall

26 on the back side of the city

27 the Lamaniy or the guards of the Lamaniy

28 by night are drunk

29 therefore let us send a proclamation

30 among all this people

31 that they gather together

32 their flocks and herds

33 that they may drive them

1   into the wilderness by night
2   and I will go
3   according to your command
4   and pay the last tribute of wine to the Lamaniy
5   and they will be drunk
6   and we will pass through the secret pass
7   on the left of their camp
8   when they are drunk and asleep
9   thus we will depart
10 with our women and our children
11 our flocks and our herds into the wilderness
12 and we will travel around the land of Shilom"
13
14 And it came to pass
15 that the king listened and followed the words of Gid`on
16 and king Lemhi caused
17 that his people should gather their flocks together
18 and he sent the tribute of wine to the Lamaniy
19 and he also sent more wine as a present unto them
20 and they did drink freely of the wine
21 which king Lemhi did send unto them
22
23 And it came to pass
24 that the people of king Lemhi did depart
25 by night into the wilderness
26 with their flocks and their herds
27 and they went round about the land of Shilom
28 in the wilderness
29 and bent their course towards the land of Zarahemla
30 being led by Ammon and his brothers
31 and they had taken all their gold and silver
32 and their precious things
33 which they could carry

1   and also their provisions with them
2   into the wilderness
3   and they pursued their journey
4   and after being many days in the wilderness
5   they arrived in the land of Zarahemla
6   and joined Mosheyahu 's people
7   and became his subjects
8
9   And it came to pass
10 that Mosheyahu received them with joy
11 and he also received their records
12 and also the records
13 which had been found
14 by the people of Lemhi
15
16 And now it came to pass
17 when the Lamaniy had found
18 that the people of Lemhi had departed out
19 of the land by night
20 that they sent an army
21 into the wilderness to pursue them
22 and after they had pursued them two days
23 they could no longer follow their tracks
24 therefore they were lost in the wilderness
25
26 An account of Almah and the people of YHVH
27 who were driven into the wilderness
28 by the people of King Noach
29
30 Now Almah having been warned of YHVH
31 that the armies of king Noach would come upon them
32 and having made it known to his people
33 therefore they gathered together

1 their flocks and took of their grain

2 and departed into the wilderness

3 before the armies of king Noach

4 and YHVH did strengthen them

5 that the people of king Noach

6 could not overtake them to destroy them

7 and they fled eight days journey into the wilderness

8 and they came to a land

9 yes even a very beautiful and pleasant land

10 a land of pure water

11 and they pitched their tents

12 and began to till the ground

13 and began to build buildings

14 yes they were industrious

15 and did labor exceedingly

16 and the people desired

17 that Almah should be their king

18 for he was beloved by his people

19 but he said unto them

20

21 "Behold it is not necessary

22 that we should have a king

23 for thus says YHVH

24

25 "You shall not esteem one flesh above another

26 or one man shall not think himself above another

27 therefore I say unto you it is not expedient

28 that you should have a king

29 nevertheless if it were possible

30 that you could always have just men

31 to be your kings it would be well

32 for you to have a king

33 but remember the lawlessness

1   of king Noach and his kohanim
2   and I myself was caught in a snare
3   and did many things
4   which were abominable in the sight of YHVH
5   which caused me sore repentance
6   nevertheless after much tribulation YHVH did hear my cries
7   and did answer my prayers
8   and has made me an instrument in his hands
9   in bringing so many of you
10 to a knowledge of his truth
11 nevertheless in this I do not glory
12 for I am unworthy to glory of myself
13
14 And now I say unto you
15 you have been oppressed by king Noach
16 and have been in bondage to him
17 and his kohanim
18 and have been brought
19 into lawlessness by them
20 therefore you were bound
21 with the bands of lawlessness
22
23 And now as you have been delivered
24 by the power of Elohiym out of these bonds
25 yes even out of the hands of king Noach
26 and his people
27 and also from the bonds of lawlessness
28 even so I desire that you should stand fast
29 in this liberty
30 in which you have been made free
31 and that you trust no man
32 to be a king over you
33 and also trust no one

1   to be your moreh

2   nor your kohen

3   except he be a man of Elohiym

4   walking in his ways

5   and keeping his mitzvot"

6

7   Thus did Almah teach his people

8   that every man

9   should love his neighbor as himself

10   that there should be no contention

11   among them

12   and now Almah was their Kohen Gadol

13   he being the founder

14   of their assembly

15

16   And it came to pass

17   that none received authority

18   to preach or to teach

19   except it were by him from Elohiym

20   therefore he set apart

21   all their kohanim

22   and all their morim

23   and none were set apart

24   except they were just men

25   therefore they did watch over their people

26   and did nourish them

27   with things pertaining to righteousness

28

29   And it came to pass

30   that they began

31   to prosper exceedingly in the land

32   and they called the land Helam

33

1 And it came to pass
2 that they did multiply and prosper exceedingly
3 in the land of Helam
4 and they built a city
5 which they called the city of Helam
6 nevertheless YHVH sees fit
7 to correct his people
8 yes he tries their patience
9 and their faith
10 nevertheless whoever puts his trust
11 in him the same
12 shall be lifted up at the last day
13 yes and thus it was with this people
14 for behold I will show unto you
15 that they were brought into bondage
16 and none could deliver them
17 but YHVH their Elohiym
18 yes even the Eloah of Avraham
19 and Yitzchak
20 and of Yacov
21
22 And it came to pass
23 that he did deliver them
24 and he did show forth his mighty power unto them
25 and great were their rejoicings
26
27 For behold it came to pass
28 that while they were in the land of Helam
29 yes in the city of Helam
30 while tilling the land round about
31 behold an army of the Lamaniy was
32 in the borders of the land
33

1   Now it came to pass
2   that the brothers of Almah fled
3   from their fields
4   and gathered themselves together
5   in the city of Helam
6   and they were much frightened
7   because of the appearance of the Lamaniy
8   but Almah went forth and stood among them
9   and exhorted them
10 that they should not be frightened
11 but that they should remember YHVH their Elohiym
12 and he would deliver them
13 therefore they hushed their fears
14 and began to cry unto YHVH
15 that he would soften the hearts of the Lamaniy
16 that they would spare them
17 and their wives and their children
18
19 And it came to pass
20 that YHVH did soften the hearts
21 of the Lamaniy
22 and Almah and his brothers went forth
23 and delivered themselves up into their hands
24 and the Lamaniy took possession
25 of the land of Helam
26 now the armies of the Lamaniy
27 which had followed
28 after the people of king Lemhi
29 had been lost in the wilderness
30 for many days
31 and behold they had found
32 those kohanim of king Noach
33 in a place which they called Amulon

1 and they had started to possess the land of Amulon
2 and had started to till the ground
3 now the name of the leader
4 of those kohanim was Amulon
5
6 And it came to pass
7 that Amulon did plead with the Lamaniy
8 and he also sent forth their wives
9 who were the daughters of the Lamaniy
10 to plead with their brothers
11 that they should not destroy their husbands
12 and the Lamaniy had compassion
13 on Amulon and his brothers
14 and did not destroy them
15 because of their wives
16 and Amulon and his brothers did join the Lamaniy
17 and they were traveling in the wilderness
18 in search of the land of Nephi
19 when they discovered the land of Helam
20 which was possessed
21 by Almah and his brothers
22
23 And it came to pass
24 that the Lamaniy promised
25 unto Almah and his brothers
26 that if they would show them the way
27 which led to the land of Nephi
28 that they would grant unto them
29 their lives and their liberty
30 but after Almah had shown them the way
31 that led to the land of Nephi
32 the Lamaniy would not keep their promise
33 but they set guards round about the land of Helam

1   over Almah and his brothers

2   and the remainder of them went

3   to the land of Nephi

4   and a part of them returned

5   to the land of Helam

6   and also brought with them the wives and the children

7   of the guards who had been left in the land

8   and the king of the Lamaniy had granted unto Amulon

9   that he should be a king and a ruler over his people

10   who were in the land of Helam

11   nevertheless he should have no power

12   to do anything contrary

13   to the will of the king of the Lamaniy

14

15   And it came to pass

16   that Amulon did gain favor

17   in the eyes of the king of the Lamaniy

18   therefore the king of the Lamaniy granted

19   unto him and his brothers

20   that they should be appointed morim

21   over his people

22   yes even over the people

23   who were in the land of Shemlon

24   and in the land of Shilom

25   and in the land of Amulon

26   for the Lamaniy had taken possession

27   of all these lands

28   therefore the king of the Lamaniy had appointed kings

29   over all these lands

30   and now the name of the king of the Lamaniy was Laman

31   being called after the name of his father

32   and therefore he was called king Laman

33   and he was king over a numerous people

1 and he appointed morim
2 of the brothers of Amulon in every land
3 which was possessed by his people
4 and thus the language of Nephi began
5 to be taught among all the people of the Lamaniy
6 and they were a people friendly one with another
7 nevertheless they knew not Elohiym
8 neither did the brothers of Amulon teach them anything
9 concerning YHVH their Elohiym
10 neither the Torah of Moshe
11 nor did they teach them the words of Abinadi
12 but they taught them
13 that they should keep their record
14 and that they might write one to another
15 and thus the Lamaniy began
16 to increase in riches
17 and began to trade one with another
18 and grow great
19 and began to be a cunning and a wise people
20 as to the wisdom of the world
21 yes a very cunning people delighting
22 in all manner of wickedness and plunder
23 except it were among their own brothers
24
25 And now it came to pass
26 that Amulon began to exercise authority
27 over Almah and his brothers
28 and began to persecute him
29 and cause that his children
30 should persecute their children
31 for Amulon knew Almah
32 that he had been one of the king's kohanim
33 and that it was he that believed the words of Abinadi

1   and was driven out before the king

2   and therefore he was angry with him

3   for he was subject to king Laman

4   yet he exercised authority over them

5   and put tasks upon them

6   and put taskmasters over them

7

8   And it came to pass

9   that so great were their afflictions

10   that they began to cry mightily to Elohiym

11   and Amulon commanded them

12   that they should stop their cries

13   and he put guards over them to watch them

14   that whoever should be found calling upon Elohiym

15   should be put to death

16   and Almah and his people did not raise their voices

17   to YHVH their Elohiym

18   but did pour out their hearts to him

19   and he did know the thoughts of their hearts

20

21   And it came to pass

22   that the voice of YHVH came

23   to them in their afflictions saying

24

25   "Lift up your heads

26   and be of good comfort

27   for I know of the covenant

28   which you have made unto me

29   and I will covenant with my people

30   and deliver them out of bondage

31   and I will also ease the burdens

32   which are put upon your shoulders

33   that even you cannot feel them upon your backs

1 even while you are in bondage
2 and this will I do
3 that you may stand as witnesses for me hereafter
4 and that you may know of a certainty
5 that I YHVH Elohiym do visit my people
6 in their afflictions"
7
8 And now it came to pass
9 that the burdens which were laid
10 upon Almah and his brothers were made light
11 yes YHVH did strengthen them
12 that they could bear up their burdens with ease
13 and they did submit cheerfully
14 and with patience
15 to all the will of YHVH
16
17 And it came to pass
18 that so great was their faith
19 and their patience
20 that the voice of YHVH came
21 unto them again saying
22
23 "Be of good comfort
24 for on the next day
25 I will deliver you out of bondage"
26
27 and he said unto Almah
28
29 "You shall go before this people
30 and I will go with you
31 and deliver this people out of bondage"
32 Now it came to pass
33 that Almah and his people

1   in the night-time gathered their flocks together

2   and also of their grain

3   yes even all the nighttime were

4   they gathering their flocks together

5   and in the morning YHVH caused a deep sleep

6   to come upon the Lamaniy

7   yes and all their task-masters were in a profound sleep

8   and Almah and his people departed

9   into the wilderness

10   and when they had traveled all day

11   they pitched their tents in a valley

12   and they called the valley Almah

13   because he led their way in the wilderness

14   yes and in the valley of Almah

15   they poured out their thanks to Elohiym

16   because he had been merciful unto them

17   and eased their burdens

18   and had delivered them out of bondage

19   for they were in bondage

20   and none could deliver them

21   except it were YHVH their Elohiym

22   and they gave thanks to Elohiym

23   yes all their men and all their women

24   and all their children

25   that could speak lifted their voices

26   in the praises of their Elohiym

27

28   and now YHVH said unto Almah

29

30   "Be swift and get you

31   and this people out of this land

32   for the Lamaniy have awakened

33   and do pursue you

1 therefore get you out of this land
2 and I will stop the Lamaniy in this valley
3 that they come no further
4 in pursuit of this people"
5
6 And it came to pass
7 that they departed out of the valley
8 and took their journey
9 into the wilderness
10 and after they had been in the wilderness twelve days
11 they arrived in the land of Zarahemla
12 and king Mosheyahu did also receive them with joy
13 and now king Mosheyahu caused
14 that all the people should be gathered together
15 now there were not so many
16 of the children of Nephi
17 or so many of those
18 who were descendants of Nephi
19 as there were of the people of Zarahemla
20 who was a descendant of Mulek
21 and those who came with him
22 into the wilderness
23 and there were not so many
24 of the people of Nephi
25 and of the people of Zarahemla
26 as there were of the Lamaniy
27 yes they were not half so numerous
28 and now
29 all the people of Nephi were assembled together
30 and also all the people of Zarahemla
31 and they were gathered together
32 in two bodies
33

1   And it came to pass
2   that Mosheyahu did read
3   and caused to be read the records
4   of Zeniff to his people
5   yes he read the records
6   of the people of Zeniff
7   from the time they left the land of Zarahemla
8   until they returned again
9   and he also read the account of Almah
10 and his brothers
11 and all their afflictions
12 from the time they left the land of Zarahemla
13 until the time they returned again
14 and now when Mosheyahu had made an end
15 of reading the records his people
16 who stayed in the land were struck
17 with wonder and amazement
18 for they knew not what to think
19 for when they beheld those
20 that had been delivered out of bondage
21 they were filled
22 with exceedingly great joy
23
24 And again
25 when they thought of their brothers
26 who had been killed by the Lamaniy
27 they were filled with sorrow
28 and even shed many tears of sorrow
29 and again
30 when they thought
31 of the immediate goodness of Elohiym
32 and his power
33 in delivering Almah and his brothers

1 out of the hands of the Lamaniy

2 and of bondage

3 they did raise their voices and give thanks to Elohiym

4 and again

5 when they thought upon the Lamaniy

6 who were their brothers

7 of their sinful and polluted state

8 they were filled

9 with pain and anguish

10 for the welfare of their souls

11

12 And it came to pass

13 that those who were the children

14 of Amulon and his brothers

15 who had taken to wife the daughters of the Lamaniy

16 were displeased with the conduct of their fathers

17 and they would no longer be called

18 by the names of their fathers

19 therefore they took upon themselves the name of Nephi

20 that they might be called the children of Nephi

21 and be numbered among those who were called Nephiy

22 and now

23 all the people of Zarahemla were numbered with the Nephiy

24 and this because the kingdom had been conferred upon none

25 but those who were descendants of Nephi

26

27 And now it came to pass

28 that when Mosheyahu had made an end of speaking

29 and reading to the people he desired

30 that Almah should also speak to the people

31 and Almah did speak unto them

32 when they were assembled together in large bodies

33 and he went from one body to another preaching

1 unto the people repentance
2 and faith on YHVH
3 and he did exhort the people of Lemhi
4 and his brothers
5 all those that had been delivered out of bondage
6 that they should remember
7 that it was YHVH that did deliver them
8
9 And it came to pass
10 that after Almah had taught the people many things
11 and had made an end of speaking to them
12 that king Lemhi desired
13 that he might be immersed
14 and all his people desired
15 that they might be immersed also
16 therefore Almah did go forth into the water
17 and did immerse them
18 yes he did immerse them
19 after the manner he did his brothers
20 in the waters of Mur'mon
21 yes and as many as he did immerse did belong
22 to the assembly of Elohiym
23 and this because of their belief
24 on the words of Almah
25
26 And it came to pass
27 that king Mosheyahu granted unto Almah
28 that he might establish assemblies
29 throughout all the land of Zarahemla
30 and gave him power
31 to decree kohanim and morim
32 over every assembly
33 now this was done

1 because there were so many people

2 that they could not all be governed

3 by one moreh

4 neither could they all hear the word of Elohiym

5 in one assembly

6 therefore they did assemble themselves together

7 in different bodies being called assemblies

8 every assembly having

9 their kohanim and their morim

10 and every kohen preaching the word

11 according as it was delivered to him

12 by the mouth of Almah

13 and thus notwithstanding there being many assemblies

14 they were all one assembly

15 yes even the assembly of Elohiym

16 for there was nothing preached

17 in all the assemblies

18 except it were repentance and faith in Elohiym

19 and now there were seven assemblies

20 in the land of Zarahemla

21

22 And it came to pass

23 that whoever desired

24 to take upon them the name

25 of Mashiach or of Elohiym

26 they did join the assemblies of Elohiym

27 and they were called the people of Elohiym

28 and YHVH did pour out his Ruach upon them

29 and they were blessed and prospered

30 in the land

31

32 Now it came to pass

33 that there were many of the rising generation

1   that could not understand the words

2   of king Benyamin

3   being little children at the time he spoke unto his people

4   and they did not believe the tradition

5   of their fathers

6   they did not believe

7   what had been said

8   concerning the resurrection of the dead

9   neither did they believe

10   concerning the coming of Mashiach

11   and now because of their unbelief

12   they could not understand the word of Elohiym

13   and their hearts were hardened

14   and they would not be immersed

15   neither would they join the assembly

16   and they were a separate people

17   as to their faith

18   and remained so ever after

19   even in their carnal and sinful state

20   for they would not call upon YHVH their Elohiym

21   and now in the reign of Mosheyahu

22   they were not half so numerous

23   as the people of Elohiym

24   but because of the disagreements

25   among the brothers

26   they became more numerous

27

28   For it came to pass

29   that they did deceive many

30   with their flattering words

31   who were in the assembly

32   and did cause them to commit many sins

33   therefore it became necessary

1 that those who committed sin
2 that were in the assembly
3 should be warned by the assembly
4
5 And it came to pass
6 that they were brought before the kohanim
7 and delivered up unto the kohanim
8 by the morim
9 and the kohanim brought them before Almah
10 who was the Kohen Gadol
11 now king Mosheyahu had given Almah the authority
12 over the assembly
13 And it came to pass
14 that Almah did not know concerning them
15 but there were many witnesses against them
16 yes the people stood and testified
17 of their lawlessness in abundance
18 now there had not any such thing happened before
19 in the assembly
20 therefore Almah was troubled in his being
21 and he caused that they should be brought before the king
22 and he said unto the king
23
24 "behold here are many
25 whom we have brought before you
26 who are accused of their brothers
27 yes and they have been taken
28 in various kinds of lawlessness
29 and they do not repent of their lawlessness
30 therefore we have brought them before you
31 that you may judge them
32 according to their crimes
33 but king Mosheyahu said unto Almah

1
2   "behold I judge them not
3   therefore I deliver them
4   into your hands to be judged"
5
6   and now the being of Almah was again troubled
7   and he went and inquired of YHVH
8   what he should do concerning this matter
9   for he feared that he should do wrong
10 in the sight of Elohiym
11
12 And it came to pass
13 that after he had poured out
14 his whole nefesh to Elohiym
15 the voice of YHVH came to him saying
16
17 " Blessed are you Almah
18 and blessed are they
19 who were immersed in the waters of Mur'mon
20 you are blessed
21 because of your exceeding faith
22 in the words alone of my servant Abinadi
23 and blessed are they
24 because of their exceeding faith
25 in the words alone
26 which you hast spoken unto them
27 and blessed are you
28 because you have established
29 an assembly among this people
30 and they shall be established
31 and they shall be my people
32 yes blessed is this people
33 who are willing to bear my name

1 for in my name shall they be called
2 and they are mine
3 and because you have inquired of me
4 concerning the rebel you are blessed
5 you are my servant
6 and I covenant with you
7 that you shall have eternal life
8 and you shall serve me
9 and go forth in my name
10 and shall gather together my sheep
11 and he that will hear my voice
12 shall be my sheep
13 and him shall you receive into the assembly
14 and him will I also receive
15 for behold this is my assembly
16 whoever is immersed
17 shall be immersed unto repentance
18 and whoever you receive
19 shall believe in my name
20 and him will I freely forgive
21 for it is I that takes upon me the sins of the world
22 for it is I that has created them
23 and it is I that grants unto him
24 that believes unto the end a place
25 at my right hand
26
27 For behold
28 in my name are they called
29 and if they know me
30 they shall come forth
31 and shall have a place eternally
32 at my right hand
33

1 And it shall come to pass

2 that when the second trump shall sound

3 then shall they that never knew me come forth

4 and shall stand before me

5 and then shall they know

6 that I am YHVH their Elohiym

7 that I am their Redeemer

8 but they would not be redeemed

9 and then I will confess unto them

10 that I never knew them

11 and they shall depart into everlasting fire

12 prepared for the evil one and his angels

13

14 Therefore I say unto you

15 that he that will not hear my voice the same

16 shall you not receive into my assembly

17 for him I will not receive at the last day

18 therefore I say unto you

19 go and whoever rebels against me him

20 shall you judge

21 according to the sins which he has committed

22 and if he confess his sins

23 before you and me

24 and repents in the sincerity of his heart him

25 shall you forgive

26 and I will forgive him also

27 yes and as often as my people repent will I forgive them

28 their violations against me

29 and you shall also forgive one another your violations

30 for verily I say unto you he

31 that forgives not his neighbor's violations

32 when he says that he repents the same has

33 brought himself under condemnation

1 now I say unto you Go
2 and whoever will not repent of his sins the same
3 shall not be numbered among my people
4 and this shall be observed
5 from this time forward"
6
7 And it came to pass
8 when Almah had heard these words
9 he wrote them down
10 that he might have them
11 and that he might judge the people of that assembly
12 according to the mitzvot of Elohiym
13
14 And it came to pass
15 that Almah went and judged those
16 that had been taken in lawlessness
17 according to the word of YHVH
18 and whoever repented of their sins
19 and did confess them
20 them he did number
21 among the people of the assembly
22
23 And those that would not confess
24 their sins and repent of their lawlessness
25 the same were not numbered
26 among the people of the assembly
27 and their names were blotted out
28
29 And it came to pass
30 that Almah did regulate
31 all the affairs of the assembly
32 and they began again to have peace
33 and to prosper exceedingly

1   in the affairs of the assembly walking circumspectly
2   before Elohiym receiving many
3   and immersing many
4   and now all these things did Almah
5   and his fellow laborers do
6   who were over the assembly walking in all diligence
7   teaching the word of Elohiym in all things
8   suffering all manner of afflictions
9   being persecuted by all those
10 who did not belong to the assembly of Elohiym
11 and they did admonish their brothers
12 and they were also admonished every one
13 by the word of Elohiym
14 according to his sins
15 or to the sins which he had committed
16 being commanded of Elohiym
17 to pray without ceasing
18 and to give thanks in all things
19
20 And now it came to pass
21 that the persecutions
22 which were inflicted on the assembly
23 by the unbelievers became so great
24 that the assembly began
25 to complain and complain to their leaders
26 concerning the matter
27 and they did complain to Almah
28 and Almah laid the case before their king Mosheyahu
29 and Mosheyahu consulted with his kohanim
30
31 And it came to pass
32 that king Mosheyahu sent a proclamation
33 throughout the land round about

1 that there should not any unbeliever persecute any
2 of those who belonged to the assembly of Elohiym
3 and there was a strict command
4 throughout all the assemblies
5 that there should be no persecutions among them
6 that there should be an equality among all men
7 that they should let no pride
8 nor arrogance disturb their peace
9 that every man should esteem his neighbor
10 as himself laboring with their own hands
11 for their support
12 yes and all their kohanim and morim
13 should labor with their own hands
14 for their support in all cases
15 except it were in sickness
16 or in much want
17 and doing these things they did abound
18 in the grace of Elohiym
19 and there began to be much peace again in the land
20 and the people began to be very numerous
21 and began to scatter abroad upon the face of the earth
22 yes on the north and on the south
23 on the east and on the west
24 building large cities and villages
25 in all quarters of the land
26 and YHVH did visit them and prosper them
27 and they became a large and wealthy people
28
29 Now the sons of Mosheyahu were numbered
30 among the unbelievers
31 and also one of the sons of Almah was numbered
32 among them he being called Almah
33 after his father

1 nevertheless he became a very wicked
2 and an idolatrous man
3 and he was a man of many words
4 and did speak much flattery to the people
5 therefore he led many of the people to do
6 after the manner of his lawlessness
7 and he became a great hinderance
8 to the prosperity of the assembly of Elohiym
9 stealing away the hearts of the people
10 causing much dissension among the people
11 giving a chance for the enemy of Elohiym
12 to exercise his power over them
13
14 And now it came to pass
15 that while he was going about
16 to destroy the assembly of Elohiym
17 for he did go about secretly
18 with the sons of Mosheyahu
19 seeking to destroy the assembly
20 and to lead astray the people of YHVH contrary
21 to the mitzvot of Elohiym
22 or even the king
23 and as I said unto you
24 as they were going about rebelling against Elohiym
25 behold the angel of YHVH appeared unto them
26 and he descended as it were in a cloud
27 and he spoke as it were with a voice of thunder
28 which caused the earth to shake upon which they stood
29 and so great was their astonishment
30 that they fell to the earth
31 and understood not the words
32 which he spoke unto them
33 nevertheless he cried again saying

1
2 "Almah arise and stand forth
3 for why persecute you the assembly of Elohiym
4 for YHVH has said
5 This is my assembly
6 and I will establish it
7 and nothing shall overthrow it s
8 except it is the rebellion of my people"
9
10 and again the angel said
11
12 "Behold YHVH has heard the prayers of his people
13 and also the prayers of his servant Almah
14 who is your father
15 for he has prayed
16 with much faith concerning you
17 that you might be brought
18 to the knowledge of the truth
19 therefore for this purpose have I come
20 to convince you
21 of the power and authority of Elohiym
22 that the prayers of his servants might be answered
23 according to their faith
24 and now behold
25 can you dispute the power of Elohiym
26 for behold does not my voice shake the earth
27 and can you not also behold me before you
28 and I am sent from Elohiym
29 now I say unto you
30 go and remember the captivity of your fathers
31 in the land of Helam
32 and in the land of Nephi
33 and remember how great things he has done for them

1 for they were in bondage
2 and he has delivered them
3 and now I say unto you Almah go your way
4 and seek to destroy the assembly no more
5 that their prayers may be answered
6 and this even if you will of yourself be cast off'
7
8 And now it came to pass
9 that these were the last words
10 which the angel spoke unto Almah
11 and he departed
12 and now Almah
13 and those that were with him fell again
14 to the earth
15 for great was their astonishment
16 for with their own eyes
17 they had beheld an angel of YHVH
18 and his voice was as thunder
19 which shook the earth
20 and they knew that there was nothing
21 except the power of Elohiym
22 that could shake the earth
23 and cause it to tremble
24 as though it would part asunder
25 and now the astonishment of Almah was so great
26 that he became dumb
27 that he could not open his mouth
28 yes and he became weak
29 even that he could not move his hands
30 therefore he was taken by those that were with him
31 and carried helpless
32 even until he was laid before his father
33 and they rehearsed unto his father

1   all that had happened unto them
2   and his father rejoiced
3   for he knew
4   that it was the power of Elohiym
5   and he caused
6   that a multitude should be gathered together
7   that they might witness what YHVH had done for his son
8   and also for those that were with him
9   and he caused
10 that the kohanim should assemble themselves together
11 and they began
12 to fast and to pray to YHVH their Elohiym
13 that he would open the mouth of Almah
14 that he might speak
15 and also that his limbs might receive their strength
16 that the eyes of the people might be opened
17 to see and know of the goodness and glory of Elohiym
18
19 And it came to pass
20 after they had fasted and prayed
21 for the space of two days and two nights
22 the limbs of Almah received their strength
23 and he stood up
24 and began to speak unto them bidding them
25 to be of good comfort:
26 for said he
27
28 "I have repented of my sins
29 and have been redeemed of YHVH
30 behold I am born of the Ruach Elohiym"
31
32 and YHVH said unto me
33 'Marvel not that all mankind

1 yes men and women

2 all nations tribes tongues and people

3 must be born again

4 yes born of Elohiym changed

5 from their carnal and fallen state

6 to a state of righteousness

7 being redeemed of Elohiym

8 becoming his sons and daughters

9 and thus they become new creatures

10 and unless they do this

11 they can in not in any degree inherit the kingdom of Elohiym

12 I say unto you

13 unless this be the case

14 they must be cast off'

15

16 and this I know

17 because I was like to be cast off

18 nevertheless after wading

19 through much tribulation

20 repenting near unto death YHVH

21 in mercy has seen fit

22 to snatch me out of an everlasting burning

23 and I am born of Elohiym

24 my soul has been redeemed

25 from a malignant mind and the bonds of lawlessness

26 I was in the darkest abyss

27 but now I behold the marvelous light of Elohiym

28 my soul was racked with eternal torment

29 but I am snatched

30 and my soul is pained no more

31 I rejected my Redeemer

32 and denied that

33 which had been spoken of by our fathers

1 but now that they may foresee that he will come

2 and that he remembers every creature of his creating

3 he will make himself manifest unto all

4 yes every knee shall bow

5 and every tongue confess before him

6 yes even at the last day

7 when all men shall stand to be judged of him

8 then shall they confess

9 that he is Elohiym

10 then shall they confess

11 who live without Elohiym in the world

12 that the judgment of an everlasting punishment

13 is just upon them

14 and they shall quake and tremble and shrink

15 beneath the glance of his all searching eye"

16

17 And now it came to pass

18 that Almah began from this time forward

19 to teach the people

20 and those who were with Almah

21 at the time the angel appeared

22 unto them traveling round about

23 through all the land publishing

24 to all the people the things

25 which they had heard and seen

26 and preaching the word of Elohiym

27 in much tribulation

28 being greatly persecuted

29 by those who were unbelievers

30 being struck down by many of them

31 but notwithstanding all this

32 they did impart much consolation to the assembly

33 confirming their faith

1   and exhorting them with longsuffering

2   and much painful labor

3   to keep the mitzvot of Elohiym

4   and four of them were the sons of Mosheyahu

5   and their names were Ammon and Aharon

6   and Omner and Himni

7   these were the names of the sons of Mosheyahu

8   and they traveled throughout

9   all the land of Zarahemla and among all the people

10   who were under the reign of king Mosheyahu zealously striving

11   to repair all the injuries

12   which they had done to the assembly confessing all their sins

13   and publishing all the things which they had seen

14   and explaining the prophecies and the scriptures

15   to all who desired to hear them

16   and thus they were instruments

17   in the hands of Elohiym

18   in bringing many to the knowledge of the truth

19   yes to the knowledge of their Redeemer

20   and how blessed are they

21   for they did publish peace

22   they did publish good tidings of good

23   and they did declare unto the people

24   that YHVH reigns

25

26   Now it came to pass

27   that after the sons of Mosheyahu had done

28   all these things

29   they took a small number with them

30   and returned to their father the king

31   and desired of him

32   that he would grant unto them

33   that they might with these

1 whom they had selected go up
2 to the land of Nephi
3 that they might preach the things
4 which they had heard
5 and that they might impart the word of Elohiym
6 to their brothers the Lamaniy
7 that perhaps they might bring them
8 to the knowledge of YHVH their Elohiym
9 and convince them of the lawlessness of their fathers
10 and that perhaps they might cure them
11 of their hatred towards the Nephiy
12 that they might also be brought
13 to rejoice in YHVH their Elohiym
14 that they might become friendly to one another
15 and that there should be no more contentions
16 in all the land
17 which YHVH their Elohiym had given them
18 now they desired that salvation should be declared
19 to every creature
20 for they could not bear
21 that any human soul should perish
22 yes even the very thoughts that any soul
23 should endure endless torment did cause them
24 to quake and tremble
25 and thus did the Ruach YHVH work upon them
26 for they were the very vilest of sinners
27 and YHVH saw fit in his infinite mercy
28 to spare them
29 nevertheless they suffered much anguish of soul
30 because of their lawlessness
31 suffering much and fearing
32 that they should be cast off forever
33

1 And it came to pass
2 that they did plead with their father many days
3 that they might go up to the land of Nephi
4 and king Mosheyahu went and inquired of YHVH
5 if he should let his sons go up
6 among the Lamaniy to preach the word
7 and YHVH said unto Mosheyahu
8 "Let them go up
9 for many shall believe on their words
10 and they shall have eternal life
11 and I will deliver your sons out
12 of the hands of the Lamaniy"
13
14 And it came to pass
15 that Mosheyahu granted
16 that they might go and do
17 according to their request
18 and they took their journey
19 into the wilderness
20 to go up to preach the word
21 among the Lamaniy
22 and I shall give an account
23 of their proceedings hereafter
24 now king Mosheyahu had no one
25 to confer the kingdom upon
26 for there was not any of his sons
27 who would accept of the kingdom
28 therefore he took the records
29 which were engraved on the plates of brass
30 and also the plates of Nephi
31 and all the things
32 which he had kept and preserved
33 according to the mitzvot of Elohiym

1 after having translated
2 and caused to be written the records
3 which were on the plates of gold
4 which had been found by the people of Lemhi
5 which were delivered to him by the hand of Lemhi
6 and this he did
7 because of the great anxiety of his people
8 for they desired beyond measure
9 to know concerning those people
10 who had been destroyed
11 and now he translated them
12 by the means of those two stones
13 which were fastened into the two rims of a bow
14
15 Now these things were prepared
16 from the beginning
17 and were handed down
18 from generation to generation
19 for the purpose of interpreting languages
20 and they have been kept and preserved
21 by the hand of YHVH
22 that he should reveal to every creature
23 who should possess the land the lawlessness
24 and abominations of his people
25 and whoever has these things is called seer
26 after the manner of old times
27 now after Mosheyahu had finished translating these records
28 behold it gave an account of the people
29 who were destroyed
30 from the time that they were destroyed back
31 to the building of the great tower
32 at the time YHVH confounded the language of the people
33 and they were scattered abroad

1   upon the face of all the earth
2   yes and even from that time back
3   until the creation of Adam
4   now this account did cause the people of Mosheyahu
5   to mourn exceedingly
6   yes they were filled with sorrow
7   nevertheless it gave them much knowledge
8   in the which they did rejoice
9   and this account
10 shall be written hereafter
11 for behold it is necessary that all people
12 should know the things
13 which are written in this account
14
15 And now as I said unto you
16 that after king Mosheyahu had done these things
17 he took the plates of brass
18 and all the things which he had kept
19 and conferred them upon Almah
20 who was the son of Almah
21 yes all the records and also the interpreters
22 and conferred them upon him
23 and commanded him
24 that he should keep and preserve them
25 and also keep a record of the people handing them down
26 from one generation to another
27 even as they had been handed down
28 from the time that Lechi left Yerushalayim
29 now when Mosheyahu had done this he sent out
30 throughout all the land
31 among all the people desiring
32 to know their will
33 concerning who should be their king

1
2   And it came to pass
3   that the voice of the people came saying
4
5   "We desire that Aharon your son
6   should be our king and our ruler"
7
8   Now Aharon had gone up to the land of Nephi
9   therefore the king could not confer the kingdom upon him
10 neither would Aharon take upon him the kingdom
11 neither were any of the sons of Mosheyahu willing
12 to take upon them the kingdom
13 therefore king Mosheyahu sent again
14 among the people
15 yes even a written word sent he
16 among the people
17 and these were the words
18 that were written saying:
19
20 "Behold O you my people
21 or my brothers
22 for I esteem you as such I desire
23 that you should consider the cause
24 which you are called to consider
25 for you desire to have a king
26
27 Now I declare unto you that he
28 to whom the kingdom does rightly belong has declined
29 and will not take upon him the kingdom
30 and now if there should be another appointed in his place
31 behold I fear there would rise contentions among you
32 and who knows but what my son
33 to whom the kingdom does belong

1 should turn to be angry

2 and draw away a part of this people after him

3 which would cause wars and contentions among you

4 which would be the cause of shedding much blood

5 and perverting the way of YHVH

6 yes and destroy the souls of many people

7 now I say unto you

8 let us be wise and consider these things

9 for we have no right to destroy my son

10 neither should we have any right to destroy another

11 if he should be appointed in his place

12 and if my son should turn again

13 to his pride and vain things he would recall the things

14 which he had said

15 and claim his right to the kingdom

16 which would cause him

17 and also this people to commit much sin

18 and now let us be wise

19 and look forward to these things

20 and do that which will make

21 for the peace of this people

22 therefore I will be your king the remainder of my days

23 nevertheless let us appoint judges to judge this people

24 according to our mishpatim

25 and we will newly arrange the affairs of this people

26 for we will appoint wise men

27 to be judges that will judge this people

28 according to the mitzvot of Elohiym

29

30 Now it is better

31 that a man should be judged of Elohiym than of man

32 for the judgments of Elohiym are always just

33 but the judgments of man are not always just

1 therefore if it were possible
2 that you could have just men to be your kings
3 who would establish the mitzvot of Elohiym
4 and judge this people according to his mitzvot
5 yes if you could have men for your kings
6 who would do even as my father Benyamin did
7 for this people
8 I say unto you
9 if this could always be the case
10 then it would be necessary
11 that you should always have kings
12 to rule over you
13 and even I myself have labored
14 with all the power and faculties which I have possessed
15 to teach you the mitzvot of Elohiym
16 and to establish peace throughout the land
17 that there should be no wars nor contentions
18 no stealing nor plundering
19 nor murdering nor any manner of lawlessness
20 and whoever has committed lawlessness him have I punished
21 according to the crime which he has committed
22 according to the Torah which has been given to us
23 by our fathers
24
25 Now I say unto you
26 that because all men are not just it is not necessary
27 that you should have a king or kings
28 to rule over you
29 for behold
30 how much lawlessness does one wicked king cause to be committed
31 yes and what great destruction
32 yes remember king Noach his wickedness and his abominations
33 and also the wickedness and abominations of his people

1   behold what great destruction did come upon them
2   and also because of their lawlessness
3   they were brought into bondage
4   and were it not for the intervention
5   of their all wise Creator
6   and this because of their sincere repentance
7   they must unavoidably remain in bondage until now
8   but behold he did deliver them
9   because they did humble themselves before him
10 and because they cried mightily
11 unto him he did deliver them out of bondage
12 and thus does YHVH work with his power in all cases
13 among the children of men
14 extending the arm of mercy towards them
15 that put their trust in him
16 and behold
17 now I say unto you
18 you cannot dethrone a lawless king
19 except it be through much contention
20 and the shedding of much blood
21 for behold
22 he has his friends in lawlessness
23 and he keeps his guards about him
24 and he tears up the laws of those
25 who have reigned in righteousness before him
26 and he tramples under his feet the mitzvot of Elohiym
27 and he enacts mishpatim and sends them forth among his people
28 yes mishpatim after the manner of his own wickedness
29 and whoever does not obey his mishpatim
30 he causes to be destroyed
31 and whoever does rebel against him
32 he will send his armies against them to war
33 and if he can he will destroy them

1 and thus an unrighteous king does pervert the ways

2 of all righteousness

3

4 And now behold

5 I say unto you

6 it is not necessary

7 that such abominations

8 should come upon you

9 therefore choose you

10 by the voice of this people judges

11 that you may be judged

12 according to the mishpatim

13 which have been given you by our fathers which are correct

14 and which were given them by the hand of YHVH

15

16 Now it is not common

17 that the voice of the people desires anything contrary

18 to that which is right

19 but it is common

20 for the lesser part of the people

21 to desire that which is not right

22 therefore this shall you observe

23 and make it your chuk

24 to do your business

25 by the voice of the people

26

27 And if the time comes

28 that the voice of the people does choose lawlessness

29 then is the time

30 that the judgments of Elohiym will come upon you

31 yes then is the time he will visit you

32 with great destruction

33 even as he has previously visited this land

1 and now if you have judges

2 and they do not judge you

3 according to Torah

4 which has been given you can cause

5 that they may be judged of a higher judge

6 If your higher judges do not judge righteous judgments

7 you shall cause

8 that a small number of your lower judges

9 should be gathered together

10 and they shall judge your higher judges

11 according to the voice of the people

12 and I command you to do these things

13 in the wisdom of YHVH

14 and I command you to do these things

15 and that you have no king

16 that if these people commit sins and lawlessness

17 they shall be answered upon their own heads

18

19 For behold I say unto you the sins

20 of many people have been caused

21 by the lawlessness of their kings

22 therefore their lawlessness are answered

23 upon the heads of their kings

24 and now I desire

25 that this inequality should be no more in this land

26 especially among this my people

27 but I desire that this land be a land of liberty

28 and every man may enjoy his rights and privileges alike

29 so long as YHVH sees fit

30 that we may live and inherit the land

31 yes even as long as any of our posterity remains

32 upon the face of the land"

33

1 And many more things
2 did king Mosheyahu write unto them
3 unfolding unto them
4 all the trials and troubles of a righteous king
5 yes all the painful labor of soul for their people
6 and also all the complaining of the people to their king
7 and he explained it all unto them
8 and he told them
9 that these things ought not to be
10 but that the burden should come upon all the people
11 that every man might bear his part
12 and he also unfolded unto them
13 all the disadvantages they labored under
14 by having an unrighteous king to rule over them
15 yes all his lawlessness and abominations
16 and all the wars and contentions
17 and bloodshed and the stealing
18 and the plundering and the committing of whoredoms
19 and all manner of lawlessness
20 which cannot be enumerated telling them
21 that these things ought not to be
22 that they were expressly opposite
23 to the mitzvot of Elohiym
24
25 And now it came to pass
26 after king Mosheyahu had sent
27 these things forth
28 among the people
29 they were convinced
30 of the truth of his words
31 therefore they relinquished
32 their desires for a king
33 and became exceedingly anxious

1   that every man should have an equal chance
2   throughout all the land
3   yes and every man expressed a willingness
4   to answer for his own sins
5
6   Therefore it came to pass
7   that they assembled themselves together
8   in bodies throughout the land
9   to cast in their voices
10   concerning who should be their judges
11   to judge them according to the Torah
12   which had been given them
13   and they were exceedingly happy
14   because of the liberty
15   which had been granted unto them
16   and they did grow strong in love
17   towards Mosheyahu
18   yes they did esteem him more
19   than any other man
20   for they did not look upon him
21   as a tyrant who was seeking for gain
22   yes for that lust for riches
23   which does corrupt the soul
24   for he had not exacted riches of them
25   neither had he delighted in the shedding of blood
26   but he had established peace in the land
27   and he had granted unto his people
28   that they should be delivered
29   from all manner of bondage
30   therefore they did esteem him
31   yes exceedingly beyond measure
32
33   And it came to pass

1 that they did appoint judges

2 to rule over them

3 or to judge them

4 according to Torah

5 and this they

6 did throughout all the land

7

8 And it came to pass

9 that Almah was appointed

10 to be the first chief judge he being

11 also the Kohen Gadol his father

12 having conferred the office upon him

13 and having given him the charge

14 concerning all the affairs of the assembly

15

16 And now it came to pass

17 that Almah did walk

18 in the ways of YHVH

19 and he did keep his mitzvot

20 and he did judge righteous judgments

21 and there was continual peace

22 through the land

23 and thus commenced the reign of the judges

24 throughout all the land of Zarahemla

25 among all the people

26 who were called the Nephiy

27 and Almah was the first

28 and chief judge

29

30 And now it came to pass

31 that his father died

32 being eighty and two years old having lived

33 to fulfil the mitzvot of Elohiym

1
2 And it came to pass
3 that Mosheyahu died also
4 in the thirty and third year of his reign
5 being sixty and three years old making
6 in the whole five hundred and nine years
7 from the time Lechi left Yerushalayim
8 and thus ended the reign of the kings
9 over the people of Nephi
10 and thus ended the days of Almah
11 who was the founder of their assembly
12
13
14
15
16
17
18
19
20
21
22
23
24
25
26
27
28
29
30
31
32
33
34

1
2   **SEFER ALMAH**
3
4
5   The account of Alma
6   who was the son of Alma the first and chief judge
7   over the people of Nephi
8   and also the Kohen Gadol over the assembly
9   an account of the reign of the judges
10   and the wars and contentions among the people
11   and also an account of a war between the Nephiy and the Lamaniy
12   according to the record of Alma the first and chief judge
13
14
15
16
17
18
19
20
21
22
23
24
25
26
27
28
29
30
31
32
33

3-WARING A GOOD WAR

1
2 Now it came to pass
3 that in the first year of the reign of the judges
4 over the people of Nephi
5 from this time forward king Mosheyahu having gone the way
6 of all the earth having warred a good warfare walking uprightly
7 before Elohiym leaving none to reign in his stead
8 nevertheless he had established the mishpatim
9 and they were acknowledged by the people
10 therefore they were obliged to abide by the mishpatim
11 which he had made
12
13 And it came to pass
14 that in the first year of the reign of Alma in the judgment seat
15 there was a man brought before him to be judged a man
16 who was large and was noted for his much strength
17 and he had gone about among the people preaching to them
18 that which he termed to be the word of Elohiym bearing down
19 against the assembly declaring unto the people
20 that every priest and teacher ought to become popular
21 and they ought not to labor with their hands
22 but that they ought to be supported by the people
23 and he also testified unto the people
24 that all mankind should be saved at the last day
25 and that they need not fear nor tremble
26 but that they might lift up their heads and rejoice
27 for YHVH had created all men and had also redeemed all men
28 and in the end all men should have eternal life
29
30 And it came to pass that
31 he did teach these things so much
32 that many did believe on his words even so many
33 that they began to support him and give him money

1 and he began to be lifted up in the pride of his heart

2 and to wear very costly apparel

3 yes and even began to establish a assembly

4 after the manner of his preaching

5

6 And it came to pass

7 as he was going to preach to those

8 who believed on his word he met a man

9 who belonged to the assembly of Elohiym

10 yes even one of their teachers

11 and he began to contend with him sharply

12 that he might lead away the people of the assembly

13 but the man withstood him admonishing him

14 with the words of Elohiym

15 now the name of the man was Gideon

16 and it was he who was an instrument in the hands of Elohiym

17 in delivering the people of Limhi out of bondage

18 now because Gideon withstood him

19 with the words of Elohiym he was wroth with Gideon

20 and drew his sword and began to smite him

21 now Gideon being stricken with many years

22 therefore he was not able to withstand his blows

23 therefore he was killed by the sword

24 and the man who killed him was taken by the people of the assembly

25 and was brought before Alma to be judged

26 according to the crimes which he had committed

27

28 And it came to pass

29 that he stood before Alma

30 and pled for himself with much boldness

31 but Alma said unto him

32

33 "Behold this is the first time that priestcraft

1. has been introduced among this people
2. and behold you are not only guilty of priestcraft
3. but have endeavored to enforce it by the sword
4. and were priestcraft to be enforced among this people
5. it would prove their entire destruction
6. and you have shed the blood of a righteous man
7. yes a man who has done much good among this people
8. and were we to spare you his blood would come upon us
9. for vengeance
10. therefore you are condemned to die according to the mishpatim
11. which has been given us by Mosheyahu our last king
12. and it has been acknowledged by this people
13. therefore this people must abide by the Mishpatim"
14.
15. And it came to pass
16. that they took him and his name was Nachor
17. and they carried him upon the top of the hill Manti
18. and there he was caused or rather did acknowledge
19. between the heavens and the earth
20. that what he had taught to the people was contrary
21. to the word of Elohiym
22. and there he suffered an dishonorable death
23. nevertheless this did not put an end
24. to the spreading of priestcraft through the land
25. for there were many who loved the vain things of the world
26. and they went forth preaching false teachings
27. and this they did for the sake of riches and honor
28. nevertheless they did not lie if it were known for fear of the mishpatim
29. for liars were punished
30. therefore they pretended to preach according to their belief
31. and now the Torah could have no power on any man for his belief
32. and they did not steal for fear of the mishpatim
33. for such were punished neither did they rob

1 nor murder for he that murdered was punished unto death

2

3 But it came to pass

4 that whoever did not belong to the assembly of Elohiym

5 began to persecute those that did belong to the assembly of Elohiym

6 and had taken upon them the name of Mashiach

7 yes they did persecute them and afflict them

8 with all manner of words

9 and this because of their humility

10 because they were not proud in their own eyes

11 and because they did impart the word of Elohiym one with another

12 without money and without price

13 now there was a strict chukkim among the people of the assembly

14 that there should not any man belonging to the assembly arise

15 and persecute those that did not belong to the assembly

16 and that there should be no persecution among themselves

17 nevertheless there were many among them who began to be proud

18 and began to contend warmly with their adversaries even unto blows

19 yes they would strike one another with their fists

20 now this was in the second year of the reign of Alma

21 and it was a cause of much affliction to the assembly

22 yes it was the cause of much trial with the assembly

23 for the hearts of many were hardened

24 and their names were blotted out

25 that they were remembered no more

26 among the people of Elohiym

27 and also many withdrew themselves from among them

28

29 Now this was a great trial

30 to those that did stand fast in the faith

31 nevertheless they were steadfast and immovable

32 in keeping the mitzvot of Elohiym

33 and they bore with patience the persecution

1 which was heaped upon them
2 and when the priests left their labor to impart the word of Elohiym
3 unto the people the people also left their labors to hear the word of Elohiym
4 and when the priest had imparted unto them the word of Elohiym
5 they all returned again diligently unto their labors
6 and the priest not esteeming himself above his hearers
7 for the preacher was no better than the hearer
8 neither was the teacher any better than the learner
9 and thus they were all equal
10 and they did all labor every man according to his strength
11 and they did impart of their substance every man
12 according to that which he had
13 to the poor and the needy and the sick and the afflicted
14 and they did not wear costly apparel
15 yet they were clean and pleasant to look upon
16 and thus they did establish the affairs of the assembly
17 and thus they began to have continual peace again
18 notwithstanding all their persecutions
19 and now because of the steadiness of the assembly
20 they began to be exceedingly rich having abundance
21 of all things whatsoever they stood in need
22 an abundance of flocks and herds and fatlings of every kind
23 and also abundance of grain and of gold and of silver
24 and of precious things and abundance of silk and finely spun linen
25 and all manner of good plain cloth
26 and thus in their prosperous circumstances
27 they did not send away any who were naked or that were hungry
28 or that were thirsty or that were sick or that had not been nourished
29 and they did not set their hearts upon riches
30 therefore they were liberal to all
31 both old and young both bond and free
32 both male and female whether out of the assembly
33 or in the assembly having no respect to persons

1 as to those who stood in need
2 and thus they did prosper and become far more wealthy
3 than those who did not belong to their assembly
4 for those who did not belong to their assembly did indulge themselves
5 in sorceries and in idolatry or idleness
6 and in babblings and in envyings and strife wearing costly apparel
7 being lifted up in the pride of their own eyes
8 persecuting
9 lying
10 thieving
11 robbing
12 committing whoredoms
13 and murdering and all manner of wickedness
14 nevertheless the mishpatim were put in force upon all those
15 who did transgress it inasmuch as it was possible
16
17 And it came to pass
18 that by thus exercising the mishpatim upon them
19 every man suffering according to that which he had done
20 they became more stable and did not depart from the Torah
21 if it were known
22 therefore there was much peace among the people of Nephi
23 until the fifth year of the reign of the judges
24
25 And it came to pass
26 in the commencement of the fifth year of their reign
27 there began to be a contention among the people
28 for a certain man being called Amlici
29 he being a very cunning man
30 yes a wise man as to the wisdom of the world he
31 being after the order of the man that killed Gideon by the sword
32 who was executed according to the Torah
33 now this Amlici had by his cunning drawn away much people after him

1   even so much that they began to be very powerful

2   and they began to endeavor to establish Amlici

3   to be a king over the people

4   now this was alarming to the people of the assembly

5   and also to all those who had not been drawn away

6   after the persuasions of Amlici

7   for they knew that according to the Torah

8   that such things must be established by the voice of the people

9   therefor if it were possible

10 that Amlici should gain the voice of the people he

11 being a wicked man would deprive them

12 of their rights and privileges of the assembly

13 for it was his intent to destroy the assembly of Elohiym

14

15 And it came to pass

16 that the people assembled themselves together throughout all the land

17 every man according to his mind

18 whether it were for or against Amlici in separate bodies having

19 much dispute and wonderful contentions one with another

20 and thus they did assemble themselves together

21 to cast in their voices concerning the matter

22 and they were laid before the judges

23

24 And it came to pass

25 that the voice of the people came against Amlici

26 that he was not made king over the people

27 now this did cause much joy in the hearts of those who were against him

28 but Amlici did stir up those who were in his favor

29 to anger against those who were not in his favor

30

31 And it came to pass

32 that they gathered themselves together

33 and did consecrate Amlici to be their king

1   now when Amlici was made king over them he commanded them

2   that they should take up arms against their brothers

3   and this he did that he might subject them to him

4   now the people of Amlici were distinguished by the name of Amlici being

5   called Amliciy

6   and the remainder were called Nephiy or the people of Elohiym

7   therefor the people of the Nephiy were aware of the intent of the Amliciy

8   and therefore they did prepare to meet them

9   yes they did arm themselves

10   with swords and with cimeters

11   and with bows and with arrows

12   and with stones and with slings

13   and with all manner of weapons of war of every kind

14   and thus they were prepared to meet the Amliciy at the time of their coming

15   and there were appointed captains and higher captains and chief captains

16   according to their numbers

17

18   And it came to pass

19   that Amlici did arm his men

20   with all manner of weapons of war of every kind

21   and he also appointed rulers and leaders over his people

22   to lead them to war against their brothers

23

24   And it came to pass

25   that the Amliciy came upon the hill Amnihu

26   which was east of the river Tzidon

27   which ran by the land of Zarahemla

28   and there they began to make war with the Nephiy

29   now Alma being the chief judge and the governor of the people of Nephi

30   therefore he went up with his people

31   yes with his captains and chief captains

32   yes at the head of his armies against the Amliciy to battle

33   and they began to slay the Amliciy upon the hill east of Tzidon

1 and the Amliciy did contend with the Nephiy with great strength
2 insomuch that many of the Nephiy did fall before the Amliciy
3 nevertheless YHVH did strengthen the hand of the Nephiy
4 that they killed the Amliciy with great slaughter
5 that they began to flee before them
6
7 And it came to pass
8 that the Nephiy did pursue the Amliciy all that day
9 and did slay them with much slaughter
10 insomuch that there were slain of the Amliciy
11 twelve thousand five hundred thirty and two souls
12 and there were slain of the Nephiy
13 six thousand five hundred sixty and two souls
14
15 And it came to pass
16 that when Alma could pursue the Amliciy no longer he caused
17 that his people should pitch their tents
18 in the valley of Gideon the valley being called
19 after that Gideon who was slain
20 by the hand of Nachor with the sword
21 and in this valley the Nephiy did pitch their tents for the night
22 and Alma sent spies to follow the remnant of the Amliciy
23 that he might know of their plans and their plots
24 whereby he might guard himself against them
25 that he might preserve his people from being destroyed
26 now those whom he had sent out to watch the camp
27 of the Amliciy were called Zeram and Amnor
28 and Manti and Limher
29 these were they who went out with their men
30 to watch the camp of the Amliciy
31
32 And it came to pass
33 that on the next day they returned

1 into the camp of the Nephiy

2 in great haste being greatly astonished

3 and struck with much fear saying

4

5 "behold we followed the camp of the Amliciy

6 and to our great astonishment in the land of Minon

7 above the land of Zarahemla in the course

8 of the land of Nephi we saw a numerous host of the Lamaniy

9 and behold the Amliciy have joined them

10 and they are upon our brothers in that land

11 and they are fleeing before them with their flocks

12 and their wives and their children towards our city

13 and except we are quick they obtain possession of our city

14 and our fathers and our wives and our children be killed"

15

16 And it came to pass

17 that the people of Nephi took their tents

18 and departed out of the valley of Gideon

19 towards their city

20 which was the city of Zarahemla

21 and behold as they were crossing the river Tzidon

22 the Lamaniy and the Amliciy being as numerous

23 almost as it were as the sands of the sea came upon them

24 to destroy them

25 nevertheless the Nephiy being strengthened

26 by the hand of YHVH having prayed mightily to him

27 that he would deliver them out of the hands of their enemies

28 therefore YHVH did hear their cries and did strengthen them

29 and the Lamaniy and the Amliciy did fall before them

30

31 And it came to pass

32 that Alma fought with Amlici with the sword face to face

33 and they did contend mightily one with another

1

2 And it came to pass

3 that Alma being a man of Elohiym being exercised

4 with much faith cried saying

5

6 "O YHVH have mercy and spare my life

7 that I may be an instrument in your hands

8 to save and preserve this people"

9

10 Now when Alma had said these words

11 he contended again with Amlici

12 and he was strengthened insomuch

13 that he slew Amlici with the sword

14 and he also contended with the king of the Lamaniy

15 but the king of the Lamaniy fled back from before Alma

16 and sent his guards to contend with Alma

17 but Alma with his guards contended with the guards of the king of the

18 Lamaniy

19 until he slew and drove them back

20 and thus he cleared the ground or rather the bank

21 which was on the west of the river Tzidon throwing the bodies

22 of the Lamaniy who had been slain into the waters of Tzidon

23 that thereby his people might have room to cross

24 and contend with the Lamaniy and the Amliciy

25 on the west side of the river Tzidon

26

27 And it came to pass

28 that when they had all crossed the river Tzidon

29 that the Lamaniy and the Amliciy began to flee before them

30 notwithstanding they were so numerous

31 that they could not be numbered

32 and they fled before the Nephiy towards the wilderness

33 which was west and north away beyond the borders of the land

1 and the Nephiy did pursue them with their might

2 and did slay them

3 yes they were met on every hand and slain

4 and driven until they were scattered on the west and on the north

5 until they had reached the wilderness

6 which was called Har Mountz

7 and it was that part of the wilderness

8 which was infested by wild and ravenous beasts

9

10 And it came to pass

11 that many died in the wilderness of their wounds

12 and were devoured by those beasts

13 and also the vultures of the air

14 and their bones have been found

15 and have been heaped up on the earth

16

17 And it came to pass that the Nephiy who were not slain

18 by the weapons of war after having buried those who had been slain

19 now the number of the slain were not numbered

20 because of the greatness of their number

21 after they had finished burying their dead

22 they all returned to their lands

23 and to their houses and their wives and their children

24 now many women and children had been slain with the sword

25 and also many of their flocks and their herds

26 and also many of their fields of grain were destroyed

27 for they were trodden down by the armies of men

28 and now as many of the Lamaniy and the Amliciy

29 who had been slain upon the bank of the river Tzidon were cast

30 into the waters of Tzidon

31 and behold their bones are in the depths of the sea

32 and they are many

33 and the Amliciy were distinguished from the Nephiy

1 for they had marked themselves with red in their foreheads
2 after the manner of the Lamaniy
3 nevertheless they had not shorn their heads
4 like unto the Lamaniy
5 now the heads of the Lamaniy were shorn and they were naked
6 except it were skin which was girded about their loins
7 and also their armor which was girded about them
8 and their bows and their arrows
9 and their stones and their slings and so forth
10 and the skins of the Lamaniy were dark according to the mark
11 which was set upon their fathers
12 which was a curse upon them
13 because of their transgression and their rebellion
14 against their brothers who consisted of Nephi Yacov
15 and Yoseph and Shem who were just and holy men
16 and their brothers sought to destroy them
17 therefore they were cursed
18 and YHVH Elohiym set a mark upon them
19 yes upon Laman and Lemuel
20 and also the sons of Ishmael and Ishmaelitish women
21 and this was done that their seed might be distinguished from the seed
22 of their brothers that thereby YHVH Elohiym might preserve his people
23 that they might not mix and believe in incorrect traditions
24 which would prove their destruction
25
26
27 And it came to pass
28 that whoever did mingle his seed with
29 that of the Lamaniy did bring the same curse upon his seed
30 therefor whoever suffered himself to be led away
31 by the Lamaniy was called under that head
32 and there was a mark set upon him
33

1   And it came to pass

2   that whosoever would not believe in the tradition of the Lamaniy

3   but believed those records

4   which were brought out of the land of Yerushalayim

5   and also in the tradition of their fathers

6   which were correct

7   who believed in the mitzvot of Elohiym

8   and kept them were called the Nephiy

9   or the people of Nephi from that time forth

10   and it is they who have kept the records

11   which are true of their people

12   and also of the people of the Lamaniy

13   now we will return again to the Amliciy

14   for they also had a mark set upon them

15   yes they set the mark upon themselves

16   yes even a mark of red upon their foreheads

17   thus the word of Elohiym is fulfilled

18   for these are the words which he said to Nephi

19

20   "Behold the Lamaniy have I cursed

21   and I will set a mark on them that they

22   and their seed may be separated from you and your seed

23   from this time forward and forever

24   except they repent of their wickedness

25   and turn to me that I may have mercy upon them

26   and again I will set a mark upon him

27   that mingles his seed with your brothers

28   that they may be cursed also

29   and again I will set a mark upon him

30   that fights against you and your seed

31   and again I say he that departs from you

32   shall no more be called your seed

33   and I will bless you and whoever shall be called your seed

1   from this time forward and forever
2   and these were the promises of YHVH unto Nephi and to his seed"
3
4   Now the Amliciy knew not
5   that they were fulfilling the words of Elohiym
6   when they began to mark themselves in their foreheads
7   nevertheless they had come out
8   in open rebellion against Elohiym
9   therefore it was necessary that the curse should fall upon them
10 now I would that you should see
11 that they brought upon themselves the curse
12 and even so does every man that is cursed
13 bring upon himself his own condemnation
14
15 Now it came to pass
16 that not many days after the battle
17 which was fought in the land of Zarahemla
18 by the Lamaniy and the Amliciy
19 that there was another army of the Lamaniy came in
20 upon the people of Nephi in the same place
21 where the first army met the Amliciy
22
23 And it came to pass
24 that there was an army sent
25 to drive them out of their land
26 now Alma himself being afflicted
27 with a wound did not go up
28 to battle at this time against the Lamaniy
29 but he sent up a numerous army against them
30 and they went up and killed many of the Lamaniy
31 and drove the remainder of them
32 out of the borders of their land
33 and then they returned again

1　and began to establish peace in the land being troubled no more

2　for a time with their enemies

3　now all these things were done

4　yes all these wars and contentions were commenced

5　and ended in the fifth year of the reign of the judges

6　and in one year were thousands and tens of thousands of souls sent

7　to the eternal world that they might reap their rewards

8　according to their works

9　whether they were good or whether they were bad

10　to reap eternal happiness or eternal misery

11　according to the ruach which they enlisted to obey

12　whether it be a good ruach or a bad one

13　for every man receives wages of him whom he enlists to obey

14　and this according to the words of the ruach of prophecy

15　therefore let it be according to the truth

16　and thus ends the fifth year of the reign of the judges

17

18　Now it came to pass

19　in the sixth year of the reign of the judges over the people of Nephi

20　there were no contentions nor wars in the land of Zarahemla

21　but the people were afflicted

22　yes greatly afflicted for the loss of their brothers

23　and also for the loss of their flocks and herds

24　and also for the loss of their fields of grain

25　which were trodden under foot and destroyed by the Lamaniy

26　and so great were their afflictions

27　that every soul had cause to mourn

28　and they believed that it was the judgments of Elohiym sent upon them

29　because of their wickedness and their abominations

30　therefore they were awakened to a remembrance of their duty

31　and they began to establish the assembly more fully

32　yes and many were immersed in the waters of Tzidon

33　and were joined to the assembly of Elohiym

1   yes they were immersed by the hand of Alma
2   who had been consecrated the high priest
3   over the people of the assembly
4   by the hand of his father Alma
5
6
7   And it came to pass
8   in the seventh year of the reign of the judges
9   there were about three thousand five hundred souls
10 that united themselves to the assembly of Elohiym
11 and were immersed
12 and thus ended the seventh year of the reign of the judges
13 over the people of Nephi
14 and there was continual peace in all that time
15
16 And it came to pass
17 in the eighth year of the reign of the judges
18 that the people of the assembly began to wax proud
19 because of their exceeding riches
20 and their fine silks and their fine-twined linen
21 and because of their many flocks and herds
22 and their gold and their silver
23 and all manner of precious things
24   which they had obtained by their industry
25 and in all these things were they lifted up
26 in the pride of their eyes
27 for they began to wear very costly apparel
28 now this was the cause of much affliction to Alma
29 yes and to many of the people whom Alma had set apart
30 to be morim and kohanim and elders over the assembly
31 yes many of them were sorely grieved for the wickedness
32 which they saw beginning to be among their people
33 for they saw and beheld with great sorrow

1 that the people of the assembly began to be lifted up
2 in the pride of their eyes
3 and to set their hearts upon riches
4 and upon the vain things of the world
5 that they began to be scornful one towards another
6 and they began to persecute those that did not believe
7 according to their own will and pleasure
8 and thus in this eighth year of the reign of the judges
9 there began to be great contentions
10 among the people of the assembly
11 yes there was envying and strife
12 and malice and persecutions
13 and pride even to exceed the pride of those
14 who did not belong to the assembly of Elohiym
15 and thus ended the eighth year of the reign of the judges
16 and the wickedness of the assembly was a great stumbling block
17 to those who did not belong to the assembly
18 and thus the assembly began to fail in its progress
19
20 And it came to pass
21 in the commencement of the ninth year
22 Alma saw the wickedness of the assembly
23 and he saw also that the example of the assembly
24 began to lead those who were unbelievers on
25 from one manner of lawlessness to another
26 thus bringing on the destruction of the people
27 yes he saw great inequality among the people
28 some lifting themselves up
29 with their pride despising others turning their backs
30 upon the needy and the naked
31 and those who were hungry and those who were thirsty
32 and those who were sick and afflicted
33 now this was a great cause for weeping among the people

1   while others were abasing themselves

2   helping those who stood in need of their help

3   such as imparting their substance to the poor and the needy

4   feeding the hungry and suffering all manner of afflictions following Mashiach

5   who should come according to the ruach of prophecy

6   looking forward to that day

7   thus retaining a remission of their sins being filled with great joy

8   because of the resurrection of the dead

9   according to the will and power

10 and deliverance of Yehoshua Mashiach

11 from the bands of death

12

13 And now it came to pass

14 that Alma having seen the afflictions

15 of the humble followers of Elohiym

16 and the persecutions which were heaped upon them

17 by the remainder of his people

18 and seeing all their inequality

19 began to be very sorrowful

20 nevertheless the Ruach of YHVH did not fail him

21 and he selected a wise man

22 who was among the elders of the assembly

23 and gave him power according to the voice of the people

24 that he might have power to enact laws

25 according to the laws which had been given

26 and to put them in force

27 according to the wickedness and the crimes of the people

28 now this man's name was Nephiyahu

29 and he was appointed chief judge

30 and he sat in the judgment seat

31 to judge and to govern the people

32 now Alma did not grant unto him the office

33 of being high priest over the assembly

1 but he retained the office of high priest unto himself
2 but he delivered the judgment seat unto Nephiyahu
3 and this he did that he himself might go forth among his people
4 or among the people of Nephi
5 that he might preach the word of Elohiym unto them
6 to stir them up in remembrance of their duty
7 and that he might pull down by the word of Elohiym
8 all the pride and craftiness and all the contentions
9 which were among his people seeing no way
10 that he might reclaim them
11 except it were in bearing down
12 in pure testimony against them
13 and thus in the commencement
14 of the ninth year of the reign of the judges
15 over the people of Nephi
16 Alma delivered up the judgment seat to Nephiyahu
17 and confined himself wholly
18 to the high priesthood of the holy order of Elohiym
19 to the testimony of the word
20 according to the ruach of revelation and prophecy
21
22
23
24
25
26
27
28
29
30
31
32
33
34

4-THE MANNER OF ELOHIYM

3 **The words which Almah the Kohen Gadol**
4 **after the holy manner of Elohiym delivered**
5 **to the people in their cities and villages**
6 **throughout the land**

9 Now it came to pass
10 that Almah began to deliver the word of Elohiym
11 unto the people first in the land of Zarahemla
12 and from thence throughout all the land
13 and these are the words which he spoke to the people in the assembly
14 which was established in the city of Zarahemla
15 according to his own record saying

17 "I Almah having been set apart
18 by my father Almah to be a Kohen Gadol
19 over the assembly of Elohiym
20 he having power and authority from Elohiym
21 to do these things
22 behold I say unto you
23 that he began to establish an assembly
24 in the land which was in the borders of Nephi
25 yes the land which was called the land of Mor'amon
26 yes and he did immerse his brothers in the waters of Mor'amon
27 and behold I say unto you they were delivered out of the hands
28 of the people of king Noach by the mercy and power of Elohiym

30 And behold after that they were brought into bondage
31 by the hands of the Lamaniy in the wilderness
32 yes I say unto you they were in captivity
33 and again YHVH did deliver them out of bondage by the power of his word

1 and we were brought into this land

2 and here we began to establish the assembly of Elohiym

3 throughout this land also

4 and now behold I say unto you my brothers you

5 that belong to this assembly have you sufficiently retained

6 in remembrance the captivity of your fathers

7 yes and have you sufficiently retained in remembrance his mercy

8 and long-suffering towards them

9 and moreover have you sufficiently retained in remembrance

10 that he has delivered their souls from sheol

11

12 Behold he changed their hearts

13 yes he awakened them out of a deep sleep

14 and they awoke unto Elohiym

15 behold they were in the midst of darkness

16 nevertheless their souls were illuminated

17 by the light of the everlasting word

18 yes they were encircled about

19 by the bands of death and the chains of Sheol

20 and an everlasting destruction did await them

21 and now I ask of you my brothers were they destroyed

22 behold I say unto you No they were not

23

24 And again I ask were the bands of death broken and the chains of sheol

25 which encircled them about were they loosed I say unto you

26 yes they were loosed and their souls did expand

27 and they did sing redeeming love

28 and I say unto you that they are saved

29 and now I ask of you on what conditions are they saved

30 yes what grounds had they to hope for salvation

31 What is the cause of their being loosed from the bands of death

32 yes and also the chains of Sheol

33

1   Behold I can tell you did not my father Almah believe
2   in the words which were delivered by the mouth of Abinadi
3   and was he not a holy prophet
4   did he not speak the words of Elohiym
5   and my father Almah believe them
6   and according to his faith
7   there was a mighty change worked in his heart
8   behold I say unto you that this is all true
9   and behold he preached the word unto your fathers
10   and a mighty change was also worked in their hearts
11   and they humbled themselves
12   and put their trust in the true and living Elohiym
13   and behold they were faithful until the end
14   therefore they were saved
15

16   And now behold I ask of you
17   my brothers of the assembly have you spiritually been born of Elohiym
18   have you received his image in your countenances
19   have you experienced this mighty change in your hearts
20   do you exercise faith in the redemption of him who created you
21   do you look forward with an eye of faith
22   and view this mortal body raised in immortality
23   and this corruption raised in incorruption
24   to stand before Elohiym to be judged according to the deeds
25   which have been done in the mortal body
26   I say unto you can you imagine to yourselves
27   that you hear the voice of YHVH saying unto you
28   in that day
29

30   'Come unto me you blessed
31   for behold your works have been the works
32   of righteousness upon the face of the earth'
33

1 Or do you imagine to yourselves that you can lie
2 unto YHVH in that day and say
3
4 'Adonai our works have been righteous works
5 upon the face of the earth'
6
7 And that he will save you
8 or otherwise can you imagine yourselves
9 brought before the council of Elohiym with your souls filled
10 with guilt and remorse having a remembrance of all your guilt
11 yes a perfect remembrance of all your wickedness
12 yes a remembrance that you have set at defiance the mitzvot of Elohiym
13 I say unto you can you look up to Elohiym at that day
14 with a pure heart and clean hands
15 I say unto you can you look up having the image of Elohiym engraved
16 upon your countenances
17 I say unto you can you think of being saved
18 when you have yielded yourselves to become subjects to the evil one
19 I say unto you you will know at that day
20 that you cannot be saved for there can no man be saved
21 except his garments are washed white
22 yes his garments must be purified
23 until they are cleansed from all stain
24 through the blood of him of whom it has been spoken by our fathers
25 who should come to redeem his people from their sins
26 and now I ask of you my brothers
27 how will any of you feel if you shall stand
28 before the porch of Elohiym having your garments stained
29 with blood and all manner of filthiness
30 behold what will these things testify against you
31 behold will they not testify that you are murderers
32 yes and also that you are guilty of all manner of wickedness
33 behold my brothers do you suppose

1   that such an one can have a place to sit down

2   in the kingdom of Elohiym

3   with Avraham with Yitzchak and with Yacov

4   and also all the holy prophets whose garments are cleansed

5   and are without blemish pure and white

6

7   I say unto you

8   No except you make our Creator a liar from the beginning

9   or suppose that he is a liar from the beginning

10   you cannot suppose that such can have place

11   in the kingdom of heaven

12   but they shall be cast out

13   for they are the children of the kingdom of the evil one

14

15   And now behold I say unto you my brothers

16   if you have experienced a change of heart

17   and if you have felt to sing the song of redeeming love[2]

18   I would ask can you feel so now

19   have you walked keeping yourselves blameless

20   before Elohiym could you say

21   if you were called to die at this time within yourselves

22   that you have been sufficiently humble

23   that your garments have been cleansed and made white

24   through the blood of Mashiach

25   who will come to redeem his people from their sins

26

27   behold are you stripped of pride

28   I say unto you if you are not you are not prepared to meet Elohiym

29   behold you must prepare quickly

30   for the kingdom of heaven is soon at hand

31   and such an one has not eternal life

32

---

[2] Shemot (Exodus) 15:

1   Behold I say is there one among you

2   who is not stripped of envy

3   I say unto you that such an one is not prepared

4   and I would that he should prepare quickly

5   for the hour is close at hand and he knows not

6   when the time shall come

7   for such an one is not found guiltless

8   and again I say unto you is there one among you

9   that does make mock his brother

10   or that heaps upon him persecutions

11   OY unto such an one

12   for he is not prepared and the time is at hand

13   that he must repent or he cannot be saved

14   yes even OY unto all you workers of lawlessness Repent Repent

15   for YHVH Elohiym has spoken it

16

17   Behold he sends an invitation unto all men

18   for the arms of mercy are extended towards them

19   and he says

20

21   "Repent and I will receive you"

22

23   yes he says

24

25   "Come unto me and you shall partake

26   of the fruit of the tree of life

27   yes you shall eat and drink

28   of the bread and the waters of life freely

29   yes come unto me

30   and bring forth works of righteousness

31   and you shall not be cut down

32   and cast into the fire"

33

1 For behold the time is at hand
2 that whoever brings forth not good fruit
3 or whosoever does not the works
4 of righteousness the same have cause to wail and mourn
5 O you workers of lawlessness
6 you that are puffed up in the vain things of the world
7 you that have professed to have known the ways of righteousness
8 nevertheless have gone astray as sheep having no shepherd
9 notwithstanding a shepherd has called after you
10 and is still calling after you
11 but you will not listen to and obey his voice
12
13 Behold I say unto you that the good shepherd does call you
14 yes and in his own name he does call you
15 which is the name of Mashiach
16 and if you will not listen to and obey the voice of the good shepherd
17 to the name by which you are called
18 behold you are not the sheep of the good shepherd
19 and now if you are not the sheep of the good shepherd
20 of what fold are you
21 behold I say unto you that the evil one is your shepherd
22 and you are of his fold
23 and now who can deny this
24 behold I say unto you
25 whoever denies this is a liar
26 and a child of the evil one
27
28 For I say unto you
29 that whatever is good comes from Elohiym
30 and whatever is evil cometh from the evil one
31 therefore if a man brings forth good works he listens and obeys
32 unto the voice of the good shepherd
33 and he does follow him

1 but whosoever brings forth evil works the same

2 becomes a child of the evil one

3 for he listens to and obeys his voice and does follow him

4 and whosoever does this must receive his wages of him

5 therefore for his wages he receives death

6 as to things pertaining unto righteousness being dead

7 unto all good works

8

9 And now my brothers I would that you should hear me

10 for I speak in the energy of my soul

11 for behold I have spoken unto you plainly

12 that you cannot go astray

13 or have spoken according to the mitzvot of Elohiym

14 for I am called to speak after this manner

15 according to the holy manner of Elohiym

16 which is in Mashiach Yehoshua

17 yes I am commanded to stand and testify unto this people the things

18 which have been spoken by our fathers

19 concerning the things which are to come

20

21 And this is not all

22 do you not suppose that I know of these things myself

23 behold I testify unto you that I do know

24 that these things whereof I have spoken are true

25 and how do you suppose that I know of their surety

26 behold I say unto you

27 they are made known unto me by the Ruach of Elohiym

28 behold I have fasted and prayed many days

29 that I might know these things of myself

30 and now I do know of myself that they are true

31 for YHVH Elohiym has made them manifest unto me by his Ruach

32 and this is the ruach of revelation which is in me

33

1 and moreover I say unto you
2 that it has thus been revealed unto me
3 that the words which have been spoken by our fathers are true
4 even so according to the spirit of prophecy which is in me
5 which is also by the manifestation of the Ruach of Elohiym
6 I say unto you that I know of myself
7 that whatsoever I shall say unto you
8 concerning that which is to come is true
9 and I say unto you that I know that Yehoshua Mashiach shall come
10 yes the Son the chosen of the Father
11 full of grace and mercy and truth
12 and behold it is he that comes to take away
13 the sins of the world
14 yes the sins of every man who unwaveringly believes on his name
15
16 And now I say unto you
17 that this is the order after which I am called
18 yes to preach unto my beloved brothers
19 yes and every one that dwells in the land
20 yes to preach unto all
21 both old and young both bond and free
22 yes I say unto you the aged and also the middle aged
23 and the rising generation
24 yes to cry unto them
25 that they must repent and be born again
26
27 yes thus says the Ruach
28
29 "Repent all you ends of the earth
30 for the kingdom of heaven is soon at hand
31 yes the Son of Elohiym comes in his glory
32 in his might majesty power and dominion"
33

1 Yes my beloved brothers I say unto you
2 that the Ruach says
3 "behold the glory of the King of all the earth
4 and also the King of heaven
5 shall very soon shine forth
6 among all the children of men"
7
8 And also the Ruach says unto me
9 yes cries unto me with a mighty voice saying
10
11 "Go forth and say unto this people repent
12 for except you repent you can not inherit the kingdom of heaven"
13
14 And again I say unto you the Ruach says
15
16 "behold the ax is laid at the root of the tree
17 therefore every tree that brings not forth good fruit
18 shall be cut down and cast into the fire
19 yes a fire which cannot be consumed
20 even an unquenchable fire"
21
22 Behold and remember the Holy One has spoken it
23
24 And now my beloved brothers
25 I say unto you can you withstand these sayings
26 yes can you lay aside these things
27 and trample the Holy One under your feet
28 yes can you be puffed up in the pride of your hearts
29 yes will you still persist in the wearing of costly apparel
30 and setting your hearts upon the vain things of the world
31 upon your riches
32 yes will you persist in thinking
33 that you are better one than another

1   yes will you persist in the persecution of your brothers

2   who humble themselves

3   and do walk after the holy manner of Elohiym

4   in that they have been brought into this assembly

5   having been set apart by the Ruach Elohiym

6   and they do bring forth works which are the results of repentance

7   yes and will you persist in turning your backs

8   upon the poor and the needy

9   and in withholding your substance from them

10   and finally all you that will persist in your wickedness

11   I say unto you that these are they who shall be cut down

12   and cast into the fire except they quickly repent

13

14   And now I say unto you

15   all you that are desire to follow the voice of the good shepherd come you out

16   from those who depart from the Torah and be you separate

17   and touch not their unclean things

18   and behold their names shall be blotted out

19   that the names of those who depart from the Torah

20   shall not be numbered among the names of the righteous

21   that the word of Elohiym may be fulfilled which says

22

23   "The names of those who depart from the Torah

24   shall not be mingled with the names of my people

25   for the names of the righteous shall be written in the book of life

26   and unto them will I grant an inheritance at my right hand"

27

28   And now my brothers

29   what have you to say against this

30   I say unto you if you speak against it it matters not

31   for the word of Elohiym must be fulfilled

32   for what shepherd is there among you having many sheep does not watch over

33   them

1 that the wolves enter not and devour his flock

2 and behold if a wolf enter his flock does he not drive him out

3 yes and at the last if he can he will destroy him

4 and now I say unto you

5 that the good shepherd does call after you

6 and if you will listen to and obey his voice he will bring you

7 into his fold and you are his sheep

8 and he commands you

9 that you suffer no ravenous wolf to enter among you

10 that you may not be destroyed

11

12 And now I Almah do command you

13 in the language of him who has commanded me

14 that you observe to do the words

15 which I have spoken unto you

16 I speak by way of command unto you that belong to the assembly

17 and unto those who do not belong to the assembly

18 I speak by way of invitation saying

19 come and be immersed unto repentance

20 that you also may be partakers of the fruit

21 of the etz chaim

22

23 And now it came to pass

24 that after Almah had made an end of speaking

25 unto the people of the assembly

26 which was established in the city of Zarahemla he ordained priests

27 and elders by laying on his hands according to the manner of Elohiym

28 to preside and watch over the assembly

29

30 And it came to pass

31 that whoever did not belong to the assembly

32 who repented of their sins were immersed unto repentance

33 and were received into the assembly

1
2 and it also came to pass
3 that whosoever did belong to the assembly
4 that did not repent of their wickedness
5 and humble themselves before Elohiym
6 I mean those who were lifted up
7 in the pride of their hearts the same were rejected
8 and their names were blotted out
9 that their names were not numbered among those of the righteous
10 and thus they began to establish the manner of the assembly
11 in the city of Zarahemla
12 now I would that you should understand
13 that the word of Elohiym was liberal unto all
14 that none were deprived of the privilege of assembling themselves together
15 to hear the word of Elohiym
16 nevertheless the children of Elohiym were commanded
17 that they should gather themselves together often
18 and join in fasting and mighty prayer
19 in behalf of the welfare of the souls
20 of those who knew not Elohiym
21
22 And now it came to pass
23 that when Almah had made these regulations he departed from them
24 yes from the assembly which was in the city of Zarahemla
25 and went over upon the east of the river Tzidon
26 into the valley of Gideon there having been a city built
27 which was called the city of Gid'on
28 which was in the valley that was called Gid'on being called
29 after the man who was slain by the hand of Nachor with the sword
30 and Almah went and began to declare the word of Elohiym
31 unto the assembly which was established in the valley of Gideon
32 according to the revelation of the truth of the word
33 which had been spoken by his fathers

1 and according to the ruach of prophecy which was in him

2 according to the testimony of Yehoshua Mashiach the Son of Elohiym

3 who should come to redeem his people from their sins

4 and the holy manner by which he was called

5 and thus it is written

6 Amein

7

8

9

10

11

12 **The words of Almah**

13 **which he delivered to the people in Gideon**

14 **according to his own record**

15

16

17 Behold my beloved brothers seeing

18 that I have been permitted to come unto you

19 therefore I attempt to address you in my language

20 yes by my own mouth seeing that it is the first time

21 that I have spoken unto you by the words of my mouth

22 I having been wholly confined to the judgment seat having had much business

23 that I could not come unto you

24 and even I could not have come now at this time were it not

25 that the judgment seat has been given to another to rule in my stead

26 and YHVH in much mercy has granted that I should come unto you

27

28 And behold I have come having great hopes and much desire

29 that I should find that you had humbled yourselves before Elohiym

30 and that you had continued in the petitioning of his grace

31 that I should find that you were blameless before him

32 that I should find that you were not in the awful dilemma

33 that our brothers were in at Zarahemla

1. but blessed be the name of Elohiym
2. that he hath given me to know
3. yes has given unto me the exceedingly great joy of knowing
4. that they are established again in the way of his righteousness
5. and I trust according to the Ruach Elohiym which is in me
6. that I shall also have joy over you
7. nevertheless I do not desire that my joy over you should come
8. by the cause of so much afflictions and sorrow
9. which I have had for the brothers at Zarahemla
10. for behold my joy comes over them
11. after wading through much affliction and sorrow
12.
13. But behold I trust that you are not in a state of so much unbelief
14. as were your brothers
15. I trust that you are not lifted up in the pride of your hearts
16. yes I trust that you have not set your hearts upon riches
17. and the vain things of the world
18. yes I trust that you do not worship idols
19. but that you do worship the true and the living Elohiym
20. and that you look forward for the remission of your sins
21. with an everlasting faith which is to come
22. for behold I say unto you
23. there be many things to come
24. and behold there is one thing which is of more importance than they all
25. for behold the time is not far distant
26. that the Redeemer lives and comes among his people
27.
28. Behold I do not say
29. that he will come among us
30. at the time of his dwelling in his mortal tabernacle
31. for behold the Ruach has not said unto me that this should be the case
32. now as to this thing I do not know
33. but this much I do know that YHVH Elohiym has power to do all things

1 which are according to his word

2 but behold the Ruach has said this much

3 unto me saying

4

5 "Cry unto this people saying repent you

6 and prepare the way of YHVH

7 and walk in his paths which are straight

8 for behold the kingdom of heaven is at hand

9 and the Son of Elohiym comes

10 upon the face of the earth"

11

12 And behold he shall be born of Miryam at Yerushalayim

13 which is the land of our forefathers

14 she being a young woman

15 a precious and chosen vessel

16 who shall be covered and conceive

17 by the power of the Ruach Elohiym

18 and bring forth a son

19 yes even the Chosen Son of Elohiym

20 and he shall go forth suffering pains and afflictions

21 and temptations of every kind

22 and this that the word might be fulfilled which says

23

24 "He will take upon him the pains and the sicknesses of his people"

25

26 And he will take upon him death

27 that he may loose the bands of death which bind his people

28 and he will take upon him their infirmities

29 that his bowels may be filled with mercy according to the flesh

30 that he may know according to the flesh how

31 to deliver his people according to their infirmities

32 now the Ruach knows all things

33 nevertheless the Son of Elohiym suffers according to the flesh

1   that he might take upon him the sins of his people

2   that he might wipe away their rebellion

3   according to the power of his deliverance

4   and now behold this is the testimony which is in me

5

6   Now I say unto you

7   that you must repent and be born again

8   for the Ruach says

9

10   "If you are not born again you cannot inherit the kingdom of heaven"

11

12   Therefore come and be immersed unto repentance

13   that you may be washed from your sins

14   that you may have faith on the Lamb of Elohiym

15   who taketh away the sins of the world

16   who is mighty to save

17   and to cleanse from all unrighteousness

18   yes I say unto you come and fear not

19   and lay aside every sin

20   which easily does surround you

21   which does bind you down to destruction

22   yes come and go forth

23   and show unto your Elohiym

24   that you are willing to repent of your sins

25   and enter into a covenant with him

26   to keep his mitzvot

27   and witness it unto him this day

28   by going into the waters of mikveh

29   and whoever does this

30   and guards the mitzvot of Elohiym

31   from that time forward the same will remember

32   that I say unto him

33   yes he will remember

1   that I have said unto him

2   'he shall have eternal life'

3   according to the testimony of the Ruach Elohiym

4   which testifies in me

5

6   And now my beloved brothers

7   do you believe these things

8   behold I say unto you

9   yes I know that you believe them

10   and the way that I know that you believe them is

11   by the manifestation of the Ruach which is in me

12   and now because your faith is strong concerning that

13   yes concerning the things which I have spoken great is my joy

14   for as I said unto you from the beginning

15   that I had much desire

16   that you were not in the state of dilemma like your brothers

17   even so I have found that my desires have been gratified

18   for I perceive that you are in the paths of righteousness

19   I perceive that you are in the path which leads to the kingdom of Elohiym

20   yes I perceive that you are making his paths straight

21   I perceive that it has been made known unto you

22   by the testimony of his word

23   that he cannot walk in crooked paths

24   neither does he vary from that which he has said

25   neither has he a shadow of turning

26   from the right to the left

27   or from that which is right to that which is wrong

28   therefore his course is one eternal round

29   and he does not dwell in unholy temples

30   neither can filthiness or anything which is unclean

31   be received into the kingdom of Elohiym

32   therefore I say unto you the time shall come

33   yes and it shall be at the last day

1   that he who is filthy shall remain in his filthiness

2

3   And now my beloved brothers I have said these things unto you

4   that I might awaken you to a sense of your duty to Elohiym

5   that you may walk blameless before him

6   that you may walk after the holy manner of Elohiym

7   after which you have been received

8   and now I would

9   that you should be humble and be submissive

10   and gentle easy to be entreated

11   full of patience and long suffering

12   being temperate in all things

13   being diligent in keeping the mitzvot of Elohiym

14   at all times asking for whatever things you stand in need

15   both spiritual and temporal always returning thanks unto Elohiym

16   for whatever things you do receive

17   and see that you have faith hope and tzedekah

18   and then you will always abound in good works

19   and may YHVH bless you and keep your garments without blemish

20   that you may at last be brought to sit down

21   with Avraham Yitzchak and Yacov

22   and the holy prophets who have been

23   ever since the world began having your garments spotless

24   even as their garments are spotless in the kingdom of heaven

25   to go no more out

26

27   And now my beloved brothers

28   I have spoken these words unto you

29   according to the Ruach which testifies in me

30   and my soul does exceedingly rejoice

31   because of the exceeding diligence and regard

32   which you have given unto my word

33   and now may the peace of Elohiym rest upon you

1 and upon your houses and lands

2 and upon your flocks and herds

3 and all that you possess your women and your children

4 according to your faith and good works

5 from this time forth and forever

6 and thus I have spoken

7 Amein

8

9

10 And now it came to pass

11 that Almah returned from the land of Gid'on

12 after having taught the people of Gideon many things

13 which cannot be written having established the manner of the assembly

14 according as he had before done in the land of Zarahemla

15 yes he returned to his own house at Zarahemla

16 to rest himself from the labors which he had performed

17 and thus ended the ninth year of the reign of the judges over the people of

18 Nephi

19

20 And it came to pass

21 in the commencement of the tenth year of the reign of the judges over the

22 people of Nephi that Almah departed from there and took his journey over

23 into the land of Melek

24 on the west of the river Tzidon on the west

25 by the borders of the wilderness

26 and he began to teach the people in the land of Melek

27 according to the holy manner of Elohiym by which he had been called

28 and he began to teach the people throughout all the land of Melek

29

30 And it came to pass

31 that the people came to him throughout all the borders of the land

32 which was by the wilderness side

33 and they were immersed throughout all the land

1   so that when he had finished his work at Melek he departed from there

2   and traveled three days' journey on the north of the land of Melek

3   and he came to a city which was called Ammoniyah

4   now it was the custom of the people of Nephi to call their lands

5   and their cities and their villages

6   yes even all their small villages

7   after the name of him who first possessed them

8   and thus it was with the land of Ammoniyah

9

10   And it came to pass

11   that when Almah had come

12   to the city of Ammoniyah he began

13   to preach the word of Elohiym unto them

14   now the evil one had gotten great hold

15   upon the hearts of the people of the city of Ammoniyah

16   therefore they would not listen to and obey the words of Almah

17   nevertheless Almah labored much in the spirit

18   wrestling with Elohiym in mighty prayer

19   that he would pour out his Ruach upon the people who were in the city

20   that he would also grant

21   that he might immerse them unto repentance

22   nevertheless they hardened their hearts saying unto him

23

24   "behold we know that you are Almah

25   and we know that you are Kohen Gadol over the assembly

26   which you hast established in many parts of the land

27   according to your tradition

28   and we are not of your assembly

29   and we do not believe in such foolish traditions

30   and now we know

31   that because we are not of your assembly we know

32   that you have no power over us

33   and you have delivered up the judgment seat unto Nephiyah

1 therefore you are not the chief judge over us"

2

3 Now when the people had said this

4 and withstood all his words and denounced him and spit upon him

5 and caused that he should be cast out of their city he departed from there

6 and took his journey towards the city which was called Aharon

7

8 And it came to pass

9 that while he was journeying there being weighed down

10 with sorrow wading through much tribulation

11 and anguish of soul because of the wickedness of the people

12 who were in the city of Ammoniyah

13 it came to pass

14 while Almah was thus weighed down with sorrow

15 behold an angel of YHVH appeared unto him saying

16

17 "Blessed are you Almah

18 therefore lift up your head and rejoice

19 for you have great cause to rejoice

20 for you have been faithful in keeping the mitzvot of Elohiym

21 from the time which you received your first message from him

22 behold I am he that delivered it unto you

23 and behold I am sent to command you

24 that you return to the city of Ammoniyah

25 and preach again unto the people of the city

26 yes preach unto them

27 yes say unto them except they repent YHVH Elohiym will destroy them

28 for behold they do study at this time

29 that they may destroy the liberty of your people"

30 'For thus says YHVH'

31 which is contrary to the chukkim and mishpatim and mitzvot

32 which he has given unto his people"

33

1 Now it came to pass

2 that after Almah had received his message

3 from the angel of YHVH he returned quickly to the land of Ammoniyah

4 and he entered the city by another way

5 yes by the way which is on the south of the city of Ammoniyah

6 and as he entered the city he was hungry

7 and he said to a man

8

9 "Will you give to an humble servant of Elohiym something to eat"

10

11 And the man said unto him I am Nephiy

12 and I know that you are a holy prophet of Elohiym

13 for you are the man whom an angel said in a vision

14

15 "You shalt receive"

16

17 therefore go with me into my house

18 and I will impart unto you of my food

19 and I know that you will be a blessing

20 unto me and my house

21

22 And it came to pass

23 that the man received him into his house

24 and the man was called Amulek

25 and he brought forth bread and meat

26 and set before Almah

27

28 And it came to pass

29 that Almah ate bread and was filled

30 and he blessed Amulek and his house

31 and he gave thanks unto Elohiym

32 and after he had eaten and was filled he said unto Amulek

33

1 "I am Almah

2 and am the Kohen Gadol over the assembly of Elohiym

3 throughout the land

4 and behold I have been called

5 to preach the word of Elohiym among all this people

6 according to the ruach of revelation and prophecy

7 and I was in this land

8 and they would not receive me

9 but they cast me out

10 and I was about to set my back towards this land forever

11 but behold I have been commanded

12 that I should turn again and prophesy unto this people

13 yes and to testify against them concerning their lawlessness

14 and now Amulek because you have fed me and taken me in

15 you are blessed for I was hungry

16 for I had fasted many days"

17

18 and Almah tarried many days with Amulek

19 before he began to preach unto the people

20

21 And it came to pass

22 that the people did descend more into lawlessness

23 and the word came to Almah saying

24

25 "Go and also say unto my servant Amulek go forth

26 and prophesy unto this people saying repent you for thus says YHVH

27 except you repent I will visit this people in my anger

28 yes and I will not turn my fierce anger away"

29

30 and Almah went forth and also Amulek among the people

31 to declare the words of Elohiym unto them

32 and they were filled with the Ruach Elohiym

33 and they had power given unto them insomuch

1   that they could not be confined in dungeons

2   neither was it possible that any man could kill them

3   nevertheless they did not exercise their power

4   until they were bound in bands and cast into prison

5   now this was done that YHVH might show forth his power in them

6

7   And it came to pass

8   that they went forth and began to preach and to prophesy

9   unto the people according to the spirit and power

10 which YHVH had given them

11

12 and again I Almah having been commanded of Elohiym

13 that I should take Amulek and go forth and preach again

14 unto this people or the people who were in the city of Ammoniyah

15 it came to pass

16 as I began to preach unto them they began to contend with me saying

17

18 "Who are you

19 do you suppose that we shall believe the testimony of one man

20 even though he should preach unto us that the earth should pass away"

21

22 now they understood not the words which they spoke

23 for they knew not that the earth should pass away

24

25 and they said also

26

27 "We will not believe your words if you should prophesy

28 that this great city should be destroyed in one day"

29

30 now they knew not that Elohiym could do such marvelous works

31 for they were a hard hearted and a stubborn people

32 and they said

33

1. "Who is Elohiym that he sends no more authority
2. than one man among this people
3. to declare unto them the truth
4. of such great and marvelous things"
5.
6. and they stood forth to lay their hands on me
7. but behold they did not
8. and I stood with boldness to declare unto them
9. yes I did boldly testify unto them saying
10.
11. "behold O you wicked and perverse generation
12. how have you forgotten the tradition of your fathers
13. yes how soon you have forgotten the mitzvot of Elohiym
14. do you not remember
15. that our father Lechi was brought out of Yerushalayim by the hand of Elohiym
16. do you not remember that they were all led by him through the wilderness
17. and have you forgotten so soon
18. how many times he delivered our fathers out of the hands of their enemies
19. and preserved them from being destroyed
20. even by the hands of their own brothers
21. yes and if it had not been for his matchless power and his mercy
22. and his long-suffering towards us we should unavoidably have been cut off
23. from the face of the earth long before this period of time
24. and perhaps been consigned to a state of endless misery and sorrow
25.
26. behold now I say unto you that he commands you to repent
27. and except you repent you can in not inherit the kingdom of Elohiym
28. but behold this is not all
29. he has commanded you to repent or he will utterly destroy you
30. from off the face of the earth
31. yes he will visit you in his anger
32. and in his fierce anger he will not turn away
33. behold do you not remember the words

1   which he spoke unto Lechi saying

2

3   "that Inasmuch as you shall keep my mitzvot you shall prosper in the land"

4

5   and again it is said

6

7   "that Inasmuch as you will not keep my mitzvot you shall be cut off

8   from the presence of YHVH"

9

10   now I would that you should remember

11   that inasmuch as the Lamaniy have not kept the mitzvot of Elohiym

12   they have been cut off from the presence of YHVH

13   now we see that the word of YHVH has been verified in this thing

14   and the Lamaniy have been cut off from his presence

15   from the beginning of their transgressions in the land

16   nevertheless I say unto you

17   that it shall be more tolerable for them in the day of judgment

18   than for you if you remain in your sins

19   yes and even more tolerable for them in this life than for you

20   except you repent

21   for there are many promises which are extended to the Lamaniy

22   for it is because of the traditions of their fathers

23   that caused them to remain in their state of ignorance

24   therefore YHVH will be merciful unto them

25   and prolong their existence in the land

26   and at some period of time they will be brought to believe in his word

27   and to know of the incorrectness of the traditions of their fathers

28   and many of them will be saved for YHVH will be merciful

29   unto all who call on his name

30

31   but behold I say unto you

32   that if you persist in your departure from the Torah

33   that your days shall not be prolonged in the land

1 for the Lamaniy shall be sent upon you

2 and if you repent not they shall come in a time when you know not

3 and you shall be visited with utter destruction

4 and it shall be according to the fierce anger of YHVH

5 for he will not allow you

6 that you shall live in your lawlessness to destroy his people

7 I say unto you No he would rather allow that the Lamaniy might destroy

8 all his people who are called the people of Nephi

9 if it were possible that they could fall into sin and rebellion

10 after having had so much light and so much knowledge given unto them

11 of YHVH their Elohiym

12 yes after having been such a highly favored people of YHVH

13 yes after having been favored

14 above every other nation kindred tongue or people

15 after having had all things made known unto them

16 according to their desires and their faith and prayers of that

17 which has been and which is and which is to come

18 Having been visited by the Ruach Elohiym

19 having conversed with angels

20 and having been spoken unto by the voice of YHVH

21 and having the spirit of prophecy

22 and the spirit of revelation

23 and also many gifts

24 the gift of speaking with languages

25 and the gift of preaching

26 and the gift of the Ruach Elohiym

27 and the gift of translation

28 yes and after having been delivered of Elohiym out of the land of

29 Yerushalayim

30 by the hand of YHVH having been saved from famine

31 and from sickness and all manner of diseases of every kind

32 and they having waxed strong in battle

33 that they might not be destroyed having been brought out

1   of bondage time after time
2   and having been kept and preserved until now
3   and they have been prospered
4   until they are rich in all manner of things
5
6   and now behold I say unto you
7   that if this people who have received so many blessings
8   from the hand of YHVH should rebel contrary to the light and knowledge
9   which they do have
10 I say unto you that if this be the case
11 that if they should fall into rebellion it would be far more tolerable
12 for the Lamaniy than for them
13 for behold the promises of YHVH are extended to the Lamaniy
14 but they are not unto you if you rebel
15 for has not YHVH expressly promised and firmly decreed
16 that if you will rebel against him that you shall utterly be destroyed
17 from off the face of the land
18 and now for this cause
19 that you may not be destroyed YHVH has sent his angel
20 to visit many of his people declaring unto them
21 that they must go forth and cry loudly
22 unto this people saying
23
24 "Repent you for the kingdom of heaven is nigh at hand"
25
26 and not many days from this time the Son of Elohiym
27 shall come in his glory
28 and his glory shall be the glory
29 of the One Chosen of the Father
30 full of grace equity and truth
31 full of patience mercy and long suffering quick
32 to hear the cries of his people
33 and to answer their prayers

1 and behold he comes to redeem those
2 who will be immersed unto repentance
3 through faith on his name
4 therefore prepare you the way of YHVH
5 for the time is at hand that all men shall harvest a reward of their works
6 according to that which they have been
7 if they have been righteous they shall harvest the salvation of their souls
8 according to the power and deliverance of Yehoshua Mashiach
9 and if they have been evil they shall harvest the condemnation of their souls
10 according to the power and captivation of the evil one
11 now behold this is the voice of the angel crying unto the people
12 and now my beloved brothers
13 for you are my brothers
14 and you should to be chosen
15 and you should to bring forth works which demonstrate repentance seeing
16 that your hearts have been grossly hardened against the word of Elohiym
17 and seeing that you are a lost and a fallen people
18
19 Now it came to pass
20 that when I Almah had spoken these words
21 behold the people were angry with me
22 because I said unto them that they were a hard hearted and a stubborn people
23 and also because I said unto them
24 that they were a lost and a fallen people
25 they were angry with me and sought to lay their hands upon me
26 that they might cast me into prison
27
28 But it came to pass
29 that YHVH did not allow them
30 that they should take me at that time
31 and cast me into prison
32
33 And it came to pass

1 that Amulek went and stood forth
2 and began to preach unto them also
3 and now the words of Amulek are not all written
4 nevertheless a part of his words are written in this book
5
6 now these are the words which Amulek preached
7 unto the people who were in the land of Ammoniyah saying
8
9 "I am Amulek I am the son of Gid'onah
10 who was the son of Yishma'el who was a descendant of Aminadi
11 and it was that same Aminadi who interpreted the writing
12 which was upon the wall of the temple
13 which was written by the finger of Elohiym
14 and Aminadi was a descendant of Nephi who was the son of Lechi
15 who came out of the land of Yerushalayim
16 who was a descendant of Menashsheh who was the son of Yoseph
17 who was sold into Egypt by the hands of his brothers
18
19 and behold I am also a man of no small reputation
20 among all those who know me yes
21 and behold I have many relatives and friends
22 and I have also acquired much riches by the hand of my industry
23 nevertheless after all this I never have known much of the ways of YHVH
24 and his mysteries and marvelous power
25 I said I never had known much of these things
26 but behold I mistake for I have seen much
27 of his mysteries and his marvelous power
28 yes even in the preservation of the lives of this people
29 nevertheless I did harden my heart
30 for I was called many times
31 and I would not hear
32 therefore I knew concerning these things
33 yet I would not know

1 therefore I went on rebelling against Elohiym in departing from Torah in my

2 heart

3 even until the fourth day of this seventh month

4 which is in the tenth year of the reign of the judges

5 As I was journeying to see a very close family

6 behold an angel of YHVH appeared unto me and said

7

8 "Amulek return to thine own house

9 for you shalt feed a prophet of YHVH

10 yes a holy man who is a chosen man of Elohiym

11 for he has fasted many days because of the sins of this people

12 and he is hungry and you shall receive him into your house and feed him

13 and he shall bless you and your house

14 and the blessing of YHVH shall rest upon you and your house"

15

16 And it came to pass

17 that I obeyed the voice of the angel

18 and returned towards my house

19 and as I was going there I found the man whom the angel said unto me

20 "You shalt receive into your house"

21 and behold it was this same man who has been speaking unto you

22 concerning the things of Elohiym

23 and the angel said unto me 'he is a holy man'

24 wherefore I know he is a holy man

25 because it was said by an angel of Elohiym

26 and again I know that the things whereof he has testified are true

27 for behold I say unto you that as YHVH lives

28 even so has he sent his angel

29 to make these things manifest unto me

30 and this he has done while this Almah has dwelt at my house

31 for behold he hath blessed mine house

32 he has blessed me and my women

33 and my children and my father and my relatives

1 yes even all my relatives has he blessed

2 and the blessing of YHVH has rested upon us

3 according to the words which he spoke

4

5 and now when Amulek had spoken these words the people

6 began to be astonished seeing there was more than one witness

7 who testified of the things that they were accused of

8 and also of the things which were to come

9 according to the ruach of prophecy which was in them

10 nevertheless there were some among them

11 who thought to question them

12 that by their cunning devices

13   they might catch them in their words

14 that they might find witness against them

15 that they might deliver them to their judges

16 that they might be judged according to the law

17 and that they might be killed or cast into prison

18 according to the crime which they could make appear

19 or witness against them

20 now it was those men who sought to destroy them

21 who were lawyers who were hired or appointed by the people

22 to administer the law at their times of trials

23 or at the trials of the crimes of the people before the judges

24 now these lawyers were learned in all the arts and cunning of the people

25 and this was to enable them that they might be skillful in their profession

26

27 And it came to pass

28 that they began to question Amulek

29 that thereby they might make him cross his words

30 or contradict the words which he should speak

31 now they knew not that Amulek could know of their designs

32

33 But it came to pass

1   as they began to question him he perceived their thoughts

2   and he said unto them

3   "O you wicked and perverse generation

4   you lawyers and hypocrites

5   for you are laying the foundations of the evil one

6   for you are laying traps and snares

7   to catch the holy ones of Elohiym

8   You are laying plans to pervert the ways of the righteous

9   and to bring down the anger of Elohiym upon your heads

10 even to the utter destruction of this people

11 yes well did Mosiah say

12 who was our last king

13 when he was about to deliver up the kingdom having no one to confer it upon

14 causing

15 that this people should be governed by their own voices

16 yes well did he say

17 that if the time should come

18 that the voice of this people should choose lawlessness

19 that is if the time should come that this people should fall into rebellion

20 they would be ripe for destruction

21 and now I say unto you

22 that well does YHVH judge of your lawlessness

23 well does he cry unto this people by the voice of his angels

24 'Repent you repent for the kingdom of heaven is at hand'

25 yes well does he cry by the voice of his angels

26 that 'I will come down among my people with equity and justice in my hands'

27 yes and I say unto you

28 that if it were not for the prayers of the righteous who are now in the land

29 that you would even now be visited with utter destruction

30 yet it would not be by flood as were the people in the days of Noah

31 but it would be by famine and by pestilence and the sword

32 but it is by the prayers of the righteous that you are spared now

33 therefore if you will cast out the righteous from among you

1 then will not YHVH stay his hand
2 but in his fierce anger he will come out against you
3 then you shall be struck by famine and by pestilence and by the sword
4 and the time is soon at hand
5 except you repent
6
7 And now it came to pass
8 that the people were more angry with Amulek
9 and they cried out saying
10
11 "This man does revile against our laws which are just
12 and our wise lawyers whom we have selected"
13
14 but Amulek stretched forth his hand
15 and shouted the mightier unto them saying
16
17 "O you wicked and perverse generation
18 why has the evil one got such great hold upon your hearts
19 why will you yield yourselves unto him
20 that he may have power over you to blind your eyes
21 that you will not understand the words
22 which are spoken according to their truth
23
24 For behold have I testified against your law
25 You do not understand
26 you say that I have spoken against your law
27 but I have not
28 but I have spoken in favor of your law
29 to your condemnation
30 and now behold I say unto you
31 that the foundation of the destruction
32 of this people is beginning to be laid
33 by the unrighteousness of your lawyers and your judges"

1

2 And now it came to pass

3 that when Amulek had spoken these words

4 the people cried out against him saying

5

6 "now we know that this man is a child of the evil one

7 for he has lied unto us

8 for he hath spoken against our law

9 and now he says that he has not spoken against it

10 and again he has reviled against our lawyers and our judges"

11

12 And it came to pass

13 that the lawyers put it into their hearts

14 that they should remember these things against him

15 and there was one among them whose name was Zeezrom

16 now he was the foremost to accuse Amulek and Almah he being one

17 of the most expert among them having much business

18 to do among the people

19 now the object of these lawyers was to get gain

20 and they got gain according to their employ

21 now it was in the law of Mosheyahu

22 that every man who was a judge of the law

23 or those who were appointed to be judges should receive wages

24 according to the time which they labored to judge

25 those who were brought before them to be judged

26 now if a man owed another

27 and he would not pay that which he did owe he was complained of

28 to the judge and the judge executed authority

29 and sent forth officers that the man should be brought before him

30 and he judged the man according to the Torah

31 and the evidence which was brought against him

32 and thus the man was compelled to pay that which he owed

33 or be stripped or be cast out from among the people

1   as a thief and a robber

2   and the judge received for his wages

3   according to his time

4   a senine of gold for a day

5   or a senum of silver

6   which is equal to a senine of gold

7   and this is according to the law which was given

8

9   now these are the names of the different pieces

10   of their gold and of their silver

11   according to their value

12   and the names are given by the Nephiy

13   for they did not reckon after the manner of the Yehudim

14   who were at Yerushalayim

15   neither did they measure after the manner of the Yehudim

16   but they altered their reckoning and their measure

17   according to the minds and the circumstances

18   of the people in every generation until the reign of the judges

19   they having been established by king Moshiyahu

20

21   now the reckoning is thus

22   a senine of gold a seon of gold a shum of gold and a limnah of gold

23   a senum of silver an amnor of silver an ezrom of silver and an onti of silver

24   a senum of silver was equal to a senine of gold

25   and either for a measure of barley

26   and also for a measure of every kind of grain

27   now the amount of a seon of gold was twice the value of a senine

28   and a shum of gold was twice the value of a seon

29   and a limnah of gold was the value of them all

30   and an amnor of silver was as great as two senums

31   and an ezrom of silver was as great as four senums

32   and an onti was as great as them all

33

1 now this is the value of the lesser numbers of their reckoning
2 a shiblon is half of a senum
3 therefore a shiblon for half a measure of barley
4 and a shiblum is a half of a shiblon
5 and a leah is the half of a shiblum
6 now this is their number according to their reckoning
7 now an antion of gold is equal to three shiblons
8
9 now it was for the sole purpose to get gain
10 because they received their wages according to their employ
11 therefore they did stir up the people to rioting
12 and all manner of disturbances and to depart from the Torah
13 that they might have more work
14 that they might get money according to the lawsuits
15 which were brought before them
16 therefore they did stir up the people against Almah and Amulek
17 and this Zeezrom began to question Amulek saying
18
19 "Will you answer me a few questions
20 which I shall ask you"
21
22 now Zeezrom was a man who was expert in the devices of the evil one
23 that he might destroy that which was good
24 therefore he said unto Amulek
25
26 'Will you answer the questions which I shall ask you'
27
28 and Amulek said unto him
29
30 "Yes if it be according to the Ruach YHVH which is in me
31 for I shall say nothing which is contrary to the Ruach YHVH"
32
33 and Zeezrom said unto him

1
2 "behold here are six onties of silver
3 and all these will I give you
4 if you will deny the existence of Elohiym"
5
6 now Amulek said
7 "O you child of sheol why tempt you me know you
8 that the righteous yield to no such temptations believe you
9 that there is no Elohiym
10 I say unto you no you know
11 that there is an Elohiym
12 but you love that money more than him
13 and now you have lied before Elohiym unto me
14 You said unto me
15 'behold these six onties which are of great worth I will give unto you' when
16 you had it
17 in your heart to retain them from me
18 and it was only your desire that I should deny the true and living Elohiym
19 that you might have cause to destroy me
20 and now behold for this great evil you shall have your reward"
21
22 and Zeezrom said unto him
23
24 "You say there is a true and living Elohiym"
25
26 and Amulek said
27
28 "yes there is a true and living Elohiym"
29
30 now Zeezrom said
31
32 "Is there more than one Elohiym"
33

1 and he answered

2

3 "No"

4

5 now Zeezrom said unto him again

6

7 "how know you these things"

8

9 and he said

10

11 "An angel has made them known unto me"

12

13 and Zeezrom said again

14

15 "Who is he that shall come is it the Son of Elohiym"

16

17 and he said unto him

18

19 "yes"

20

21 and Zeezrom said again

22

23 "Shall he save his people in their sins"

24

25 and Amulek answered and said unto him

26

27 "I say unto you he shall not

28   for it is impossible for him to deny his word"

29

30 now Zeezrom said unto the people

31

32 "See that you remember these things

33 for he said there is but one Eloah

1 yet he says that the Son of Elohiym shall come
2 but he shall not save his people
3 as though he had authority to command Elohiym"
4
5 now Amulek said again unto him
6
7 "behold you have lied for you say that I have spoken
8 as though I had authority to command Elohiym
9 because I said he shall not save his people in their sins
10 and I say unto you again that he cannot save them in their sins
11 for I cannot deny his word
12 and he has said that no unclean thing can inherit the kingdom of heaven
13 therefore how can you be saved except you inherit the kingdom of heaven
14 therefore you cannot be saved in your sins"
15
16 now Zeezrom said again unto him
17
18 "Is the Son of Elohiym the very Kedem Elohiym
19
20 and Amulek said unto him
21
22 "Yes he is the very Kedem Elohiym of heaven and of earth
23 and all things which in them are
24 he is the beginning and the end
25 the alef and the tav
26 and he shall come into the world to redeem his people
27 and he shall take upon him the rebellion of those who believe on his name
28 and these are they that shall have eternal life
29 and salvation comes to none else
30 therefore the evil remain as though there had been no redemption made
31 except it be the loosing of the bands of death
32 for behold the day comes that all shall rise from the dead
33 and stand before Elohiym

1 and be judged according to their works

2

3 now there is a death which is called a temporal death

4 and the death of Mashiach shall loose the bands of this temporal death

5 that all shall be raised from this temporal death the spirit

6 and the body shall be reunited again in its perfect form

7 both limb and joint shall be restored to its proper frame

8 even as we now are at this time

9 and we shall be brought to stand before Elohiym knowing

10 even as we know now

11 and have a bright recollection of all our guilt

12

13 now this restoration shall come to all

14 both old and young

15 both bond and free

16 both male and female

17 both the evil and the righteous

18 and even there shall not so much as a hair of their heads be lost

19 but everything shall be restored to its perfect frame

20 as it is now or in the body

21 and shall be brought and be arraigned before the porch of Mashiach the son

22 and the Kedem Elohiym and the Ruach Elohiym

23 which is one Kedem Elohiym

24 to be judged according to their works

25 whether they be good or whether they be evil

26

27 now behold I have spoken unto you

28 concerning the death of the mortal body

29 and also concerning the resurrection of the mortal body

30 I say unto you that this mortal body is raised to an immortal body

31 that is from death

32 even from the first death unto life

33 that they can die no more their spirits uniting

1   with their bodies never to be divided

2   thus the whole becoming spiritual and immortal

3   that they can no more see corruption"

4

5   now when Amulek had finished these words the people

6   began again to be astonished

7   and also Zeezrom began to tremble

8   and thus ended the words of Amulek

9   or this is all that I have written

10

11   now Almah seeing that the words of Amulek had silenced Zeezrom

12   for he beheld that Amulek had caught him

13   in his lying and deceiving to destroy him

14   and seeing that he began to tremble

15   under a consciousness of his guilt he opened his mouth

16   and began to speak unto him

17   and to establish the words of Amulek

18   and to explain things beyond

19   or to unfold the scriptures beyond that

20   which Amulek had done

21

22   now the words that Almah spoke unto Zeezrom were heard

23   by the people round about

24   for the multitude was great and he spoke after this manner

25

26   "now Zeezrom seeing that you have been taken

27   in your lying and craftiness

28   for you hast not lied unto men only

29   but you have lied unto Elohiym

30   for behold he knows all your thoughts

31   and you see that your thoughts are made known unto us by his Ruach

32   and you see that we know that your plan was a very subtle plan

33   as to the subtlety of the evil one

1   for to lie and to deceive this people

2   that you might set them against us

3   to revile us and to cast us out

4   now this was a plan of thine adversary

5   and he has exercised his power in you

6

7   now I would that you should remember

8   that what I say unto you I say unto all

9   and behold I say unto you all

10   that this was a snare of the adversary

11   which he has laid to catch this people

12   that he might bring you into subjection unto him

13   that he might encircle you about with his chains

14   that he might chain you down to everlasting destruction

15   according to the power of his captivity

16

17   now when Almah had spoken these words Zeezrom

18   began to tremble more exceedingly

19   for he was convinced more and more of the power of Elohiym

20   and he was also convinced that Almah and Amulek had a knowledge of him

21   for he was convinced that they knew the thoughts and intents of his heart

22   for power was given unto them that they might know of these things

23   according to the spirit of prophecy

24   and Zeezrom began to inquire of them diligently

25   that he might know more concerning the kingdom of Elohiym

26   and he said unto Almah

27

28   "What does this mean which Amulek has spoken

29   concerning the resurrection of the dead

30   that all shall rise from the dead

31   both the just and the unjust

32   and are brought to stand before Elohiym

33   to be judged according to their works"

1
2 and now Almah began to expound these things
3 unto him saying
4
5 "It is given unto many to know the mysteries of Elohiym
6 nevertheless they are laid under a strict mitzvah
7 that they shall not impart only according to the portion of his word
8 which he does grant unto the children of men
9 according to the regard and diligence which they give unto him
10 and therefore he that will harden his heart the same receives the lesser portion
11 of the word
12 and he that will not harden his heart to him is given the greater portion of the
13 word
14 until it is given unto him to know the mysteries of Elohiym
15 until he know them in full
16
17 and they that will harden their hearts
18 to them is given the lesser portion of the word
19 until they know nothing concerning his mysteries
20 and then they are taken captive by the devil
21 and led by his will down to destruction
22 now this is what is meant by the chains of Sheol
23 and Amulek hath spoken plainly concerning death
24 and being raised from this mortality to a state of immortality
25 and being brought before the bar of Elohiym
26 to be judged according to our works
27 then if our hearts have been hardened
28 yes if we have hardened our hearts against the word insomuch
29 that it has not been found in us
30 then will our state be awful
31 for then we shall be condemned
32 for our words will condemn us
33 yes all our works will condemn us we shall not be found spotless

1 and our thoughts will also condemn us

2 and in this awful state we shall not dare to look up to our Elohiym

3 and we would rejoice and be glad

4 if we could command the rocks and the mountains

5 to fall upon us to hide us from his presence

6 but this cannot be we must come forth and stand before him

7 in his glory and in his power

8 and in his might majesty and dominion

9 and acknowledge to our everlasting shame

10 that all his judgments are just

11 that he is just in all his works

12 and that he is merciful unto the children of men

13 and that he has all power to save every man that believes on his name

14 and brings forth fruit demonstrating repentance

15

16 and now behold I say unto you

17 then comes a death

18 even a second death

19 which is a spiritual death

20 then is a time that whoever dies in his sins

21 as to a temporal death

22 shall also die a spiritual death

23 yes he shall die as to things pertaining unto righteousness

24 then is the time when their torments shall be as a lake of fire and brimstone

25 whose flame ascend up forever and ever

26 and then is the time that they shall be chained down

27 to an everlasting destruction

28 according to the power and captivity of the evil one he having subjected them

29 according to his will

30 then I say unto you

31 they shall be as though there had been no redemption made

32 for they cannot be redeemed according to Elohiym's justice

33 and they cannot die seeing there is no more corruption

1
2 Now it came to pass
3 that when Almah had made an end of speaking
4 these words the people began to be more astonished
5 but there was one Antionah
6 who was a chief ruler among them came forth
7 and said unto him
8
9 "What is this that you have said that man should rise from the dead
10 and be changed from this mortal to an immortal state
11 that the soul can never die
12 What does the scripture mean
13 which says that Elohiym placed k'ruvim and a flaming sword
14 on the east of the garden of Eden
15 for fear that our first parents should enter and partake
16 of the fruit of the tree of life and live forever
17 and thus we see that there was no possible chance
18 that they should live forever"
19
20 now Almah said unto him
21
22 "This is the thing which I was about to explain
23 now we see that Ahdam did fall by the partaking
24 of the fruit of the Tree of Knowledge good and evil
25 according to the word of Elohiym
26 and thus we see that by his fall
27 all mankind became a lost and fallen people
28
29 and now behold I say unto you
30 that if it had been possible for Ahdam to have partaken
31 of the fruit of the tree of life at that time
32 there would have been no death
33 and the word would have been void making Elohiym a liar

1   for he said

2

3   "If you eat you shalt surely die"[3]

4

5   and we see that death comes upon mankind

6   yes the death which has been spoken of by Amulek

7   which is the temporal death

8   nevertheless there was a space granted unto man

9   in which he might repent

10 therefore this life became a probationary state

11 a time to prepare to meet Elohiym

12 a time to prepare for that endless state

13 which has been spoken of by us

14 which is after the resurrection of the dead

15 now if it had not been for the plan of redemption

16 which was planned from the creation of the world

17 there could have been no resurrection of the dead

18 but there was a plan of redemption planned

19 which shall bring to pass the resurrection of the dead

20 of which has been spoken

21

22 and now behold if it were possible

23 that our first parents could have gone forth and partaken of the Etz Chaim

24 they would have been forever miserable having no preparatory state

25 and thus the plan of redemption would have been frustrated

26 and the word of Elohiym would have been void taking none effect

27 but behold it was not so

28 but it was appointed unto men

29 that they must die

30 and after death

31 they must come to judgment

32 even that same judgment

---

[3] Beresheit (Genesis) 2:17

1   of which we have spoken which is the end
2   and after Elohiym had appointed that these things should come unto man
3   behold then he saw that it was necessary that man should know
4   concerning the things that he had appointed unto them
5   therefore he sent angels to converse with them
6   who caused men to behold of his glory
7
8   and they began from that time forth to call on his name
9   therefore Elohiym conversed with men
10   and made known unto them the plan of redemption
11   which had been prepared from the creation of the world
12   and this he made known unto them
13   according to their faith and repentance and their holy works
14   therefore he gave mitzvot unto men
15   they having first rebelled the first mitzvot
16   as to things which were temporal
17   and becoming as elohiym knowing good from evil placing themselves
18   in a state to act or being placed in a state to act
19   according to their wills and pleasures
20   whether to do evil or to do good
21   therefore Elohiym gave unto them mitzvoth
22   after having made known unto them the plan of redemption
23   that they should not do evil the penalty thereof being a second death
24   which was an everlasting death
25   as to things pertaining unto righteousness
26   for on such the plan of redemption could have no power
27   for the works of justice could not be destroyed
28   according to the great goodness of Elohiym
29
30   but Elohiym did call on men
31   in the name of his Chosen Son
32   this being the plan of redemption
33   which was planned saying

1
2 "If you will repent and harden not your hearts
3 then will I have mercy upon you
4 through my One Chosen Son
5 therefore whoever repents and hardens not his heart he
6 shall have claim on mercy through my One Chosen Son
7 unto a remission of his sins
8 and these shall enter into my rest
9 and whoever will harden his heart and will do lawlessness
10 behold I swear in my anger
11 that he shall not enter into my rest"
12
13 and now my brothers behold I say unto you
14 that if you will harden your hearts you
15 shall not enter into the rest of YHVH
16 therefore your lawlessness provokes him
17 that he sends down his anger upon you
18 as in the first provocation
19 yes according to his word in the last provocation
20 as well as the first
21 to the everlasting destruction of your souls
22 therefore according to his word
23 unto the last death as well as the first
24 `and now my brothers seeing we know these things
25 and they are true let us repent and harden not our hearts
26 that we provoke not YHVH our Elohiym
27 to pull down his anger upon us
28 in these his second mitzvot
29 which he has given unto us
30 but let us enter into the rest of Elohiym
31 which is prepared according to his word
32
33 and again my brothers I would cite your minds forward

1   to the time when YHVH Elohiym gave these mitzvot unto his children
2   and I would that you should remember
3   that YHVH Elohiym ordained kohanim after his set apart manner
4   which was after the manner of his Chosen Son
5   to teach these things unto the people
6
7   and those kohanim were prepared
8   after the manner of his Chosen Son
9   in a manner that thereby the people might know
10 in what manner to look forward to his Chosen Son
11 for redemption
12 and this is the manner after which they were prepared
13 being called and prepared
14 from the creation of the world
15 according to the foreknowledge of Elohiym
16 on account of their exceeding faith and good works
17 in the first place being left to choose good or evil
18 therefore they having chosen good
19 and exercising exceedingly great faith are called
20 with a holy calling
21 yes with that holy calling
22 which was prepared with
23 and according to a preparatory redemption for such
24 and thus they have been called to this holy calling
25 on account of their faith
26 while others would reject the Ruach Elohiym
27 on account of the hardness of their hearts
28 and blindness of their minds
29 while if it had not been for this
30 they might have had as great privilege as their brothers
31 or in sum
32 in the first place
33 they were on the same standing with their brothers

1 thus this holy calling being prepared from the creation of the world

2 for such as would not harden their hearts being in

3 and through the atonement of the One Chosen Son

4 who was prepared

5 and thus being called by this holy calling

6 and prepared for the High Service[4] after the holy manner of Elohiym

7 to teach his mitzvot unto the children of men

8 that they also might enter into his rest

9 This High Service being after the manner of his Chosen Son

10 which manner was from the creation of the world

11 or in other words being without beginning of days or end of years

12 being prepared from eternity to all eternity

13 according to his foreknowledge of all things

14

15 now they were prepared after this manner

16 being called with a holy calling

17 and prepared with a holy ordinance

18 and taking upon them the High Service after the holy manner

19 which calling and ordinance and High Service is without beginning or end

20 thus they become kohanim g'dolim forever

21 after the order of the Son the One Chosen of the Father

22 who is without beginning of days or end of years

23 who is full of grace equity and truth

24 and thus it is

25 Amein

26

27 now as I said concerning the holy manner or this high service

28 there were many who were prepared

29 and became kohanim g'dolim of Elohiym

30 and it was on account of their exceeding faith and repentance

31 and their righteousness before Elohiym

32 they choosing to repent and work righteousness

---

[4] Kehunah Gadol- High service, priesthood

1 rather than to perish

2 therefore they were called after this holy manner

3 and were set apart and their garments were washed white

4 through the blood of the Lamb

5 now they after being set apart by the Ruach Elohiym having their garments

6 made white

7 being pure and spotless before Elohiym could not look upon sin

8 except it were with abhorrence

9 and there were many exceedingly great many

10 who were made pure and entered into the rest of YHVH their Elohiym

11

12 and now my brothers I would

13 that you should humble yourselves before Elohiym

14 and bring forth fruit demonstrating repentance

15 that you may also enter into that rest

16 yes humble yourselves even as the people in the days of Malki-Tzedek

17 who was also a Kohen Gadol after this same manner which I have spoken

18 who also took upon him the high service forever

19 and it was this same Malki-Tzedek to whom Avraham paid tithes

20 yes even our father Avraham paid tithes

21 of one tenth part of all he possessed

22

23 Aow these ordinances were given after this manner

24 that thereby the people might look forward on the Chosen Son of Elohiym

25 it being a mark of his manner or it being his manner

26 and this that they might look forward to him

27 for a remission of their sins

28 that they might enter into the rest of YHVH

29

30 now this Malki-Tzedek was a king over the land of Shalem

31 and his people had grown strong in lawlessness and abomination

32 yes they had all gone astray they were full of all manner of wickedness

33 but Malki-Tzedek having exercised mighty faith

1 and received the office of the high service
2 according to the holy manner of Elohiym did preach repentance
3 unto his people
4 and behold they did repent
5 and Malki-Tzedek did establish peace in the land in his days
6 therefore he was called the sar shalom[5]
7 for he was the king of Shalem
8 and he did reign under his father
9 now there were many before him
10 and also there were many afterwards
11 but none were greater
12 therefore of him they have more particularly made mention
13 now I need not rehearse the matter
14 what I have said may suffice
15 behold the scriptures are before you
16 if you will twist them it shall be to your own destruction"
17
18 And now it came to pass
19 that when Almah had said these words
20 unto them he stretched forth his hand unto them
21 and cried with a mighty voice saying
22
23 "now is the time to repent for the day of salvation draws near
24 yes and the voice of YHVH by the mouth of angels does declare it unto all
25 nations
26 yes does declare it that they may have glad tidings of great joy
27 yes and he does sound these glad tidings among all his people
28 yes even to them that are scattered abroad upon the face of the earth
29 therefore they have come unto us
30 and they are made known unto us in plain terms
31 that we may understand
32 that we cannot go astray

---

[5] Sar shalom – prince of peace

1   and this because of our being wanderers in a strange land

2   therefore we are thus highly favored

3   for we have these glad tidings declared unto us

4   in all parts of our vineyard

5   for behold angels are declaring it unto many at this time in our land

6   and this is for the purpose of preparing the hearts of the children of men

7   to receive his word at the time of his coming in his glory

8   and now we only wait to hear the joyful news declared unto us

9   by the mouth of angels of his coming

10   for the time comes we know not how soon

11   would to Elohiym that it might be in my day

12   but let it be sooner or later in it I will rejoice

13   and it shall be made known unto just and holy men

14   by the mouth of angels at the time of his coming

15   that the words of our fathers may be fulfilled

16   according to that which they have spoken concerning him

17   which was according to the ruach of prophecy which was in them

18

19   and now my brothers I wish from the inmost part of my heart

20   yes with great anxiety even unto pain

21   that you would listen to and obey my words

22   and cast off your sins

23   and not procrastinate the day of your repentance

24   but that you would humble yourselves before YHVH

25   and call on his holy name and watch

26   and pray continually that you may not be tempted above that

27   which you can bear

28   and thus be led by the Ruach Elohiym

29   becoming humble

30   meek

31   submissive

32   patient

33   full of love

1 and all long-suffering

2 having faith on YHVH having a hope

3 that you shall receive eternal life having the love of Elohiym

4 always in your hearts

5 that you may be lifted up at the last day

6 and enter into his rest

7 and may YHVH grant unto you repentance

8 that you may not bring down his wrath upon you

9 that you may not be bound down by the chains of Sheol

10 that you may not suffer the second death

11 and Almah spoke many more words unto the people

12 which are not written in this book

13

14 And it came to pass

15 after he had made an end of speaking unto the people

16 many of them did believe on his words

17 and began to repent and to search the scriptures

18 but the more part of them desired

19 that they might destroy Almah and Amulek

20 for they were angry with Almah

21 because of the plainness of his words unto Zeezrom

22 and they also said that Amulek had lied unto them

23 and had reviled against their law

24 and also against their lawyers and judges

25 and they were also angry with Almah and Amulek

26 and because they had testified so plainly against their wickedness

27 they sought to put them away secretly

28

29 But it came to pass

30 that they did not

31 but they took them and bound them with strong cords

32 and took them before the chief judge of the land

33 and the people went forth and witnessed against them testifying

1   that they had reviled against the law and their lawyers

2   and judges of the land and also of all the people that were in the land

3   and also testified that there was but one Elohiym

4   and that he should send his Chosen Son among the people

5   but he should not save them

6   and many such things did the people testify against Almah and Amulek

7   now this was done before the chief judge of the land

8

9   And it came to pass

10 that Zeezrom was astonished at the words which had been spoken

11 and he also knew concerning the blindness of the minds

12 which he had caused among the people by his lying words

13 and his soul began to be broken up under a consciousness of his own guilt

14 yes he began to be encircled about by the pains of Sheol

15

16 And it came to pass

17 that he began to cry unto the people saying

18

19 "behold I am guilty and these men are spotless before Elohiym"

20

21 and he began to plead for them from that time forth

22 but they reviled him saying

23

24 "Are you also possessed with the evil one"

25 and they spit upon him and cast him out from among them

26 and also all those who believed in the words

27 which had been spoken by Almah and Amulek

28 and they cast them out

29 and sent men to cast stones at them

30 and they brought their wives and children together

31 and whoever believed or had been taught to believe in the word of Elohiym

32 they caused that they should be cast into the fire

33 and they also brought forth their records

1   which contained the holy scriptures

2   and cast them into the fire also

3   that they might be burned and destroyed by fire

4

5   And it came to pass

6   that they took Almah and Amulek

7   and carried them forth to the place of execution

8   that they might witness the destruction of those

9   who were consumed by fire

10 and when Amulek saw the pains of the women and children

11 who were being consumed in the fire he also was pained

12 and he said unto Almah

13

14 "how can we witness this awful scene

15 therefore let us stretch forth our hands

16 and exercise the power of Elohiym which is in us

17 and save them from the flames"

18

19 but Almah said unto him

20

21 "The Ruach constrains me

22 that I must not stretch forth my hand

23 for behold YHVH receives them up unto himself in glory

24 and he does allow that they may do this thing

25 or that the people may do this thing unto them

26 according to the hardness of their hearts

27 that the judgments

28 which he shall exercise upon them in his anger may be just

29 and the blood of the innocent shall stand as a witness against them

30 yes and cry mightily against them at the last day"

31

32 now Amulek said unto Almah

33

1   "behold perhaps they will burn us also"

2

3   and Almah said

4

5   "Be it according to the will of YHVH

6   but behold our work is not finished

7   therefore they burn us not"

8

9   Now it came to pass

10 that when the bodies of those who had been cast

11 into the fire were consumed and also the records

12 which were cast in with them the chief judge of the land came

13 and stood before Almah and Amulek as they were bound

14 and he struck them with his hand upon their cheeks

15 and said unto them

16

17 "After what you have seen will you preach again unto this people

18 that they shall be cast into a lake of fire and brimstone

19 behold you see that you had not power to save those

20 who had been cast into the fire

21 neither has Elohiym saved them

22 because they were of your faith"

23

24 and the judge struck them again

25 upon their cheeks and asked

26

27 "What say you for yourselves"

28

29 now this judge was after the manner and faith

30 of Nachor who slew Gideon

31

32 And it came to pass

33 that Almah and Amulek answered him nothing

1 and he struck them again

2 and delivered them to the officers

3 to be cast into prison

4 and when they had been cast into prison three days

5 there came many lawyers and judges

6 and priests and teachers

7 who were of the profession of Nachor

8 and they came in unto the prison to see them

9 and they questioned them about many words

10 but they answered them nothing

11

12 And it came to pass

13 that the judge stood before them and said

14

15 "Why do you not answer the words of this people

16 Know you not

17 that I have power to deliver you up

18 unto the flames"

19

20 and he commanded them to speak

21 but they answered nothing

22

23 And it came to pass

24 that they departed and went their ways

25 but came again on the next day

26 and the judge also struck them again on their cheeks

27 and many came forth also and struck them saying

28

29 "Will you stand again and judge this people

30 and condemn our law

31 If you have such great power

32 why do you not deliver yourselves"

33

1 and many such things did they say unto them

2 gnashing their teeth upon them and spitting upon them

3 and saying

4

5 "how shall we look when we are condemned"

6

7 and many such things

8 yes all manner of such things did they say unto them

9 and thus they did mock them for many days

10 and they did withhold food from them

11 that they might hunger

12 and water that they might thirst

13 and they also did take from them their clothes

14 that they were naked

15 and thus they were bound with strong cords

16 and confined in prison

17

18 And it came to pass

19 after they had thus suffered for many days

20 and it was on the twelfth day in the tenth month

21 in the tenth year of the reign of the judges over the people of Nephi

22 that the chief judge over the land of Ammoniyah

23 and many of their teachers and their lawyers went in unto the prison

24 where Almah and Amulek were bound with cords

25

26 and the chief judge stood before them

27 and struck them again

28 and said unto them

29

30 "If you have the power of Elohiym deliver yourselves from these bands

31 and then we will believe that YHVH will destroy this people

32 according to your words"

33

1 And it came to pass
2 that they all went forth
3 and struck them saying the same words even until the last
4 and when the last had spoken unto them
5 the power of Elohiym was upon Almah and Amulek
6 and they rose and stood upon their feet
7 and Almah cried saying
8
9 "how long shall we suffer these great afflictions O YHVH
10 O YHVH give us strength
11 according to our faith which is in Mashiach
12 even unto deliverance"
13
14 and they broke the cords with which they were bound
15 and when the people saw this they began to flee
16 for the fear of destruction had come upon them
17
18 And it came to pass
19 that so great was their fear that they fell to the earth
20 and did not obtain the outer door of the prison
21 and the earth shook mightily
22 and the walls of the prison were torn in two so that they fell to the earth
23 and the chief judge and the lawyers
24 and priests and teachers who struck
25 upon Almah and Amulek were killed by the fall thereof
26 and Almah and Amulek came forth out of the prison
27 and they were not hurt for YHVH had granted unto them power
28 according to their faith which was in Mashiach
29 and they straightway came forth out of the prison
30 and they were loosed from their bands
31 and the prison had fallen to the earth
32 and every soul within the walls thereof
33 except it were Almah and Amulek was skilled

1 and they straightway came forth into the city

2 now the people having heard a great noise came running

3 together by multitudes to know the cause of it

4 and when they saw Almah and Amulek coming forth out of the prison

5 and the walls thereof had fallen to the earth

6 they were struck with great fear

7 and fled from the presence of Almah and Amulek

8 even as a goat flees with her young from two lions

9 and thus they did flee from the presence of Almah and Amulek

10

11 And it came to pass

12 that Almah and Amulek were commanded

13 to depart out of that city

14 and they departed

15 and came out even into the land of Sidom

16 and behold there they found all the people

17 who had departed out of the land of Ammoniyah

18 who had been cast out and stoned

19 because they believed in the words of Almah

20 and they related unto them all that had happened

21 unto their wives and children

22 and also concerning themselves

23 and of their power of deliverance

24 and also Zeezrom lay sick at Sidom with a burning fever

25 which was caused by the great tribulations of his mind

26 on account of his wickedness

27 for he supposed that Almah and Amulek were no more

28 and he supposed that they had been slain because of his lawlessness

29 and this great sin

30 and his many other sins did harrow up his mind

31 until it did become exceedingly sore having no deliverance

32 therefore he began to be scorched

33 with a burning heat

1   now when he heard
2   that Almah and Amulek were in the land of Sidom
3   his heart began to take courage
4   and he sent a message immediately unto them desiring them
5   to come unto him
6
7   And it came to pass
8   that they went immediately obeying the message
9   which he had sent unto them
10   and they went in unto the house unto Zeezrom
11   and they found him upon his bed sick
12   being very low with a burning fever
13   and his mind also was exceedingly sore
14   because of his lawlessness
15   and when he saw them he stretched forth his hand
16   and implored them that they would heal him
17
18   And it came to pass
19   that Almah said unto him taking him
20   by the hand
21
22   "Believe you in the power of Mashiach unto salvation"
23
24   and he answered
25   and said
26
27   "yes I believe all the words that you have taught"
28
29   and Almah said
30
31   "If you believe in the redemption of Mashiach
32   you can be healed"
33

1 and he said

2

3 "yes I believe

4   according to your words"

5

6 and then Almah cried

7 unto YHVH saying

8

9 "O YHVH our Elohiym have mercy on this man

10 and heal him according to his faith

11 which is in Mashiach"

12

13 and when Almah had said these words

14 Zeezrom leaped upon his feet

15 and began to walk

16 and this was done to the great astonishment of all the people

17 and the knowledge of this went forth

18 throughout all the land of Sidom

19 and Almah immersed Zeezrom unto YHVH

20 and he began from that time forth

21 to preach unto the people

22 and Almah established an assembly in the land of Sidom

23 and set apart priests and teachers in the land

24 to immerse unto YHVH

25 whoever desired to be immersed

26

27 And it came to pass

28 that they were many

29 for they did flock in from all the region round about Sidom

30 and were immersed

31 but as to the people that were in the land of Ammoniyah

32 they yet remained a hard hearted and a stubborn people

33 and they repented not of their sins

1   ascribing all the power of Almah and Amulek to the evil one
2   for they were of the profession of Nachor
3   and did not believe in the repentance of their sins
4
5   And it came to pass
6   that Almah and Amulek Amulek having forsaken
7   all his gold and silver and his precious things
8   which were in the land of Ammoniyah
9   for the word of Elohiym he being rejected
10 by those who were once his friends
11 and also by his father and his relatives
12 therefore after Almah having established the assembly
13 at Sidom seeing a great check
14 yes seeing that the people were checked
15 as to the pride of their hearts
16 and began to humble themselves before Elohiym
17 and began to assemble themselves together
18 at their sanctuaries to worship Elohiym
19 before the altar watching and praying continually
20 that they might be delivered from the evil one
21 and from death and from destruction
22 now as I said Almah having seen all these things
23 therefore he took Amulek
24 and came over to the land of Zarahemla
25 and took him to his own house
26 and did administer unto him in his tribulations
27 and strengthened him in YHVH
28 and thus ended the tenth year of the reign of the judges
29 over the people of Nephi
30
31 And it came to pass
32 in the eleventh year of the reign of the judges
33 over the people of Nephi

1   on the fifth day of the second month

2   there having been much peace in the land of Zarahemla

3   there having been no wars

4   nor contentions for a certain number of years

5   even until the fifth day of the second month in the eleventh year

6   there was a cry of war heard throughout the land

7   for behold the armies of the Lamaniy had come in

8   upon the wilderness side

9   into the borders of the land

10   even into the city of Ammoniyah

11   and began to kill the people

12   and destroy the city

13

14   And now it came to pass

15   before the Nephiy could raise a sufficient army

16   to drive them out of the land

17   they had destroyed the people

18   who were in the city of Ammoniyah

19   and also some around the borders of Noach

20   and taken others captive into the wilderness

21

22   Now it came to pass

23   that the Nephiy desired to obtain those

24   who had been carried away captive

25   into the wilderness

26   therefore he that had been appointed chief captain

27   over the armies of the Nephiy

28   and his name was Zoram

29   and he had two sons Lechi and Aha

30   now Zoram and his two sons knowing

31   that Almah was high priest over the assembly

32   and having heard that he had the ruach of prophecy

33   therefore they went unto him

1 and desired of him

2 to know where YHVH would that they should go

3 into the wilderness

4 in search of their brothers

5 who had been taken captive by the Lamaniy

6

7 And it came to pass

8 that Almah inquired of YHVH concerning the matter

9 and Almah returned and said unto them

10 behold the Lamaniy will cross the river Tzidon

11 in the south wilderness away up

12 beyond the borders of the land of Manti

13 and behold there shall you meet them

14 on the east of the river Tzidon

15 and there YHVH will deliver unto you your brothers

16 who have been taken captive by the Lamaniy

17

18 And it came to pass

19 that Zoram and his sons crossed over the river Tzidon

20 with their armies

21 and marched away beyond the borders of Manti

22 into the south wilderness

23 which was on the east side of the river Tzidon

24 and they came upon the armies of the Lamaniy

25 and the Lamaniy were scattered

26 and driven into the wilderness

27 and they took their brothers

28 who had been taken captive by the Lamaniy

29 and there was not one soul of them had been lost

30 that were taken captive

31 and they were brought by their brothers

32 to possess their own lands

33 and thus ended the eleventh year of the judges

1   the Lamaniy having been driven out of the land

2   and the people of Ammoniyah were destroyed

3   yes every living soul of the Ammoniyah'iy was destroyed

4   and also their great city

5   which they said Elohiym could not destroy

6   because of its greatness

7   but behold in one day it was left desolate

8   and the carcasses were mangled by dogs

9   and wild beasts of the wilderness

10 nevertheless after many days their dead bodies were heaped up

11 upon the face of the earth

12 and they were covered with a shallow covering

13 and now so great was the scent thereof

14 that the people did not go in to possess the land of Ammoniyah

15 for many years

16 and it was called Desolation of Nachoriy

17 for they were of the profession of Nachor who were slain

18 and their lands remained desolate

19 and the Lamaniy did not come again

20 to war against the Nephiy

21 until the fourteenth year of the reign of the judges

22 over the people of Nephi

23 and thus for three years did the people of Nephi have continual peace

24 in all the land

25 and Almah and Amulek went forth preaching repentance

26 to the people in their temples

27 and in their sanctuaries

28 and also in their synagogues

29 which were built after the manner of the Yehudim

30 and as many as would hear their words

31 unto them they did impart the word of Elohiym

32 without any respect of persons continually

33 and thus did Almah and Amulek go forth

1 and also many more who had been chosen for the work

2 to preach the word throughout all the land

3 and the establishment of the assembly

4 became general throughout the land

5 in all the region round about

6 among all the people of the Nephiy

7 and there was no inequality among them

8 YHVH did pour out his Ruach on all the face of the land

9 to prepare the minds of the children of men

10 or to prepare their hearts to receive the word

11 which should be taught among them

12 at the time of his coming

13 that they might not be hardened against the word

14 that they might not be unbelieving

15 and go on to destruction

16 but that they might receive the word with joy

17 and as a branch be grafted into the true vine

18 that they might enter into the rest of YHVH their Elohiym

19 now those priests who did go forth among the people did preach

20 against all lying and deceiving

21 and envying and strife

22 and malice and reviling

23 and stealing robbing plundering murdering committing adultery

24 and all manner of covetousness crying

25 that these things ought not so to be

26 Holding forth things which must shortly come

27 yes holding forth the coming of the Chosen Son of Elohiym

28 his sufferings and death

29 and also the resurrection of the dead

30 and many of the people did inquire concerning the place

31 where the Chosen Son of Elohiym should come

32 and they were taught that he would appear unto them

33 after his resurrection

1   and this the people did hear
2   with great joy and gladness
3   and now after the assembly had been established
4   throughout all the land having got the victory
5   over the evil one
6   and the word of Elohiym being preached in its purity
7   in all the land
8   and YHVH pouring out his blessings upon the people
9   thus ended the fourteenth year of the reign of the judges
10 over the people of Nephi
11
12
13
14
15
16
17
18
19
20
21
22
23
24
25
26
27
28
29
30
31
32
33

5-THE SONS OF MOSHEYAHU

1
2
3 An account of the sons of Mosheyahu
4 who rejected their rights to the kingdom
5 for the word of Elohiym
6 and went up to the land of Nephi
7 to preach to the Lamaniy
8 their sufferings and deliverance
9 according to the record of Almah
10
11 And now it came to pass
12 that as Almah was journeying
13 from the land of Gid`on southward away
14 to the land of Manti
15 behold to his astonishment he met
16 with the sons of Mosheyahu journeying
17 towards the land of Zarahemla
18 now these sons of Mosheyahu were with Almah
19 at the time the angel first appeared unto him
20 therefore Almah did rejoice exceedingly to see his brothers
21 and what added more to his joy
22 they were still his brothers in YHVH
23 yes and they had waxed strong
24 in the knowledge of the truth
25 for they were men of a sound understanding
26 and they had searched the scriptures diligently
27 that they might know the word of Elohiym
28 but this is not all
29 they had given themselves
30 to much prayer and fasting
31 therefore they had the ruach of prophecy
32 and the ruach of revelation
33 and when they taught

1   they taught with power and authority of Elohiym
2   and they had been teaching the word of Elohiym
3   for the space of fourteen years
4   among the Lamaniy having had much success
5   in bringing many to the knowledge of the truth
6   yes by the power of their words
7   many were brought before the altar of Elohiym
8   to call on his name
9   and confess their sins before him
10 now these are the circumstances
11 which attended them in their journeyings
12 for they had many afflictions
13 they did suffer much both in body and in mind
14 such as hunger thirst and fatigue
15 and also much labor in the Ruach
16 now these were their journeyings
17 Having taken leave of their father Mosheyahu
18 in the first year of the judges having refused the kingdom
19 which their father desired to confer upon them
20 and also this was the minds of the people
21 nevertheless they departed out of the land of Zarahemla
22 and took their swords and their spears
23 and their bows and their arrows
24 and their slings
25 and this they did
26 that they might provide food for themselves
27 while in the wilderness
28 and thus they departed into the wilderness with their numbers
29 which they had selected to go up
30 to the land of Nephi
31 to preach the word of Elohiym
32 unto the Lamaniy
33

1 And it came to pass
2 that they journeyed many days in the wilderness
3 and they fasted much and prayed much
4 that YHVH would grant unto them a portion of his Ruach
5 to go with them and abide with them
6 that they might be an instrument
7 in the hands of Elohiym
8 to bring if it were possible their brothers the Lamaniy
9 to the knowledge of the truth
10 to the knowledge of the baseness
11 of the traditions of their fathers
12 which were not correct
13
14 And it came to pass
15 that YHVH did visit them with his Ruach
16 and said unto them
17
18 "Be comforted"
19
20   and they were comforted
21
22 and YHVH said unto them also
23 "Go forth among the Lamaniy your brothers
24 and establish my word
25 yet you shall be patient in long suffering and afflictions
26 that you may show forth good examples unto them in me
27 and I will make an instrument of you in my hands
28 unto the salvation of many souls"
29
30 And it came to pass
31 that the hearts of the sons of Mosheyahu
32 and also those who were with them took courage
33 to go forth unto the Lamaniy

1   to declare unto them the word of Elohiym

2

3   And it came to pass

4   when they had arrived in the borders

5   of the land of the Lamaniy

6   that they separated themselves

7   and departed one from another trusting in YHVH

8   that they should meet again at the close of their harvest

9   for they supposed that great was the work

10   which they had undertaken

11   and assuredly it was great

12   for they had undertaken to preach the word of Elohiym

13   to a wild and a hardened and a ferocious people

14   a people who delighted in murdering the Nephiy

15   and robbing and plundering them

16   and their hearts were set upon riches

17   or upon gold and silver and precious stones

18   yet they sought to obtain these things

19   by murdering and plundering

20   that they might not labor for them

21   with their own hands

22   thus they were a very idle people

23   many of whom did worship idols

24   and the curse of Elohiym had fallen upon them

25   because of the traditions of their fathers

26   notwithstanding the promises of YHVH were extended unto them

27   on the conditions of repentance

28   therefore this was the cause

29   for which the sons of Mosheyahu had undertaken the work

30   that perhaps they might bring them unto repentance

31   that perhaps they might bring them to know

32   of the plan of redemption

33

1 therefore they separated themselves one from another
2 and went forth among them every man alone
3 according to the word and power of Elohiym
4 which was given unto him
5 now Ammon being the chief among them
6 or rather he did administer unto them
7 and he departed from them
8 after having blessed them
9 according to their several stations
10 having imparted the word of Elohiym unto them
11 or administered unto them before his departure
12 and thus they took their several journeys throughout the land
13 and Ammon went to the land of Yishma'el the land
14 being called after the sons of Yishma'el
15 who also became Lamaniy
16 and as Ammon entered the land of Yishma'el the Lamaniy took him
17 and bound him as was their custom
18 to bind all the Nephiy who fell into their hands
19 and carry them before the king
20 and thus it was left to the pleasure of the king
21 to kill them or to retain them in captivity
22 or to cast them into prison
23 or to cast them out of his land
24 according to his will and pleasure
25 and thus Ammon was carried before the king
26 who was over the land of Yishma'el
27 and his name was Lamoni\
28 and he was a descendant of Yishma'el
29 and the king inquired of Ammon
30 if it were his desire to dwell in the land
31 among the Lamaniy or among his people
32 and Ammon said
33 unto him

1
2   "Yes I desire to dwell among this people for a time
3   yes and perhaps until the day I die"
4
5   And it came to pass
6   that king Lamoni was much pleased with Ammon
7   and caused that his bands should be loosed
8   and he would that Ammon should take one of his daughters to wife
9
10   but Ammon said
11   unto him
12
13   "No but I will be your servant"
14
15   therefore Ammon became a servant to king Lamoni
16
17   And it came to pass
18   that he was set among other servants
19   to watch the flocks of Lamoni
20   according to the custom of the Lamaniy
21   and after he had been in the service of the king three days
22   as he was with the Lamanitish servants going forth
23   with their flocks to the place of water
24   which was called the water of Sebus
25   and all the Lamaniy drive their flocks to this place
26   that they may have water
27   therefore as Ammon
28   and the servants of the king were driving forth their flocks
29   to this place of water
30   behold a certain number of the Lamaniy
31   who had been with their flocks to water stood
32   and scattered the flocks of Ammon and the servants of the king
33   and they scattered them insomuch

1 that they fled many ways

2 now the servants of the king began to complain saying

3

4 "now the king will kill us as he has our brothers

5 because their flocks were scattered

6 by the wickedness of these men"

7

8 and they began to weep exceedingly saying

9

10 "behold our flocks are scattered already"

11

12 now they wept because of the fear of being killed

13 now when Ammon saw this his heart was swollen within him with joy

14 for said he I will show forth my power

15 unto these my fellow-servants

16 or the power which is in me

17 in restoring these flocks unto the king

18 that I may win the hearts of these my fellow servants

19 that I may lead them to believe in my words

20 and now these were the thoughts of Ammon

21 when he saw the afflictions of those

22 whom he termed to be his brothers

23

24 And it came to pass

25 that he flattered them by his words saying

26

27 "My brothers be of good cheer

28 and let us go in search of the flocks

29 and we will gather them together

30 and bring them back unto the place of water

31 and thus we will preserve the flocks unto the king

32 and he will not kill us"

33

1 And it came to pass
2 that they went in search of the flocks
3 and they did follow Ammon
4 and they rushed forth with much swiftness
5 and did head the flocks of the king
6 and did gather them together again
7 to the place of water
8 and those men again stood to scatter their flocks
9 but Ammon said unto his brothers
10
11 "Encircle the flocks round about that they flee not
12 and I go and contend with these men
13 who do scatter our flocks"
14
15 Therefore they did as Ammon commanded them
16 and he went forth and stood to contend with those
17 who stood by the waters of Sebus
18 and they were in number not a few
19 therefore they did not fear Ammon
20 for they supposed that one of their men could kill him
21 according to their pleasure
22 for they knew not that YHVH had promised Mosheyahu
23 that he would deliver his sons out of their hands
24 neither did they know anything
25 concerning YHVH
26 therefore they delighted in the destruction of their brothers
27 and for this cause they stood to scatter the flocks of the king
28 but Ammon stood forth
29 and began to cast stones at them with his sling
30 yes with mighty power he did sling stones at them
31 and thus he killed a certain number of them insomuch
32 that they began to be astonished at his power
33 nevertheless they were angry

1 because of the killed of their brothers
2 and they were determined that he should fall
3 therefore seeing that they could not hit him with their stones
4 they came forth with clubs to kill him
5 but behold every man that lifted his club
6 to strike Ammon he struck off their arms
7 with his sword
8 for he did withstand their blows
9 by striking their arms with the edge of his sword
10 insomuch that they began to be astonished
11 and began to flee before him
12 yes and they were not few in number
13 and he caused them to flee by the strength of his arm
14 now six of them had fallen by the sling
15 but he killed none save it were their leader with his sword
16 and he struck off as many of their arms
17 as were lifted against him
18 and they were not a few
19 and when he had driven them afar off he returned
20 and they watered their flocks and returned them
21 to the pasture of the king
22 and then went in unto the king bearing the arms
23 which had been cut off by the sword of Ammon
24 of those who sought to kill him
25 and they were carried in unto the king
26 for a testimony of the things which they had done
27
28 And it came to pass
29 that king Lamoni caused
30 that his servants should stand forth
31 and testify to all the things which they had seen
32 concerning the matter
33 and when they had all testified

1   to the things which they had seen
2   and he had learned of the faithfulness of Ammon
3   in preserving his flocks
4   and also of his great power
5   in contending against those
6   who sought to kill him he was astonished exceedingly
7   and said
8
9   "Surely this is more than a man
10   behold is not this the Ruach Gadol
11   who does send such great punishments
12   upon this people because of their murders"
13
14   and they answered the king and said
15
16   "Whether he be the Ruach Gadol
17   or a man we know not
18   but this much we do know
19   that he cannot be killed
20   by the enemies of the king
21   neither can they scatter the king's flocks
22   when he is with us
23   because of his expertness and great strength
24   therefore we know that he is a friend to the king
25   and now O king we do not believe
26   that a man has such great power
27   for we know he cannot be killed"
28
29   and now when the king heard
30   these words he said unto them
31
32   "now I know that it is the Ruach Gadol
33   and he has come down at this time

1   to preserve your lives

2   that I might not execute you

3   as I did your brothers

4   now this is the Ruach Gadol

5   of whom our fathers have spoken"

6

7   now this was the tradition of Lamoni

8   which he had received from his father

9   that there was a Ruach Gadol

10 nevertheless they believed in a Ruach Gadol

11 they supposed that whatever they did was right

12 nevertheless Lamoni began to fear exceedingly with fear

13 for fear that he had done wrong in executing his servants

14 for he had executed many of them

15 because their brothers had scattered their flocks

16 at the place of water

17 and thus because they had had their flocks scattered

18 they were executed

19 now it was the practice of these Lamaniy

20 to stand by the waters of Sebus

21 to scatter the flocks of the people

22 that thereby they might drive away many

23 that were scattered

24 unto their own land it being a practice

25 of plunder among them

26

27 And it came to pass

28 that king Lamoni inquired of his servants saying

29

30 "Where is this man

31 that has such great power"

32

33 and they said unto him

1
2   "behold he is feeding your horses"
3
4   now the king had commanded his servants previous
5   to the time of the watering of their flocks
6   that they should prepare his horses and chariots
7   and conduct him forth to the land of Nephi
8   for there had been a great feast appointed at the land of Nephi
9   by the father of Lamoni
10   who was king over all the land
11   now when king Lamoni heard
12   that Ammon was preparing his horses and his chariots he was more astonished
13   because of the faithfulness of Ammon saying
14
15   "Surely there has not been any servant
16   among all my servants
17   that has been so faithful as this man
18   for even he does remember all my mitzvot
19   to execute them
20   now I surely know
21   that this is the Ruach Gadol
22   and I would desire him
23   that he come in unto me
24   but I dare not"
25
26   And it came to pass
27   that when Ammon had made ready the horses and the chariots
28   for the king and his servants he went in unto the king
29   and he saw that the face of the king was changed
30   therefore he was about to return out of his presence
31   and one of the king's servants said unto him
32
33   "Rabbanah"

1
2 which is being interpreted powerful or great king
3 considering their kings to be powerful
4 and thus he said unto him
5
6 "Rabbanah the king desires you to stay"
7
8 therefore Ammon turned himself unto the king
9 and said unto him
10
11 "What will you
12 that I should do for you O king"
13
14 and the king answered him not
15 for the space of an hour
16 according to their time
17 for he knew not
18 what he should say unto him
19
20 And it came to pass
21 that Ammon said unto him again
22
23 "What desire you of me"
24
25 but the king answered him not
26
27 And it came to pass
28 that Ammon being filled with the Ruach Elohiym
29 therefore he perceived the thoughts of the king
30 and he said unto him
31 "Is it because you have heard
32 that I defended your servants and your flocks
33 and killed seven of their brothers

 1 with the sling and with the sword
 2 and struck off the arms of others
 3 in order to defend your flocks and your servants
 4 behold is it this that causes your astonishment
 5 I say unto you
 6 Why is it that your astonishment is so great
 7 behold I am a man and am your servant
 8 therefore whatever you desire which is right
 9 that will I do"
10
11 now when the king had heard these words he astonished again
12 for he beheld that Ammon could discern his thoughts
13 but despite this king Lamoni did open his mouth
14 and said unto him
15
16 "Who are you art you
17 that Ruach Gadol
18 who knows all things"
19
20 Ammon answered
21 and said unto him
22
23 "I am not"
24
25 and the king said
26
27 "how know you the thoughts of my heart
28 you may speak boldly
29 and tell me concerning these things
30 and also tell me by what power you killed
31 and struck off the arms of my brothers
32 that scattered my flocks
33 and now if you will tell me concerning these things

1 whatever you desire I will give unto you
2 and if it were needed I would guard you with my armies
3 but I know that you are more powerful than all they
4 nevertheless whatever you desire of me I will grant it unto you"
5
6 now Ammon being wise
7 yet harmless he said unto Lamoni
8
9 "Will you listen to and obey my words
10 if I tell you by what power I do these things
11 for this is the thing that I desire of you"
12
13 and the king answered him
14 and said
15
16 "Yes I will believe all your words"
17
18 and thus he was caught with subtilty
19 and Ammon began to speak unto him
20 with boldness and said unto him
21
22 Believe you that there is Elohiym"
23
24 and he answered
25 and said unto him
26
27 "I do not know what that means"
28
29 and then Ammon said
30
31 "Believe you that there is a Ruach Gadol"
32
33 and he said

1
2 "Yes"
3
4 and Ammon said
5
6 "This is Elohiym"
7
8 and Ammon said unto him again
9
10 "Believe you that this Ruach Gadol
11 who is Elohiym created all things
12 which are in heaven and in the earth"
13
14 and he said
15
16 "Yes I believe that he created all things
17 which are in the earth
18 but I do not know the heavens"
19
20 and Ammon said unto him
21
22 "The heavens is a place
23 where Elohiym dwells
24 and all his holy angels"
25
26 and king Lamoni said
27
28 "Is it above the land"
29
30 and Ammon said
31
32 "Yes and he looks down
33 upon all the children of men

1 and he knows
2 all the thoughts and intents of the heart
3 for by his hand were they all created
4 from the beginning"
5
6 and king Lamoni said
7
8 "I believe all these things
9 which you have spoken
10 Are you sent from Elohiym"
11
12 Ammon said unto him
13
14 "I am a man
15 and man in the beginning was created
16 after the image of Elohiym
17 and I am called by the Ruach Elohiym
18 to teach these things unto this people
19 that they may be brought to a knowledge
20 of that which is just and true
21 and a portion of that Ruach dwells in me
22 which gives me knowledge and also power
23 according to my faith and desires
24 which are in Elohiym"
25
26 now when Ammon had said these words he began
27 at the creation of the world
28 and also the creation of Adam
29 and told him all the things concerning the fall of man
30 and rehearsed and laid before him the records
31 and the holy scriptures of the people
32 which had been spoken by the prophets
33 even down to the time that their father Lechi left Yerushalayim

1   and he also rehearsed unto them
2   for it was unto the king and to his servants
3   all the journey of their fathers in the wilderness
4   and all their suffering
5   with hunger and thirst and their travail and so forth
6   and he also rehearsed unto them
7   concerning the rebellion of Laman and Lemuel
8   and the sons of Yishma'el
9   yes all their rebellion did he relate unto them
10 and he explained unto them
11 all the records and scriptures
12 from the time that Lechi left Yerushalayim
13 down to the present time
14 but this is not all
15 for he explained unto them the plan of redemption
16 which was prepared from the foundation of the world
17 and he also made known unto them
18 concerning the coming of Mashiach
19 and all the works of YHVH
20 did he make known unto them
21
22 And it came to pass
23 that after he had said all these things
24 and explained them to the king
25 that the king believed all his words
26 and he began to cry unto YHVH saying
27
28 "O Adonai have mercy
29 according to your abundant mercy
30 which you have had upon the people of Nephi have
31 upon me and my people"
32
33 and now when he had said this he fell

1 unto the earth as if he were dead

2

3 And it came to pass

4 that his servants took him

5 and carried him in unto his wife

6 and laid him upon a bed

7 and he lay as if he were dead

8 for the space of two days and two nights

9 and his wife and his sons and his daughters mourned over him

10 after the manner of the Lamaniy greatly lamenting his loss

11

12 And it came to pass

13 that after two days and two nights

14 they were about to take his body

15 and lay it in a tomb

16 which they had made for the purpose

17 of burying their dead

18 now the queen having heard of the fame of Ammon

19 therefore she sent and desired

20 that he should come in unto her

21

22 And it came to pass

23 that Ammon did as he was commanded

24 and went in unto the queen and desired

25 to know what she would

26 that he should do

27 and she said unto him

28

29 "The servants of my husband have made it known

30 unto me that you are a prophet of a holy Elohiym

31 and that you have power

32 to do many mighty works in his name

33 therefore if this is the case I would that you should go in

1   and see my husband
2   for he has been laid upon his bed
3   for the space of two days and two nights
4   and some say that he is not dead
5   but others say that he is dead
6   and that he stinks
7   and that he ought to be placed in the tomb
8   but as for myself
9   to me he does not stink"
10   now this was what Ammon desired
11   for he knew that king Lamoni was under the power of Elohiym
12   he knew that the dark veil of unbelief was being cast away
13   from his mind
14   and the light
15   which did light up his mind
16   which was the light of the glory of Elohiym
17   which was a marvelous light of his goodness
18   yes this light had infused such joy into his soul
19   the cloud of darkness having been removed
20   and that the light of everlasting life was lit up in his soul
21   yes he knew that this had overcome his natural body
22   and he was carried away in Elohiym
23   therefore what the queen desired
24   of him was his only desire
25   therefore he went in to see the king
26   according as the queen had desired him
27   and he saw the king
28   and he knew that he was not dead
29   and he said unto the queen
30
31   "He is not dead
32   but he sleeps in Elohiym
33   and on the next day he shall rise again

1   therefore bury him not"

2

3   and Ammon said unto her

4

5   "Believe you this"

6

7   and she said unto him

8

9   "I have had no witness

10 except your word

11 and the word of our servants

12 nevertheless I believe that it shall be

13 according as you have said"

14

15 and Ammon said unto her

16

17 "Blessed are you

18 because of your exceeding faith

19 I say unto you woman

20 there has not been such great faith

21 among all the people of the Nephiy"

22

23 And it came to pass

24 that she watched over the bed of her husband

25 from that time even until that time on the next day

26 which Ammon had appointed

27 that he should rise

28

29 And it came to pass

30 that he arose according to the words of Ammon

31 and as he arose he stretched forth his hand unto the woman

32 and said

33

1   "Blessed be the name of Elohiym

2   and blessed are you

3   for as sure as you live

4   behold I have seen my Redeemer

5   and he shall come forth

6   and be born of a woman

7   and he shall redeem all mankind

8   who believe on his name"

9

10 now when he had said these words his heart was swollen within him

11 and he fell again with joy

12 and the queen also fell down

13 being overpowered by the Ruach

14 now Ammon seeing the Ruach Elohiym poured out

15 according to his prayers upon the Lamaniy his brothers

16 who had been the cause of so much mourning

17 among the Nephiy

18 or among all the people of Elohiym

19 because of their iniquities and their traditions he fell upon his knees

20 and began to pour out his soul in prayer

21 and thanksgiving to Elohiym

22 for what he had done for his brothers

23 and he was also overpowered with joy

24 and thus they all three had fallen to the earth

25 now when the servants of the king had seen that they had fallen

26 they also began to cry unto Elohiym

27 for the fear of YHVH had come upon them also

28 for it was they who had stood before the king

29 and testified unto him

30 concerning the great power of Ammon

31

32 And it came to pass

33 that they did call on the name of YHVH

1 in their might

2 even until they had all fallen to the earth

3 except it were one of the Lamaniy women

4 whose name was Abish

5 she having been converted unto YHVH

6 for many years on account

7 of a remarkable vision of her father

8 thus having been converted to YHVH

9 and never having made it known

10 therefore when she saw that all the servants of Lamoni had fallen to the earth

11 and also her mistress the queen and the king and Ammon lay prostrate upon

12 the earth

13 she knew that it was the power of Elohiym

14 and supposing that this opportunity

15 by making known unto the people

16 what had happened among them

17 that by beholding this scene it would cause them

18 to believe in the power of Elohiym

19 therefore she ran forth

20 from house to house making it known unto the people

21 and they began to assemble themselves together

22 unto the house of the king

23 and there came a multitude

24 and to their astonishment

25 they beheld the king and the queen and their servants prostrate upon the earth

26 and they all lay there as though they were dead

27 and they also saw Ammon

28 and behold he was Nephiy

29 and now the people began to complain among themselves

30 some saying that it was a great evil that had come upon them

31 or upon the king and his house

32 because he had allowed that the Nephiy

33 should remain in the land

1   but others rebuked them saying

2

3   "The king hath brought this evil upon his house

4   because he executed his servants

5   who had had their flocks scattered

6   at the waters of Sebus"

7

8   And they were also rebuked by those men

9   who had stood at the waters of Sebus

10   and scattered the flocks which belonged to the king

11   for they were angry with Ammon

12   because of the number

13   which he had killed of their brothers

14   at the waters of Sebus

15   while defending the flocks of the king

16   now one of them

17   whose brother had been killed with the sword of Ammon

18   being exceedingly angry with Ammon drew his sword

19   and went forth that he might let it fall upon Ammon to kill him

20   and as he lifted the sword to strike him

21   behold he fell dead

22   now we see that Ammon could not be killed

23   for YHVH had said unto Mosheyahu his father

24

25   "I will spare him

26   and it shall be unto him

27   according to your faith"

28

29   Therefore Mosheyahu trusted him unto YHVH

30

31   And it came to pass

32   that when the multitude beheld

33   that the man had fallen dead

1 who lifted the sword to kill Ammon fear came upon them all
2 and they did not put forth their hands to touch him
3 or any of those who had fallen
4 and they began to marvel again among themselves
5 what could be the cause of this great power
6 or what all these things could mean
7
8 And it came to pass
9 that there were many among them
10 who said that Ammon was the Ruach Gadol
11 and others said he was sent by the Ruach Gadol
12 but others rebuked them all saying
13 that he was a monster
14 who had been sent from the Nephiy
15 to torment them
16 and there were some who said
17 that Ammon was sent by the Ruach Gadol to afflict them
18 because of their lawlessness
19 and that it was the Ruach Gadol
20 that had always attended the Nephiy
21 who had ever delivered them out of their hands
22 and they said that it was this Ruach Gadol
23 who had destroyed so many of their brothers the Lamaniy
24 and thus the contention began to be exceedingly sharp among them
25 and while they were thus contending the woman servant
26 who had caused the multitude to be gathered together came
27 and when she saw the contention
28 which was among the multitude she was exceedingly sorrowful
29 even unto tears
30
31 And it came to pass
32 that she went and took the queen by the hand
33 that perhaps she might raise her from the ground

1 and as soon as she touched her hand she arose

2 and stood upon her feet

3 and cried with a loud voice saying

4

5 "O blessed Yehoshua

6 who has saved me from an awful Sheol

7 O blessed Elohiym have mercy on this people"

8

9 And when she had said this she clasped her hands

10 being filled with joy speaking many words

11 which were not understood

12 and when she had done this she took the king Lamoni by the hand

13 and behold he arose and stood upon his feet

14 and he immediately seeing the contention

15 among his people went forth

16 and began to rebuke them

17 and to teach them the words

18 which he had heard from the mouth of Ammon

19 and as many as heard his words believed

20 and were converted unto YHVH

21 but there were many among them

22 who would not hear his words

23 therefore they went their way

24

25 And it came to pass

26 that when Ammon arose he also administered unto them

27 and also did all the servants of Lamoni

28 and they did all declare unto the people the selfsame thing

29 that their hearts had been changed

30 that they had no more desire to do evil

31 and behold many did declare unto the people

32 that they had seen angels

33 and had conversed with them

1 and thus they had told them things of Elohiym

2 and of his righteousness

3

4 And it came to pass

5 that there were many that did believe in their words

6 and as many as did believe were immersed

7 and they became a righteous people

8 and they did establish an assembly among them

9 and thus the work of YHVH did commence among the Lamaniy

10 thus YHVH did begin to pour out his Ruach upon them

11 and we see that his arm is extended to all people

12 who will repent and believe on his name

13

14 And it came to pass

15 that when they had established an assembly in that land

16 that king Lamoni desired that Ammon

17 should go with him to the land of Nephi

18 that he might show him unto his father

19 and the voice of YHVH came to Ammon saying

20

21 "You shall not go up to the land of Nephi

22 for behold the king will seek your life

23 but you shall go to the land of Middiyn

24 for behold your brother Aharon and also Muloki

25 and Ammah are in prison

26

27 Now it came to pass

28 that when Ammon had heard this he said unto Lamoni

29

30 "behold my brother and brothers are in prison at Middiyn

31 and I go that I may deliver them"

32

33 Now Lamoni said unto Ammon

1 "I know in the strength of YHVH you can do all things

2 but behold I will go with you to the land of Middiyn

3 for the king of the land of Middiyn

4 whose name is Antiomno is a friend unto me

5 therefore I go to the land of Middiyn

6 that I may flatter the king of the land

7 and he will cast your brothers out of prison

8 now Lamoni said unto him

9

10 "Who told you that your brothers were in prison"

11

12 and Ammon said unto him

13

14 "No one has told me

15 except it be Elohiym

16 and he said unto me

17 go and deliver your brothers

18 for they are in prison in the land of Middiyn"

19

20 Now when Lamoni had heard this he caused

21 that his servants should make ready

22 his horses and his chariots

23 and he said unto Ammon

24

25 "Come I will go with you down

26 to the land of Middiyn

27 and there I will plead with the king

28 that he will cast your brothers out of prison"

29

30 And it came to pass

31 that as Ammon and Lamoni were journeying there

32 they met the father of Lamoni

33 who was king over all the land

1
2 And behold the father of Lamoni said unto him
3
4 "Why did you not come to the feast
5 on that great day
6 when I made a feast unto my sons
7 and unto my people"
8
9 and he also said
10
11 "Where are you going with this Nephiy
12 who is one of the children of a liar"
13
14 And it came to pass
15 that Lamoni rehearsed unto him
16 where he was going
17 for he feared to offend him
18 and he also told him all the cause
19 of his tarrying in his own kingdom
20 that he did not go unto his father
21 to the feast which he had prepared
22 and now when Lamoni had rehearsed unto him all these things
23 behold to his astonishment his father was angry with him
24 and said Lamoni
25
26 "You are going to deliver these Nephiy
27 who are sons of a liar
28 behold he robbed our fathers
29 and now his children are also come among us
30 that they may by their cunning
31 and their lying deceive us
32 that they again may rob us of our property"
33

1   Now the father of Lamoni commanded him

2   that he should kill Ammon with the sword

3   and he also commanded him t

4   hat he should not go to the land of Middiyn

5   but that he should return with him

6   to the land of Yishma'el

7   but Lamoni said unto him

8

9   "I will not kill Ammon

10   neither will I return to the land of Yishma'el

11   but I go to the land of Middiyn

12   that I may release the brothers of Ammon

13   for I know that they are just men

14   and holy prophets of the true Elohiym"

15

16   Now when his father had heard these words

17   he was angry with him

18   and he drew his sword

19   that he might strike him to the earth

20   but Ammon stood forth

21   and said unto him

22

23   "Behold you shall not kill your son

24   nevertheless it were better that he should fall than you

25   for behold he has repented of his sins

26   but if you should fall at this time

27   in your anger your soul could not be saved

28   and again it is necessary that you stop

29   for if you should kill your son

30   he being an innocent man

31   his blood would cry from the ground to YHVH his Elohiym

32   for vengeance to come upon you

33   and perhaps you would lose your soul"

1
2 Now when Ammon had said these words
3 unto him he answered him saying
4
5 "I know that if I should kill my son
6 that I should shed innocent blood
7 for it is you that has been seeking to destroy him"
8
9 And he stretched forth his hand to kill Ammon
10 but Ammon withstood his blows
11 and also struck his arm
12 that he could not use it
13 now when the king saw
14 that Ammon could kill him he began to plead with Ammon
15 that he would spare his life
16 but Ammon raised his sword
17 and said unto him
18
19 "Behold I will strike you
20 except you will grant unto me
21 that my brothers may be cast out of prison"
22
23 Now the king fearing he should lose his life said
24
25 "If you will spare me I will grant unto you
26 whatever you will ask
27 even to half of the kingdom"
28
29 Now when Ammon saw that he had prevailed
30 upon the old king
31 according to his desire he said unto him
32
33 "If you will grant that my brothers

1   may be cast out of prison
2   and also that Lamoni may retain his kingdom
3   and that you be not displeased with him
4   but grant that he may do according to his own desires
5   in whatever thing he thinks
6   then will I spare you
7   otherwise I will strike you to the earth"
8
9   now when Ammon had said
10 these words the king began
11 to rejoice because of his life
12 and when he saw that Ammon had no desire to destroy him
13 and when he also saw the great love he had
14 for his son Lamoni he was astonished exceedingly
15 and said
16
17 "Because this is all that you have desired
18 that I would release your brothers
19 and suffer that my son Lamoni
20 should retain his kingdom
21 behold I will grant unto you
22 that my son may retain his kingdom
23 from this time and forever
24 and I will govern him no more
25 and I will also grant unto you
26 that your brothers may be cast out of prison
27 and you and your brothers may come unto me in my kingdom
28 for I shall greatly desire to see you"
29
30 For the king was greatly astonished at the words
31 which he had spoken
32 and also at the words
33 which had been spoken by his son Lamoni

1 therefore he desired to learn them

2

3 And it came to pass

4 that Ammon and Lamoni proceeded on their journey

5 towards the land of Middiyn

6 and Lamoni found favor

7 in the eyes of the king of the land

8 therefore the brothers of Ammon were brought forth

9 out of prison

10 and when Ammon did meet them he was exceedingly sorrowful

11 for behold they were naked

12 and their skins were worn exceedingly

13 because of being bound with strong cords

14 and they also had suffered hunger thirst and all kinds of afflictions

15 nevertheless they were patient in all their suffering

16 and as it happened it was their lot

17 to have fallen into the hands

18 of a more hardened and a more stubborn people

19 therefore they would not listen to or obey their words

20 and they had cast them out

21 and had attacked them

22 and had driven them from house to house

23 and from place to place

24 even until they had arrived in the land of Middiyn

25 and there they were taken and cast into prison

26 and bound with strong cords

27 and kept in prison for many days

28 and were delivered by Lamoni and Ammon

29

30 **An account of the preaching**

31 **of Aharon and Muloki and their brothers**

32 **to the Lamaniy**

33

1   Now when Ammon and his brothers separated themselves
2   in the borders of the land of the Lamaniy
3   behold Aharon took his journey towards the land
4   which was called by the Lamaniy Yerushalayim calling it
5   after the land of their fathers' nativity
6   and it was away joining the borders of Mormon
7   now the Lamaniy and the Amalekiy
8   and the people of Amulon had built a great city
9   which was called Yerushalayim
10 now the Lamaniy of themselves were sufficiently hardened
11 but the Amalekiy and the Amuloniy were still harder
12 therefore they did cause the Lamaniy
13 that they should harden their hearts
14 that they should wax strong
15 in wickedness and their abominations
16
17 And it came to pass
18 that Aharon came to the city of Yerushalayim
19 and first began to preach to the Amalekiy
20 and he began to preach to them in their synagogues
21 for they had built synagogues
22 after the order of the Nachor
23 for many of the Amalekiy
24 and the Amuloniy were after the order of the Nachor
25 therefore as Aharon entered into one of their synagogues
26 to preach unto the people
27 and as he was speaking unto them
28 behold there arose an Amalekite
29 and began to contend with him saying
30
31 "What is that you have testified
32 have you seen an angel
33 why do not angels appear unto us

1 behold are not this people

2 as good as your people

3 you also say

4 except we repent we shall perish

5 how know you the thought

6 and intent of our hearts

7 how know you

8 that we have cause to repent

9 how know you

10 that we are not a righteous people

11 behold we have built holy places

12 and we do assemble ourselves together

13 to worship Elohiym

14 we do believe that Elohiym will save all men"

15 now Aharon said unto him

16

17 "Believe you that the Son of Elohiym

18 shall come to redeem mankind from their sins"

19

20 and the man said unto him

21

22

23 "We do not believe

24 that you know any such thing

25 we do not believe

26 in these foolish traditions

27 we do not believe

28 that you know of things to come

29 neither do we believe that your fathers

30 and also that our fathers did know c

31 concerning the things which they spoke

32 of that which is to come"

33

1   Now Aharon began to open the scriptures unto them

2   concerning the coming of Mashiach

3   and also concerning the resurrection of the dead

4   and that there could be no redemption for mankind

5   except it were through the death

6   and sufferings of Mashiach

7   and the atonement of his blood

8   And it came to pass

9   as he began to expound these things unto them

10   they were angry with him

11   and began to mock him

12   and they would not hear the words which he spoke

13   therefore when he saw

14   that they would not hear his words he departed out

15   of their synagogue

16   and came over to a village

17   which was called Ani Onti

18   and there he found Muloki preaching the word unto them

19   and also Ammah and his brothers

20   and they contended with many about the word

21

22   And it came to pass

23   that they saw that the people would harden their hearts

24   therefore they departed

25   and came over into the land of Middiyn

26   and they did preach the word unto many

27   and few believed on the words

28   which they taught

29   nevertheless Aharon and a certain number

30   of his brothers were taken and cast into prison

31   and the remainder of them fled out of the land of Middiyn

32   unto the regions round about

33   and those who were cast into prison suffered many things

1   and they were delivered by the hand

2   of Lamoni and Ammon

3   and they were fed and clothed

4   and they went forth again to declare the word

5   and thus they were delivered for the first time out of prison

6   and thus they had suffered

7   and they went forth wherever they were led

8   by the Ruach YHVH preaching the word of Elohiym i

9   in every synagogue of the Amalekiy

10 or in every assembly of the Lamaniy

11 where they could be admitted

12

13 And it came to pass

14 that YHVH began to bless theminsomuch

15 that they brought many

16 to the knowledge of the truth

17 yes they did convince many

18 of their sins and of the traditions of their fathers

19 which were not correct

20

21 And it came to pass

22 that Ammon and Lamoni returned

23 from the land of Middiyn

24 to the land of Yishma'el

25 which was the land of their inheritance

26 and king Lamoni would not allow

27 that Ammon should serve him

28 or be his servant

29 but he caused

30 that there should be synagogues built

31 in the land of Yishma'el

32 and he caused

33 that his people

1 or the people who were under his reign
2 should assemble themselves together
3 and he did rejoice over them
4 and he did teach them many things
5 and he did also declare unto them
6 that they were a people who were under him
7 and that they were a free people
8 that they were free from the oppressions
9 of the king his father
10 for that his father had granted unto him
11 that he might reign over the people
12 who were in the land of Yishma'el
13 and in all the land round about
14 and he also declared unto them
15 that they might have the liberty
16 of worshiping YHVH their Elohiym
17 according to their desires
18 in whatever place they were in
19 if it were in the land
20 which was under the reign of king Lamoni
21 and Ammon did preach unto the people of king Lamoni
22
23 And it came to pass
24 that he did teach them all things
25 concerning things pertaining to righteousness
26 and he did exhort them daily
27 with all diligence
28 and they gave heed unto his word
29 and they were zealous
30 for keeping the mitzvot of Elohiym
31 now as Ammon was thus teaching
32 the people of Lamoni continually
33 we will return to the account

1   of Aharon and his brothers

2   for after he departed

3   from the land of Middiyn he was led by the Ruach

4   to the land of Nephi

5   even to the house of the king

6   which was over all the land

7   except it were the land of Yishma'el

8   and he was the father of Lamoni

9

10 And it came to pass

11 that he went in unto him into the king's palace

12 with his brothers and bowed himself before the king

13 and said unto him

14

15 "behold O king

16 we are the brothers of Ammon

17 whom you have delivered out of prison

18 and now O king

19 if you will spare our lives we will be your servants"

20

21 and the king said unto them

22 "Arise

23 for I will grant unto you your lives

24 and I will not allow that you shall be my servants

25 but I will insist that you shall administer unto me

26 for I have been somewhat troubled in mind

27 because of the generosity

28 and the greatness of the words

29 of your brother Ammon

30 and I desire to know the reason

31 why he has not come up out of Middiyn with you"

32

33 and Aharon said unto the king

1
2 "behold the Ruach YHVH has called him another way
3 he has gone to the land of Yishma'el
4 to teach the people of Lamoni"
5
6 now the king said unto them
7
8 "What is this that you have said
9 concerning the Ruach YHVH
10 behold this is the thing
11 which does trouble me
12 and also what is this that Ammon said
13 'If you will repent you shall be saved
14 and if you will not repent you
15 shall be cast off at the last day'"
16 and Aharon answered him
17 and said unto him
18
19 "Believe you that there is Elohiym"
20
21 and the king said
22
23 "I know that the Amalekiy say
24 that there is Elohiym
25 and I have granted unto them
26 that they should build holy places
27 that they may assemble themselves together to worship him
28 and if now you say there is Elohiym
29 behold I will believe"
30
31 and now when Aharon heard this
32 his heart began to rejoice
33 and he said

1
2 "behold
3 assuredly as you live O king
4 there is Elohiym"
5
6 and the king said
7
8 "Is Elohiym that Ruach Gadol
9 that brought our fathers out
10 of the land of Yerushalayim"
11
12 and Aharon said unto him
13
14 "Yes he is that Ruach Gadol
15 and he created all things
16 both in heaven and in earth
17 Believe you this"
18 and he said
19
20 "Yes I believe
21 that the Ruach Gadol created all things
22 and I desire that you should tell me
23 concerning all these things
24 and I will believe your words"
25
26 And it came to pass
27 that when Aharon saw
28 that the king would believe his words he began
29 from the creation of Adam reading the scriptures unto the king
30 how Elohiym created man after his own image
31 and that Elohiym gave him mitzvot
32 and that because of rebellion man had fallen
33 and Aharon did expound unto him the scriptures

1 from the creation of Adam laying the fall of man before him

2 and their carnal state

3 and also the plan of redemption

4 which was prepared

5 from the creation of the world through Mashiach

6 for all whosoever would believe on his name

7 and since man had fallen he could not merit anything of himself

8 but the sufferings and death of Mashiach atone for their sins

9 through faith and repentance and so forth

10 and that he breaks the bands of death

11 that the grave shall have no victory

12 and that the sting of death

13 should be swallowed up in the hopes of glory

14 and Aharon did expound all these things unto the king

15

16 And it came to pass

17 that after Aharon had explained

18 these things unto him the king said

19

20 "What shall I do

21 that I may have this eternal life

22 of which you have spoken

23 Yes what shall I do

24 that I may be born of Elohiym having

25 this wicked ruach rooted out of my breast

26 and receive his Ruach

27 that I may be filled with joy

28 that I may not be cast off at the last day

29 behold"

30

31 said he

32

33 "I will give up all that I possess

1 yes I will forsake my kingdom
2 that I may receive this great joy"
3
4 but Aharon said unto him
5
6 "If you desire this thing
7 if you will bow down before Elohiym
8 yes if you will repent of all your sins
9 and will bow down before Elohiym
10 and call on his name in faith believing
11 that you shall receive
12 then shall you receive the hope[6]
13 which you desire"
14
15 And it came to pass
16 that when Aharon had said these words
17 the king did bow down before YHVH
18 upon his knees
19 yes even he did prostrate himself
20 upon the earth
21 and cried mightily saying
22
23 "O Elohiym
24 Aharon has told me that there is Elohiym
25 and if there is Elohiym
26 and if you are Elohiym
27 will you make thyself known unto me
28 and I will give away all my sins to know you
29 and that I may be raised from the dead
30 and be saved at the last day"
31
32 And now

---

[6] Ha Tikveh

1   when the king had said these words
2   he was struck as if he were dead
3
4   And it came to pass
5   that his servants ran
6   and told the queen
7   all that had happened unto the king
8   and she came in unto the king
9   and when she saw him lay
10 as if he were dead
11 and also Aharon and his brothers standing
12 as though they had been the cause of his fall
13 she was angry with them
14 and commanded that her servants
15 or the servants of the king
16 should take them and kill them
17 now the servants had seen the cause
18 of the king's fall
19 therefore they did not lay their hands
20 on Aharon and his brothers
21 and they pled with the queen saying
22
23 "Why command you
24 that we should kill these men
25 when behold one of them is mightier than us all
26 therefore we shall fall before them"
27
28 Now when the queen saw the fear
29 of the servants she also began to fear exceedingly
30 for fear that there should some evil come upon her
31 and she commanded her servants
32 that they should go and call the people
33 that they might kill Aharon and his brothers

1 now when Aharon saw the determination
2 of the queen
3 he also knowing the hardness of the hearts
4 of the people feared
5 for fear that a multitude
6 should assemble themselves together
7 and there should be a great contention
8 and a disturbance among them
9 therefore he put forth his hand
10 and raised the king from the earth
11 and said unto him
12
13 "Stand"
14
15 And he stood upon his feet receiving his strength
16 now this was done in the presence of the queen
17 and many of the servants
18 and when they saw it
19 they greatly marveled and began to fear
20 and the king stood forth
21 and began to minister unto them
22 and he did minister unto them insomuch
23 that his whole household were converted
24 unto YHVH
25 now there was a multitude gathered together
26 because of the commandment of the queen
27 and there began to be great complaining among them
28 because of Aharon and his brothers
29 but the king stood forth among them
30 and administered unto them
31 and they were pacified towards Aharon
32 and those who were with him
33

1 And it came to pass

2 that when the king saw

3 that the people were pacified he caused

4 that Aharon and his brothers

5 should stand forth in the midst of the multitude

6 and that they should preach the word unto them

7

8 And it came to pass

9 that the king sent a proclamation

10 throughout all the land

11 among all his people

12 who were in all his land

13 who were in all the regions round about

14 which was bordering

15 even to the sea

16 on the east and on the west

17 and which was divided from the land of Zarahemla

18 by a narrow strip of wilderness

19 which ran from the sea east

20 even to the sea west and round about

21 on the borders of the seashore

22 and the borders of the wilderness

23 which was on the north by the land of Zarahemla

24 through the borders of Manti

25 by the head of the river Sidon running

26 from the east towards the west

27 and thus were the Lamaniy and the Nephiy divided

28 now the more idle part of the Lamaniy lived

29 in the wilderness and dwelt in tents

30 and they were spread through the wilderness

31 on the west in the land of Nephi

32 yes and also on the west of the land of Zarahemla

33 in the borders by the seashore

1 and on the west in the land of Nephi

2 in the place of their fathers' first inheritance

3 and thus bordering along by the seashore

4 and also there were many Lamaniy on the east

5 by the seashore

6 where the Nephiy had driven them

7 and thus the Nephiy were nearly surrounded by the Lamaniy

8 nevertheless the Nephiy had taken possession

9 of all the northern parts of the land

10 bordering on the wilderness

11 at the head of the river Sidon

12 from the east to the west round about

13 on the wilderness side on the north

14 even until they came to the land

15 which they called Bountiful

16 and it bordered upon the land

17 which they called Desolation it being

18 so far northward

19 that it came into the land

20 which had been peopled

21 and been destroyed

22 of whose bones we have spoken

23 which was discovered by the people of Zarahemla

24 it being the place of their first landing

25 and they came from there up

26 into the south wilderness

27 thus the land on the northward was called Desolation

28 and the land on the southward was called Bountiful

29 it being the wilderness which is filled with all manner

30 of wild animals of every kind a part of which had come

31 from the land northward for food

32 and now it was only the distance

33 of a day and a half's journey for a Nephiy

1 on the line Bountiful
2 and the land Desolation
3 from the east to the west sea
4 and thus the land of Nephi
5 and the land of Zarahemla were
6 nearly surrounded by water
7 there being a small neck of land
8 between the land northward
9 and the land southward
10
11 And it came to pass
12 that the Nephiy had inhabited the land Bountiful
13 even from the east unto the west sea
14 and thus the Nephiy in their wisdom
15 with their guards and their armies had hemmed
16 in the Lamaniy on the south
17 that thereby they should have no more possession on the north
18 that they might not overrun the land northward
19 therefore the Lamaniy
20 could have no more possessions
21 only in the land of Nephi
22 and the wilderness round about
23 now this was wisdom in the Nephiy
24 as the Lamaniy were an enemy to them
25 they would not allow their afflictions on every hand
26 and also that they might have a country
27 where they might flee according to their desires
28 and now I after having said this return again
29 to the account of Ammon and Aharon Omner
30 and Himni and their brothers
31
32 Behold now it came to pass
33 that the king of the Lamaniy sent a proclamation

1 among all his people
2 that they should not lay their hands
3 on Ammon or Aharon
4 or Omner or Himni
5 nor either of their brothers
6 who should go forth preaching the word of Elohiym
7 in whatever place they should be
8 in any part of their land
9 Yes he sent a decree among them
10 that they should not lay their hands on them
11 to bind them or to cast them into prison
12 neither should they spit upon them
13 nor strike them nor cast them out
14 of their synagogues nor scourge them
15 neither should they cast stones at them
16 but that they should have free access to their houses
17 and also their temples and their holy places
18 and thus they might go forth
19 and preach the word
20 according to their desires
21 for the king had been converted unto YHVH
22 and all his household
23 therefore he sent his proclamation
24 throughout the land unto his people
25 that the word of Elohiym might have no obstruction
26 but that it might go forth
27 throughout all the land
28 that his people might be convinced
29 concerning the wicked traditions of their fathers
30 and that they might be convinced
31 that they were all brothers a
32 nd that they ought not to murder nor to plunder
33 nor to steal nor to commit adultery

1 nor to commit any manner of wickedness

2

3 And now it came to pass

4 that when the king had sent forth this proclamation

5 that Aharon and his brothers went forth

6 from city to city

7 and from one house of worship to another

8 establishing assemblies

9 and consecrating kohanim and teachers

10 throughout the land among the Lamaniy

11 to preach and to teach the word of Elohiym among them

12 and thus they began to have great success

13 and thousands were brought to the knowledge of YHVH

14 yes thousands were brought to believe in the traditions of the Nephiy

15 and they were taught the records and prophecies

16 which were handed down

17 even to the present time

18 and as sure as YHVH lives

19 so sure as many as believed

20 or as many as were brought

21 to the knowledge of the truth

22 through the preaching

23 of Ammon and his brothers

24 according to the ruach

25 of revelation and of prophecy

26 and the power of Elohiym working miracles in them

27 yes I say unto you as YHVH lives

28 as many of the Lamaniy as believed in their preaching

29 and were converted unto YHVH never did fall away

30 for they became a righteous people

31 they did lay down the weapons of their rebellion

32 that they did not fight against Elohiym any more

33 neither against any of their brothers

1 now these are they who were converted unto YHVH

2 the people of the Lamaniy

3 who were in the land of Yishma'el

4 and also of the people of the Lamaniy

5 who were in the land of Middiyn

6 and also of the people of the Lamaniy

7 who were in the city of Nephi

8 and also of the people of the Lamaniy

9 who were in the land of Shilom

10 and who were in the land of Shemlon

11 and in the city of L'muel

12 and in the city of Shimnilom

13 and these are the names of the cities of the Lamaniy

14 which were converted unto YHVH

15 and these are they

16 that laid down the weapons of their rebellion

17 yes all their weapons of war

18 and they were all Lamaniy

19 and the Amalekiy were not converted

20 except only one

21 neither were any of the Amuloniy

22 but they did harden their hearts

23 and also the hearts of the Lamaniy

24 in that part of the land

25 wherever they dwelt

26 yes and all their villages

27 and all their cities

28 therefore we have named all the cities of the Lamaniy

29 in which they did repent and come

30 to the knowledge of the truth

31 and were converted

32

33 And Now it came to pass

1   that the king and those who were converted desired

2   that they might have a name

3   that thereby they might be distinguished from their brothers

4   therefore the king consulted

5   with Aharon and many of their kohanim

6   concerning the name

7   that they should take upon them

8   that they might be distinguished

9

10   And it came to pass

11   that they called their name

12   Paniym Nephi Lechi[7]

13   and they were called by this name

14   and were no more called Lamaniy

15   and they began to be a very industrious people

16   yes and they were friendly with the Nephiy

17   therefore they did open a correspondence with them

18   and the curse of Elohiym did no more follow them

19

20   And it came to pass

21   that the Amalekiy

22   and the Amuloniy

23   and the Lamaniy

24   who were in the land of Amulon

25   and also in the land of Helam

26   and who were in the land of Yerushalayim

27   and in fine in all the land round about

28   who had not been converted

29   and had not taken upon them the name

30   of Paniym Nephi Lechi were stirred up

31   by the Amalekiy and by the Amuloniy

32   to anger against their brothers

---

[7] Paniym – Faces, countenance, of

1 and their hatred
2 became exceedingly inflamed against them
3 even insomuch that they began to rebel
4 against their king insomuch
5 that they would not that he should be their king
6 therefore they took up arms
7 against the people of Paniym Nephi Lechi
8
9 Now the king conferred the kingdom upon his son
10 and he called his name Paniym Nephi Lechi
11 and the king died
12 in that selfsame year
13 that the Lamaniy began
14 to make preparations for war
15 against the people of Elohiym
16 now when Ammon and his brothers
17 and all those who had come up with him
18 saw the preparations of the Lamaniy
19 to destroy their brothers
20 they came forth to the land of Midyan
21 and there Ammon met all his brothers
22 and from thence they came to the land of Yishma'el
23 that they might hold a council with Lamoni
24 and also with his brother Paniym Nephi Lechi
25 what they should do to defend themselves against the Lamaniy
26
27 Now there was not one soul
28 among all the people
29 who had been converted unto YHVH
30 that would take up arms
31 against their brothers
32 No they would not even make
33 any preparations for war

1   yes and also their king commanded them

2   that they should not

3

4   Now these are the words

5   which he said unto the people

6   concerning the matter

7

8   "I thank my Elohiym

9   my beloved people

10   that our great Elohiym has in goodness sent

11   these our brothers the Nephiy unto us

12   to preach unto us

13   and to convince us of the traditions

14   of our wicked fathers

15   and behold I thank my great Elohiym

16   that he has given us a portion of his Ruach

17   to soften our hearts

18   that we have opened a correspondence

19   with these brothers the Nephiy

20   and behold I also thank my Elohiym

21   that by opening this correspondence

22   we have been convinced of our sins

23   and of the many murders

24   which we have committed

25   and I also thank my Elohiym

26   yes my great Elohiym

27   that he has granted unto us

28   that we might repent of these things

29   and also that he has forgiven us

30   of those our many sins and murders

31   which we have committed

32   and taken away the guilt from our hearts

33   through the merits of his Son

1
2 And now behold my brothers
3 since it has been all that we could do
4 as we were the most lost of all mankind
5 to repent of all our sins and the many murders
6 which we have committed
7 and to get Elohiym
8 to take them away from our hearts
9 for it was all we could do
10 to repent sufficiently before Elohiym
11 that he would take away our stain
12
13 Now my best beloved brothers
14 since Elohiym has taken away our stains
15 and our swords have become bright
16 then let us stain our swords no more
17 with the blood of our brothers
18 behold I say unto you
19 No let us retain our swords
20 that they be not stained
21 with the blood of our brothers
22 for perhaps if we should stain our swords again
23 they can no more be washed bright
24 through the blood of the Son of our great Elohiym
25 which shall be shed for the atonement of our sins
26 and the great Elohiym has had mercy on us
27 and made these things known unto us
28 that we might not perish
29 yes and he has made these things known unto us beforehand
30 because he loves our souls
31 as well as he loves our children
32 therefore in his mercy he does visit us by his angels
33 that the plan of salvation

1   might be made known unto us
2   as well as unto future generations
3   Oh how merciful is our Elohiym
4
5   And now behold
6   since it has been as much as we could do
7   to get our stains taken away from us
8   and our swords are made bright
9   let us hide them away
10   that they may be kept bright
11   as a testimony to our Elohiym
12   at the last day or at the day
13   that we shall be brought to stand before him
14   to be judged
15   that we have not stained our swords
16   in the blood of our brothers
17   since he imparted his word unto us
18   and has made us clean thereby
19   and now my brothers
20   if our brothers seek to destroy us
21   behold we will hide away our swords
22   yes even we will bury them deep in the earth
23   that they may be kept bright as a testimony
24   that we have never used them at the last day
25   and if our brothers destroy us
26   behold we shall go to our Elohiym
27   and shall be saved"
28
29   And now it came to pass
30   that when the king had made
31   an end of these sayings
32   and all the people were assembled together
33   they took their swords

1 and all the weapons
2 which were used for the shedding of man's blood
3 and they did bury them up deep in the earth
4 and this they did it being
5 in their view a testimony to Elohiym
6 and also to men
7 that they never would use weapons again
8 for the shedding of man's blood
9 and this they did vouching and covenanting with Elohiym
10 that rather than shed the blood of their brothers
11 they would give up their own lives
12 and rather than take away from a brother
13 they would give unto him
14 and rather than spend their days in idleness
15 they would labor abundantly with their hands
16 and thus we see
17 that when these Lamaniy were brought
18 to believe and to know the truth they were firm
19 and would suffer even unto death
20 rather than commit sin
21 and thus we see that they buried their weapons of peace
22 or they buried the weapons of war for peace
23
24 And it came to pass
25 that their brothers the Lamaniy made preparations for war
26 and came up to the land of Nephi
27 for the purpose of destroying the king
28 and to place another in his place
29 and also of destroying the people of Paniym Nephi Lechi
30 out of the land
31 now when the people saw
32 that they were coming against them
33 they went out to meet them

1 and prostrated themselves before them to the earth

2 and began to call on the name of YHVH

3 and thus they were in this attitude

4 when the Lamaniy began to fall upon them

5 and began to kill them with the sword

6 and thus without meeting any resistance

7 they did kill a thousand and five of them

8 and we know that they are blessed

9 for they have gone to dwell with their Elohiym

10 now when the Lamaniy saw

11 that their brothers would not flee from the sword

12 neither would they turn aside

13 to the right hand or to the left

14 but that they would lie down and perish

15 and praised Elohiym

16 even in the very act of perishing

17 under the sword

18 now when the Lamaniy saw this

19 they did forbear from killing them

20 and there were many whose hearts had swollen in them

21 for those of their brothers who had fallen

22 under the sword

23 for they repented of the things

24 which they had done

25

26 And it came to pass

27 that they threw down their weapons of war

28 and they would not take them again

29 for they were stung for the murders

30 which they had committed

31 and they came down

32 even as their brothers relying

33 upon the mercies of those

1 whose arms were lifted to kill them

2

3 And it came to pass

4 that the people of Elohiym were joined that day

5 by more than the number who had been killed

6 and those who had been killed were righteous people

7 therefore we have no reason to doubt

8 but what they were saved

9 and there was not a wicked man killed among them

10 but there were more than a thousand

11 brought to the knowledge of the truth

12 hus we see that YHVH works in many ways

13 to the salvation of his people

14 now the greatest number

15 of those of the Lamaniy

16 who killed so many of their brothers

17 were Amalekiy and Amuloniy

18 the greatest number of whom were

19 after the order of the Nachor

20 now among those who joined the people of YHVH

21 there were none

22 who were Amalekiy or Amuloniy

23 or who were of the order of Nachor

24 but they were actual descendants of Laman and L'muel

25 and thus we can plainly discern

26 that after a people have been once enlightened

27 by the Ruach Elohiym

28 and have had great knowledge of things

29 pertaining to righteousness

30 and then have fallen away

31 into sin and transgression

32 they become more hardened

33 and thus their state becomes worse

1 than though they had never known these things

2

3 And behold now it came to pass

4 that those Lamaniy were more angry

5 because they had killed their brothers

6 therefore they swore vengeance upon the Nephiy

7 and they did no more attempt

8 to kill the people of Paniym Nephi Lechi

9 at that time

10 but they took their armies

11 and went over into the borders of the land of Zarahemla

12 and fell upon the people who were in the land of Ammoniyah

13 and destroyed them

14 and after that

15 they had many battles with the Nephiy

16 in the which they were driven and killed

17 and among the Lamaniy who were killed were

18 almost all the seed

19 of Amulon and his brothers

20 who were the Kohanim of Noach

21 and they were killed by the hands of the Nephiy

22 and the remainder having fled into the east wilderness

23 and having usurped the power and authority

24 over the Lamaniy caused

25 that many of the Lamaniy

26 should perish by fire

27 because of their belief

28 For many of them

29 after having suffered much loss

30 and so many afflictions

31 began to be stirred up

32 in remembrance of the words

33 which Aharon and his brothers had preached

1 to them in their land
2 therefore they began to disbelieve the traditions of their fathers
3 and to believe in YHVH
4 and that he gave great power unto the Nephiy
5 and thus there were many of them converted
6 in the wilderness
7
8 And it came to pass
9 that those rulers
10 who were the remnant
11 of the children of Amulon caused
12 that they should be put to death
13 yes all those that believed in these things
14 now this martyrdom caused
15 that many of their brothers
16 should be stirred up to anger
17 and there began to be contention in the wilderness
18 and the Lamaniy began to hunt the seed
19 of Amulon and his brothers
20 and began to kill them
21 and they fled into the east wilderness
22
23 And behold
24 they are hunted at this day by the Lamaniy
25 thus the words of Abinadi were brought to pass
26 which he said concerning the seed of the priests
27 who caused that he should suffer death by fire
28 For he said unto them
29
30 "What you shall do unto me
31 shall be a type of things to come"
32 and now Abinadi was the first
33 that suffered death by fire

1   because of his belief in Elohiym

2   now this is what he meant

3   that many should suffer death by fire

4   according as he had suffered

5   and he said unto the priests of Noach

6   that their seed should cause many to be put to death

7   in the like manner as he was

8   and that they should be scattered abroad

9   and killed even as a sheep having no shepherd

10 is driven and killed by wild beasts

11 and now behold

12 these words were verified

13 for they were driven by the Lamaniy

14 and they were hunted

15 and they were struck down

16

17 And it came to pass

18 that when the Lamaniy saw

19 that they could not overpower the Nephiy

20 they returned again to their own land

21 and many of them came over

22 to dwell in the land of Yishma'el

23 and the land of Nephi

24 and did join themselves to the people of Elohiym

25 who were the people of Paniym Nephi Lechi

26 and they did also bury their weapons of war

27 according as their brothers had

28 and they began to be a righteous people

29 and they did walk in the ways of YHVH

30 and did observe to keep his mitzvot and his chukkim

31 Yes and they did keep the Torah of Moshe

32 for it was necessary

33 that they should keep the Torah of Moshe as yet

1   for it was not all established

2   but not opposing the Torah of Moshe

3   they did look forward to the coming of Mashiach considering

4   that the Torah of Moshe was a type of his coming

5   and believing that they must keep those outward ma'asim

6   until the time that he should be revealed unto them

7   now they did not suppose

8   that salvation came by the Torah of Moshe

9   but the Torah of Moshe did serve

10   to strengthen their faith in Mashiach

11   and thus they did retain a hope

12   through faith unto eternal salvation relying

13   upon the ruach of prophecy

14   which spoke of those things to come

15

16   And now behold Ammon and Aharon

17   and Omner and Himni

18   and their brothers did rejoice exceedingly

19   for the success

20   which they had had among the Lamaniy seeing

21   that YHVH had granted unto them

22   according to their prayers

23   and that he had also verified his word unto them

24   in every particular

25   and now these are the words of Ammon

26   to his brothers which say thus

27

28   "My brothers and my brothers

29   behold I say unto you

30   how great reason have we to rejoice

31   for could we have supposed

32   when we started from the land of Zarahemla

33   that Elohiym would have granted unto us

1 such great blessings
2 and now I ask
3 what great blessings has he bestowed upon us
4 Can you tell
5
6 Behold I answer for you
7 for our brothers the Lamaniy were in darkness
8 yes even in the darkest abyss
9 but behold how many of them are brought
10 to behold the marvelous light of Elohiym
11 and this is the blessing
12 which has been bestowed upon us
13 that we have been made instruments
14 in the hands of Elohiym
15 to bring about this great work
16 behold thousands of them do rejoice
17 and have been brought into the fold of Elohiym
18
19 Behold the field was ripe
20 and blessed are you
21 for you did thrust in the sickle
22 and did reap with your might
23 yes all the day long did you labor
24 and behold the number of your sheaves
25 and they shall be gathered into the garners
26 that they are not wasted
27 yes they shall not be beaten down
28 by the storm at the last day
29 yes neither shall they be broken up
30 by the whirlwinds
31 but when the storm comes
32 they shall be gathered together in their place
33 that the storm cannot penetrate to them

1 yes neither shall they be driven with fierce winds

2 wherever the enemy desires to carry them

3 but behold they are in the hands of Adonai of the harvest

4 and they are his

5 and he will raise them up at the last day

6

7 Blessed be the name of our Elohiym

8 let us sing to his praise

9 yes let us give thanks to his holy name

10 for he does work righteousness forever

11 For if we had not come up out of the land of Zarahemla

12 these our dearly beloved brothers

13 who have so dearly beloved us would

14 still have been racked with hatred against us

15 yes and they would also have been strangers to Elohiym

16

17 And it came to pass

18 that when Ammon had said these words

19 his brother Aharon rebuked him saying

20

21 "Ammon I fear that your joy

22 does carry you away unto boasting"

23

24 but Ammon said unto him

25

26 "I do not boast in my own strength

27 nor in my own wisdom

28 but behold my joy is full

29 yes my heart is filled to the brim with joy

30 and I will rejoice in my Elohiym

31 Yes I know that I am nothing

32 as to my strength I am weak

33 therefore I will not boast of myself

1 but I will boast of my Elohiym
2 for in his strength I can do all things
3 yes behold many mighty miracles we
4 have performed in this land
5 for which we will praise his name forever
6 behold how many thousands of our brothers has he loosed
7 from the pains of Sheol
8 and they are brought to sing redeeming love
9 and this because of the power of his word which is in us
10 therefore have we not great reason to rejoice
11 yes we have reason to praise him forever
12 for he is El Elyon
13 and has loosed our brothers
14 from the chains of Sheol
15 yes they were encircled about
16 with everlasting darkness and destruction
17 but behold he has brought them into his everlasting light
18 yes into everlasting salvation
19 and they are encircled about
20 with the matchless bounty of his love yes
21 and we have been instruments in his hands
22 of doing this great and marvelous work
23 therefore let us glory
24 yes we will glory in YHVH
25 yes we will rejoice
26 for our joy is full
27 yes we will praise our Elohiym forever
28 behold who can glory too much in YHVH
29 yes who can say too much
30 of his great power and of his mercy
31 and of his long-suffering towards the children of men
32 behold I say unto you
33 I cannot say the smallest part which I feel

1 who could have supposed

2 that our Elohiym would have been so merciful

3 as to have snatched us

4 from our awful sinful and polluted state

5

6 Behold we went forth

7 even in anger

8 with mighty threatenings

9 to destroy his assembly

10 Oh then why did he not consign us

11 to an awful destruction

12 yes why did he not let

13 the sword of his justice fall upon us

14 and doom us to eternal despair

15

16 Oh my soul

17 almost as it were flees at the thought

18 behold he did not exercise his justice upon us

19 but in his great mercy has brought us over

20 that everlasting gulf

21 of death and misery

22 even to the salvation of our souls

23

24 And now behold my brothers

25 what natural man is there

26 that knows these things

27 I say unto you there is none

28 that knows these things

29 except it be the repentant

30 Yes he that repents

31 and exercises emunah

32 and brings forth good works

33 and prays continually without ceasing

1   unto such it is given to know the mysteries of Elohiym

2   yes unto such it shall be given to reveal things

3   which never have been revealed

4   yes and it shall be given unto such

5   to bring thousands of souls to repentance

6   even as it has been given unto us

7   to bring these our brothers to repentance

8   now do you remember my brothers

9   that we said unto our brothers

10 in the land of Zarahemla

11 we go up to the land of Nephi

12 to preach unto our brothers the Lamaniy

13 and they laughed us to scorn

14

15 For they said unto us

16

17 'Do you suppose that you can bring the Lamaniy

18 to the knowledge of the truth

19 Do you suppose that you can convince the Lamaniy

20 of the incorrectness of the traditions of their fathers

21 as stubborn a people as they are

22 whose hearts delight in the shedding of blood

23 whose days have been spent

24 in vulgar lawlessness

25 whose ways have been the ways of a rebel

26 from the beginning'

27

28 Now my brothers you remember

29 that this was their language

30 and furthermore they did say

31

32 'Let us take up arms against them

33 that we destroy them

1 and their lawlessness out of the land

2 for fear that they overrun us and destroy us'

3

4 But behold my beloved brothers

5 we came into the wilderness

6 not with the intent to destroy our brothers

7 but with the intent

8 that perhaps we might save some few of their souls

9 now when our hearts were depressed

10 and we were about to turn back

11 behold YHVH comforted us

12 and said

13 'Go among your brothers the Lamaniy

14 and bear with patience your afflictions

15 and I will give unto you success'

16

17 And now behold we have come

18 and been forth among them

19 and we have been patient in our sufferings

20 and we have suffered every hardship

21 yes we have traveled

22 from house to house relying

23 upon the mercies of the world

24 not upon the mercies of the world alone

25 but upon the mercies of Elohiym

26 and we have entered into their houses

27 and taught them

28 and we have taught them in their streets

29 yes and we have taught them upon their hills

30 and we have also entered into their temples

31 and their synagogues

32 and taught them

33 and we have been cast out

1 and mocked and spit upon

2 and struck upon our cheeks

3 and we have been stoned

4 and taken and bound with strong cords

5 and cast into prison

6 and through the power and wisdom of Elohiym

7 we have been delivered again

8 and we have suffered all manner of afflictions

9 and all this

10 that perhaps we might be the means of saving some soul

11 and we supposed that our joy would be full

12 if perhaps we could be the means of saving some

13

14 Now behold we can look forth

15 and see the fruits of our labors

16 and are they few

17 I say unto you No

18 they are many

19 yes and we can witness of their sincerity

20 because of their love towards their brothers

21 and also towards us

22 For behold they had rather sacrifice their lives

23 than even to take the life of their enemy

24 and they have buried their weapons of war

25 deep in the earth

26 because of their love towards their brothers

27 and now behold

28 I say unto you

29 has there been so great love in all the land

30 behold I say unto you No

31 there has not

32 even among the Nephiy

33 For behold they would take up arms

1 against their brothers
2 they would not allow themselves to be killed
3 but behold how many of these
4 have laid down their lives
5 and we know that they have gone to their Elohiym
6 because of their love and of their hatred to sin
7
8 Now have we not reason to rejoice
9 Yes I say unto you
10 there never were men
11 that had so great reason to rejoice as we
12 since the world began
13 yes and my joy is carried away
14 even unto boasting in my Elohiym
15 for he has
16 all power[8]
17 all wisdom[9]
18 and all understanding[10]
19 he comprehends all things
20 and he is a merciful[11] Being
21 even unto salvation
22 to those who will repent
23 and believe on his name
24
25 Now if this is boasting
26 even so will I boast
27 for this is my life and my light
28 my joy and my salvation
29 and my redemption

---

[8] gevurah
[9] chokmah
[10] Binah
[11] Chesed

1 from everlasting OY
2 yes blessed is the name of my Elohiym
3 who has been mindful of this people
4 who are a branch of the tree of Isra'el
5 and has been lost from its body
6 in a strange land
7 yes I say blessed be the name of my Elohiym
8 who has been mindful of us wanderers
9 in a strange land
10
11 Now my brothers we see that Elohiym is mindful
12 of every people
13 whatever land they may be in
14 yes he numbers his people
15 and his bowels of mercy are over
16 all the earth
17 now this is my joy
18 and my great thanksgiving
19 yes and I will give thanks unto my Elohiym forever
20 Amen"
21
22 Now it came to pass
23 that when those Lamaniy
24 who had gone to war against the Nephiy had found
25 after their many struggles to destroy
26 them that it was in vain to seek their destruction
27 they returned again to the land of Nephi
28
29 And it came to pass
30 that the Amalekiy
31 because of their loss were exceedingly angry
32 and when they saw
33 that they could not seek revenge from the Nephiy

1   they began to stir up the people in anger
2   against their brothers the people of Paniym Nephi Lechi
3   therefore they began again to destroy them
4   now this people again refused to take their arms
5   and they allowed themselves to be killed
6   according to the desires of their enemies
7
8   Now when Ammon and his brothers saw
9   this work of destruction
10 among those whom they so dearly beloved
11 and among those who had so dearly beloved them
12 for they were treated as though
13 they were angels sent from Elohiym
14 to save them from everlasting destruction
15 therefore when Ammon and his brothers saw
16 this great work of destruction
17 they were moved with compassion
18 and they said unto the king
19
20 "Let us gather together this people of YHVH
21 and let us go down to the land of Zarahemla
22 to our brothers the Nephiy
23 and flee out of the hands of our enemies
24 that we be not destroyed"
25
26 but the king said unto them
27
28 "behold the Nephiy will destroy us
29 because of the many murders and sins
30 we have committed against them"
31
32 and Ammon said
33

1   "I will go and inquire of YHVH
2   and if he say unto us
3   go down unto our brothers
4   will you go"
5
6   and the king said unto him
7
8   "Yes if YHVH says unto us go
9   we will go down unto our brothers
10   and we will be their slaves
11   until we repair unto them
12   the many murders and sins
13   which we have committed against them"
14
15   but Ammon said unto him
16
17   "It is against the mitzvot of our brothers
18   which was established by my father
19   that there should be any slaves among them
20   therefore let us go down
21   and rely upon the mercies of our brothers"
22
23   but the king said unto him
24
25   "Inquire of YHVH
26   and if he says unto us go
27   we will go
28   otherwise we will perish in the land"
29
30   And it came to pass
31   that Ammon went and inquired of YHVH
32   and YHVH said unto him
33

1   "Get this people out of this land
2   that they perish not
3   for the evil one has great hold
4   on the hearts of the Amalekiy
5   who do stir up the Lamaniy to anger
6   against their brothers
7   to kill them
8   therefore get you out of this land
9   and blessed are this people in this generation
10 for I will preserve them"
11
12 And now it came to pass
13 that Ammon went and told the king
14 all the words which YHVH had said unto him
15 and they gathered together all their people
16 yes all the people of YHVH
17 and did gather together
18 all their flocks and herds
19 and departed out of the land
20 and came into the wilderness
21 which divided the land of Nephi
22 from the land of Zarahemla
23 and came over near the borders of the land
24 And it came to pass
25 that Ammon said unto them
26 behold I and my brothers will go forth
27 into the land of Zarahemla
28 and you shall remain here until we return
29 and we will try the hearts of our brothers
30 whether they will that you shall come into their land
31
32 And it came to pass
33 that as Ammon was going forth into the land

1 that he and his brothers met Almah

2 over in the place of which has been spoken

3 and behold this was a joyful meeting

4 now the joy of Ammon was so great

5 even that he was full

6 yes he was swallowed up in the joy of his Elohiym

7 even to the exhausting of his strength

8 and he fell again to the earth

9 now was not this exceeding joy

10 behold this is joy which none receives

11 except it be the truly repentant

12 and humble seeker of happiness

13 now the joy of Almah

14 in meeting his brothers was truly great

15 and also the joy of Aharon of Omner and Himni

16 but behold their joy was not that

17 o exceed their strength

18

19 And now it came to pass

20 that Almah conducted his brothers

21 back to the land of Zarahemla

22 even to his own house

23 and they went and told the chief judge all the things

24 that had happened unto them

25 in the land of Nephi

26 among their brothers the Lamaniy

27

28 And it came to pass

29 that the chief judge sent a proclamation

30 throughout all the land

31 desiring the voice of the people

32 concerning the admitting their brothers

33 who were the people of Paniym Nephi Lechi

1

2 And it came to pass

3 that the voice of the people came saying

4

5 "behold we will give up the land of Yershon

6 which is on the east by the sea

7 which joins the land Bountiful

8 which is on the south of the land Bountiful

9 and this land Yershon is the land

10 which we will give unto our brothers for an inheritance

11 and behold we will set our armies

12 between the land Yershon

13 and the land Nephi

14 that we may protect our brothers in the land Yershon

15 and this we do for our brothers

16 on account of their fear

17 to take up arms against their brothers

18 for fear that they should commit sin

19 and this their great fear came

20 because of their sore repentance

21 which they had on account

22 of their many murders

23 and their awful wickedness

24 and now behold this will we do unto our brothers

25 that they may inherit the land Yershon

26 and we will guard them

27 from their enemies with our armies

28 on condition

29 that they will give us a portion of their substance

30 to assist us that we may maintain our armies

31

32 Now it came to pass

33 that when Ammon had heard this

1 he returned to the people of Paniym Nephi Lechi
2 and also Almah with him into the wilderness
3 where they had pitched their tents
4 and made known unto them all these things
5 and Almah also related unto them his conversion
6 with Ammon and Aharon and his brothers
7
8 And it came to pass
9 that it did cause great joy among them
10 and they went down into the land of Yershon
11 and took possession of the land of Yershon
12 and they were called by the Nephiy
13 the people of Ammon therefore
14 they were distinguished by that name ever after
15 and they were among the people of Nephi
16 and also numbered among the people
17 who were of the assembly of Elohiym
18 and they were also distinguished
19 for their zeal towards Elohiym
20 and also towards men
21 for they were perfectly honest
22 and upright in all things
23 and they were firm in the faith of Mashiach
24 even unto the end
25 and they did look upon shedding
26 the blood of their brothers
27 with the greatest abhorrence
28 and they never could be prevailed upon
29 to take up arms against their brothers
30 and they never did look upon death
31 with any degree of terror
32 for their hope and views
33 of Mashiach and the resurrection

1 therefore death was swallowed up to them
2 by the victory of Mashiach over it
3 therefore they would suffer death
4 in the most aggravating and distressing manner
5 which could be inflicted by their brothers
6 before they would take the sword or cimeter
7 to strike them
8 and thus they were
9 a zealous and beloved people
10 a highly favored people of YHVH
11
12 And now it came to pass
13 that after the people of Ammon were established
14 in the land of Yershon
15 and an assembly also established
16 in the land of Yershon
17 and the armies of the Nephiy were set
18 round about the land of Yershon
19 yes in all the borders
20 round about the land of Zarahemla
21 behold the armies of the Lamaniy had followed
22 their brothers into the wilderness
23 and thus there was a tremendous battle
24 yes even such an one
25 as never had been known
26 among all the people in the land
27 from the time Lechi left Yerushalayim
28 yes and tens of thousands of the Lamaniy were killed
29 and scattered abroad
30 Yes and also there was a tremendous slaughter
31 among the people of Nephi
32 nevertheless the Lamaniy
33 were driven and scattered

1 and the people of Nephi returned again to their land
2
3 and now this was a time
4 that there was a great mourning and lamentation heard
5 throughout all the land
6 among all the people of Nephi
7 Yes the cry of widows mourning
8 for their husbands
9 and also of fathers mourning
10 for their sons
11 and the daughter for the brother
12 yes the brother for the father
13 and thus the cry of mourning was heard
14 among all of them mourning
15 for their relatives who had been killed
16 and now certainly this was a sorrowful day
17 yes a time of solemnity
18 and a time of much fasting and prayer
19 and thus ended the fifteenth year
20 of the reign of the judges over the people of Nephi
21
22 And this is the account
23 of Ammon and his brothers
24 their journeyings in the land of Nephi
25 their sufferings in the land
26 their sorrows and their afflictions
27 and their incomprehensible joy
28 and the reception and safety of their brothers
29 in the land of Yershon
30 and now may YHVH the Redeemer of all men
31 bless their souls forever"
32

33

6-INEQUALITY OF MAN

1
2 And this is the account
3 of the wars and contentions
4 among the Nephiy
5 and also the wars
6 between the Nephiy and the Lamaniy
7 and the fifteenth year
8 of the reign of the judges is ended
9 and from the first year to the fifteenth
10 has brought to pass the destruction
11 of many thousand lives
12 yes it has brought to pass
13 an awful scene of bloodshed
14
15 And the bodies of many thousands are laid low
16 in the earth
17 while the bodies of many thousands are turning to dust in mounds
18 upon the face of the earth
19 yes and many thousands are mourning
20 for the loss of their relatives
21 because they have reason to fear
22 according to the promises of YHVH
23 that they are consigned to a state of endless OY
24 while many thousands of others truly mourn
25 for the loss of their relatives
26 yet they rejoice and to joy in the hope
27 and even know according to the promises of YHVH
28 that they are raised to dwell at the right hand of Elohiym
29 in a state of never ending happiness
30
31 And thus we see
32 how great the inequality of man is
33 because of sin and rebellion

1 and the power of the evil one
2 which comes by the cunning plans
3 which he has devised
4 to ensnare the hearts of men
5 and thus we see
6 the great call of diligence of men to labor
7 in the vineyards of YHVH
8 and thus we see
9 the great reason of sorrow
10 and also of rejoicing
11 sorrow because of death and destruction among men
12 and joy because of the light of Mashiach unto life
13
14 O that I were an angel
15 and could have the wish of my heart
16 that I might go forth and speak
17 with the trump of Elohiym
18 with a voice to shake the earth
19 and cry repentance unto every people
20 Yes I would declare unto every soul
21 as with the voice of thunder
22 repentance and the path of redemption
23 that they should repent
24 and come unto our Elohiym
25 that there might not be more sorrow
26 upon all the face of the earth
27
28 But behold I am a man
29 and do sin in my wish
30 for I ought to be content with the things
31 which YHVH has allotted unto me
32 I ought not to be distressed in my desires
33 because of the firm decree of a just Elohiym

1 for I know that he grants unto men

2 according to their desire

3 whether it be unto death or unto life

4 yes I know that he allots unto men

5 yes decrees unto them decrees

6 which are unalterable

7 according to their wills

8 whether they be unto salvation

9 or unto destruction

10 Yes and I know

11 that good and evil have come before all men

12 he that knows not good from evil is blameless

13 but he that knows good and evil

14 to him it is given according to his desires

15 whether he desires good or evil

16 life or death

17 joy or remorse of conscience

18 now seeing that I know these things

19 why should I desire more

20 than to perform the work

21 to which I have been called

22 why should I desire

23 that I were an angel

24 that I could speak

25 unto all the ends of the earth

26

27 For behold YHVH does grant unto all nations

28 of their own nation and language

29 to teach his word

30 yes in wisdom

31 all that he sees fit

32 that they should have

33 therefore we see

1   that YHVH does counsel in wisdom
2   according to that which is just and true
3   I know that which YHVH has commanded me
4   and I glory in it
5   I do not glory of myself
6   but I glory in that which YHVH hath commanded me
7   yes and this is my glory
8   that perhaps I may be an instrument
9   in the hands of Elohiym
10   to bring some soul to repentance
11   and this is my joy
12
13   And behold
14   when I see many of my brothers
15   truly repentant and coming to YHVH their Elohiym
16   then is my soul filled with joy
17   then do I remember what YHVH has done for me
18   yes even that he has heard my prayer
19   yes then do I remember his merciful arm
20   which he extended towards me
21   Yes and I also remember the captivity of my fathers
22   for I surely do know
23   that YHVH did deliver them out of bondage
24   and by this did establish his assembly
25   yes YHVH Elohiym
26   the Elohiym of Avraham
27   the Elohiym of Yitzchak
28   and the Elohiym of Yacov did deliver them out of bondage
29   Yes I have always remembered the captivity of my fathers
30   and that same Elohiym
31   who delivered them out of the hands of the Egyptians
32   did deliver them out of bondage
33   Yes and that same Elohiym

1 did establish his assembly among them

2 yes and that same Elohiym has called me

3 by a holy calling

4 to preach the word unto this people

5 and has given me much success

6 in the which my joy is full

7 but I do not joy in my own success alone

8 but my joy is more full

9 because of the success of my brothers

10 who have been up to the land of Nephi

11 behold they have labored exceedingly

12 and have brought forth much fruit

13 and how great shall be their reward

14 now when I think of the success

15 of these my brothers

16 my soul is carried away

17 even to the separation of it

18 from the body as it were

19 so great is my joy

20 and now may Elohiym grant

21 unto these my brothers

22 that they may sit down in the kingdom of Elohiym

23 yes and also all those

24 who are the fruit of their labors

25 that they may go no more out

26 but that they may praise him forever

27 and may Elohiym grant

28 that it may be done

29 according to my words

30 even as I have spoken

31 Amein

32

33 Behold now it came to pass

1   that after the people of Ammon were established

2   in the land of Yershon

3   yes and also after the Lamaniy were driven out

4   of the land

5   and their dead were buried

6   by the people of the land

7   now their dead were not numbered

8   because of the greatness of their numbers

9   neither were the dead of the Nephiy numbered

10

11   But it came to pass

12   after they had buried their dead

13   and also after the days

14   of fasting and mourning and prayer

15   and it was in the sixteenth year

16   of the reign of the judges

17   over the people of Nephi

18   there began to be continual peace

19   throughout all the land

20   Yes and the people did observe

21   to keep the mitzvot of YHVH

22   and they were strict

23   in observing the chukkim of Elohiym

24   according to the Torah of Moshe

25   for they were taught to keep the Torah of Moshe

26   until it should be fully established

27   and thus the people did have no disturbance

28   in all the sixteenth year

29   of the reign of the judges

30   over the people of Nephi

31

32   And it came to pass

33   that in the commencement of the seventeenth year

1   of the reign of the judges
2   there was continual peace
3
4   But it came to pass
5   in the latter end of the seventeenth year
6   there came a man into the land of Zarahemla
7   and he was Anti-Mashiach
8   for he began to preach unto the people
9   against the prophecies
10   which had been spoken by the prophets
11   concerning the coming of Mashiach
12   now there was no mishpat against a man's belief
13   for it was strictly contrary to the commands of Elohiym
14   that there should be a mishpat
15   which should bring men on
16   to unequal grounds
17
18   For thus says the scripture
19
20   "Choose you this day
21   whom you will serve"[12]
22
23   Now if a man desired to serve Elohiym
24   it was his privilege
25   or rather if he believed in Elohiym
26   it was his privilege to serve him
27   but if he did not believe in him
28   there was no mishpat to punish him
29   but if he murdered he was punished unto death
30   and if he robbed he was also punished
31   and if he stole he was also punished
32   and if he committed adultery he was also punished

---

[12] Yehoshua (Joshua) 24:15

1 yes for all this wickedness they were punished

2

3 For there was a mishpat

4 that men should be judged

5 according to their crimes

6 nevertheless there was no mishpat

7 against a man's belief

8 therefore a man was punished

9 only for the crimes

10 which he had done

11 therefore all men were on equal grounds

12 and this Anti-Mashiach

13 whose name was Korihor

14 and the mishpatim could have no hold upon him

15 began to preach unto the people

16 that there should be no Mashiach

17 and after this manner did he preach saying

18

19 "O you that are bound down

20 under a foolish and a vain hope

21 why do you yoke yourselves

22 with such foolish things

23 Why do you look for a Mashiach

24 For no man can know of anything

25 which is to come

26 behold these things

27 which you call prophecies

28 which you say are handed down

29   by holy prophets

30 behold they are foolish traditions

31 of your fathers

32

33 How do you know of their certainty

1 behold you cannot know of things
2 which you do not see
3 therefore you cannot know
4 that there shall be a Mashiach
5 you look forward and say
6 that you see a purification of your sin
7 but behold it is the effect of an unstable mind
8 and this derangement of your minds comes
9 because of the traditions of your fathers
10 which lead you away into a belief of things
11 which are not so"
12
13 And many more such things
14 did he say unto them telling them
15 that there could be no atonement made
16 for the sins of men
17 but every man fared in this life
18 according to the management of the creature
19 therefore every man prospered
20 according to his genius
21 and that every man conquered
22 according to his strength
23 and whatever a man did was no crime
24 and thus he did preach unto them
25 leading away the hearts of many causing them
26 to lift up their heads in their wickedness
27 yes leading away many women and also men
28 to commit whoredoms
29 telling them that when a man was dead
30 that was the end thereof
31 now this man went over to the land of Yershon also
32 to preach these things among the people of Ammon
33 who were once the people of the Lamaniy

1 but behold they were more wise
2 than many of the Nephiy
3 for they took him and bound him
4 and carried him before Ammon
5 who was a Kohen Gadol over that people
6
7 And it came to pass
8 that he caused that he should be carried out of the land
9 and he came over into the land of Gid`on
10 and began to preach unto them also
11 and here he did not have much success
12 for he was taken and bound
13 and carried before the Kohen Gadol
14 and also the chief judge over the land
15
16 And it came to pass
17 that the high priest said unto him
18
19 "Why do you go about
20 perverting the ways of YHVH
21 why do you teach this people
22 that there shall be no Mashiach
23 to interrupt their rejoicings
24 why do you speak against
25 all the prophecies of the holy prophets"
26
27 Now the Kohen Gadol's name was Giddonah
28 and Korihor said unto him
29
30 "Because I do not teach the foolish traditions of your fathers
31 and because I do not teach this people
32 to bind themselves down
33 under the foolish takanot and ma'asim

1   which are laid down by ancient kohanim
2   to usurp power and authority over them
3   to keep them in ignorance
4   that they may not lift up their heads
5   but be brought down
6   according to your words
7
8   You say that this people is a free people
9   behold I say they are in bondage
10 you say that those ancient prophecies are true
11 behold I say that you do not know that they are true
12 you say that this people is a guilty and a fallen people
13 because of the transgression of a parent
14 behold I say that a child is not guilty because of its parents
15 and you also say that Mashiach shall come
16 but behold I say that you do not know
17 that there shall be a Mashiach
18 and you say also that he shall be killed
19 for the sins of the world
20 and thus you lead away this people
21 after the foolish traditions of your fathers
22 and according to your own desires
23 and you keep them down
24 even as it were in bondage
25 that you may glut yourselves
26 with the labors of their hands
27 that they did not look up with boldness
28 and that they did not enjoy
29 their rights and privileges
30
31 Yes they did not make use of that
32 which is their own
33 for fear that they should offend their kohanim

1 who do yoke them according to their desires
2 and have brought them to believe
3 by their traditions and their dreams
4 and their whims and their visions
5 and their pretended mysteries
6 that they should
7 if they did not do according to their words
8 offend some unknown being
9 who they say is Elohiym a being
10 who never has been seen or known
11 who never was nor ever will be"
12
13 Now when the Kohen Gadol and the chief judge
14 saw the hardness of his heart
15 yes when they saw
16 that he would revile even against Elohiym
17 they would not make any reply to his words
18 but they caused that he should be bound
19 and they delivered him up
20 into the hands of the officers
21 and sent him to the land of Zarahemla
22 that he might be brought before Almah and the chief judge
23 who was governor over all the land
24 And it came to pass
25 that when he was brought before Almah and the chief judge
26 he did go on in the same manner
27 as he did in the land of Gid`on
28 yes he went on to blaspheme
29 and he did rise up in great swelling words before Almah
30 and did revile against the kohanim and morim accusing them
31 of leading away the people
32 after the silly traditions of their fathers
33 for the sake of profiting

1 on the labors of the people
2 now Almah said unto him
3
4 "You know that we do not profit ourselves
5 upon the labors of this people
6 for behold I have labored
7 even from the commencement
8 of the reign of the judges until now
9 with my own hands for my support
10 despite my many travels round about the land
11 to declare the word of Elohiym unto my people
12 and despite the many labors
13 which I have performed in the assembly
14 I have never received so much as even one senine for my labor
15 neither have any of my brothers
16 except it were in the judgments eat
17 and then we have received only according to the mishpatim for our time
18
19 And now if we do not receive anything
20 for our labors in the assembly
21 what does it profit us to labor in the assembly
22 except it were to declare the truth
23 that we may have rejoicing in the joy of our brothers
24 then why say you
25 that we preach unto this people to get gain
26 when you of thyself know that we receive no gain
27 and now believe you
28 that we deceive this people
29 that causes such joy in their hearts
30 and Korihor answered him
31
32 "Yes"
33

1   and then Almah said unto him

2

3   "Believe you that there is Elohiym"

4

5   and he answered

6

7   "No"

8

9   now Almah said unto him

10

11   "Will you deny again that there is Elohiym

12   and also deny the Mashiach

13   For behold I say unto you

14   I know there is Elohiym

15   and also that Mashiach shall come

16   and now what evidence have you

17   that there is no Elohiym

18   or that Mashiach comes not

19   I say unto you that you have none

20   except it be your word only

21

22   But behold I have all things as a testimony

23   that these things are true

24   and you also have all things as a testimony unto you

25   that they are true

26   and will you deny them

27   believe you that these things are true

28   behold I know that you believe

29   but you are possessed with a lying ruach

30   and you have put off the Ruach of Elohiym

31   that it may have no place in you

32   but the evil one has power over you

33   and he does carry you about working plans

1 that he may destroy the children of Elohiym"

2

3 and now Korihor said unto Almah

4

5 "If you will show me a sign

6 that I may be convinced that there is a Elohiym

7 yes show unto me that he has power

8 and then will I be convinced

9 of the truth of your words"

10

11 but Almah said unto him

12

13 "You have had signs enough

14 will you tempt your Elohiym

15 will you say

16 'Show unto me a sign'

17 when you have the testimony of all these your brothers

18 and also all the holy prophets

19 the scriptures are laid before you

20 yes and all things are a sign that there is Elohiym

21 yes even the earth

22 and all things that are upon the face of it

23 yes and its motion

24 yes and also all the planets

25 which move in their regular form do witness

26 that there is El Hashamayim va'erets[13]

27

28 and yet do you go about

29 leading away the hearts of this people

30 testifying unto them there is no Elohiym

31 and yet will you deny against all these witnesses"

32

---

[13] God of Heaven and Earth

1 and he said

2

3 "Yes I will deny

4 except you shall show me a sign"

5

6 And now it came to pass

7 that Almah said unto him

8

9 "Behold I am grieved

10 because of the hardness of your heart

11 yes that you will still resist the ruach of the truth

12 that your soul may be destroyed

13 but behold it is better

14 that your soul should be lost than

15 that you should be the means of bringing

16 many souls down to destruction

17 by your lying and by your flattering words

18 therefore if you shall deny again

19 behold Elohiym shall strike you

20 that you shall become dumb

21 that you shall never open your mouth any more

22 that you shall not deceive this people any more"

23

24 Now Korihor said unto him

25

26 "I do not deny the existence of Elohiym

27 but I do not believe that there is Elohiym

28 and I say also that you do not know that there is a Elohiym

29 and except you show me a sign

30 I will not believe"

31

32 now Almah said unto him

33

1 "This will I give unto you for a sign
2 that you shall be struck dumb
3 according to my words
4 and I say that in the name of Elohiym
5 you shall be struck dumb
6 that you shall no more have utterance"
7
8 Now when Almah had said these words
9 Korihor was struck dumb
10 that he could not have utterance
11 according to the words of Almah
12 and now when the chief judge saw this
13 he put forth his hand
14 and wrote unto Korihor saying
15
16 "Are you convinced of the power of Elohiym
17 In whom did you desire
18 that Almah should show forth his sign
19 Would you that he should afflict others
20 to show unto you a sign
21 behold he has showed unto you a sign
22 and now will you dispute more"
23
24 And Korihor put forth his hand
25 and wrote saying
26
27 "I know that I am dumb
28 for I cannot speak
29 and I know that nothing
30 except it were the power of Elohiym
31 could bring this upon me
32 yes and I always knew that there was Elohiym
33 but behold the evil one has deceived me

1 for he appeared unto me in the form of an angel

2 and said unto me

3 'Go and reclaim this people

4 for they have all gone astray

5 after an unknown Elohiym'

6 and he said unto me

7 There is no Elohiym

8 yes and he taught me that which I should say

9 and I have taught his words

10 and I taught them

11 because they were pleasing unto the carnal mind

12 and I taught them

13 even until I had much success insomuch

14 that I truthfully believed that they were true

15 and for this cause I withstood the truth

16 even until I have brought this great curse upon me"

17

18 Now when he had said this he implored

19 that Almah should pray unto Elohiym

20 that the curse might be taken from him

21 but Almah said unto him

22

23 "If this curse should be taken from you

24 you would again lead away the hearts of this people

25 therefore it shall be unto you even as YHVH will"

26

27 And it came to pass

28 that the curse was not taken off of Korihor

29 but he was cast out and went about

30 from house to house begging for his food

31 now the knowledge of what had happened unto Korihor

32 was immediately published throughout all the land

33 yes the proclamation was sent forth

1 by the chief judge to all the people in the land

2 declaring unto those who had believed in the words of Korihor

3 that they must speedily repent

4 for fear that the same judgments would come unto them

5

6 And it came to pass

7 that they were all convinced of the wickedness of Korihor

8 therefore they were all converted again unto YHVH

9 and this put an end to the lawlessness

10 after the manner of Korihor

11 and Korihor did go about

12 from house to house begging food for his support

13

14 And it came to pass

15 that as he went forth among the people

16 yes among a people who had separated themselves

17 from the Nephiy

18 and called themselves Zoramiy

19 being led by a man whose name was Zoram

20 and as he went forth among them

21 behold he was run upon and trampled down

22 even until he was dead

23 and thus we see the end of him

24 who perverts the ways of YHVH

25 and thus we see

26 that the evil one will not support his children at the last day

27 but does speedily drag them down to Sheol

28

29 Now it came to pass

30 that after the end of Korihor Almah having received word

31 that the Zoramiy were perverting the ways of YHVH

32 and that Zoram who was their leader

33 was leading the hearts of the people

1   to bow down to dumb idols

2   his heart again began to sicken

3   because of the lawlessness of the people

4   For it was the cause of great sorrow to Almah

5   to know of lawlessness among his people

6   therefore his heart was exceedingly sorrowful

7   because of the separation of the Zoramiy from the Nephiy

8   now the Zoramiy had gathered themselves

9   together in a land

10   which they called Antionum

11   which was east of the land of Zarahemla

12   which lay nearly bordering upon the seashore

13   which was south of the land of Yershon

14   which also bordered upon the wilderness south

15   which wilderness was full of the Lamaniy

16   now the Nephiy greatly feared

17   that the Zoramiy would enter

18   into a correspondence with the Lamaniy

19   and that it would be the means

20   of great loss on the part of the Nephiy

21

22   And now

23   as the preaching of the word had a great tendency

24   to lead the people to do that which was just

25   yes it had had more powerful effect

26   upon the minds of the people

27   than the sword or anything else which had happened unto them

28   therefore Almah thought it was necessary

29   that they should try the virtue of the word of Elohiym

30   therefore he took Ammon and Aharon

31   and Omner and Himni he did leave in the assembly in Zarahemla

32   but the former three he took with him

33   and also Amulek and Zeezrom who were at Melek

1 and he also took two of his sons

2 now the eldest of his sons he took not with him

3 and his name was Helaman

4 but the names of those whom he took

5 with him were Shiblon and Corianton

6 and these are the names of those

7 who went with him among the Zoramiy

8 to preach unto them the word

9 now the Zoramiy were dissidents from the Nephiy

10 therefore they had had the word of Elohiym preached unto them

11 but they had fallen into great errors

12 for they would not observe

13 to keep the mitzvot of Elohiym and his chukkim

14 according to the Torah of Moshe

15 neither would they observe the takanot of the assembly

16 to continue in prayer and supplication to Elohiym daily

17 that they might not enter into temptation

18 Yes in sum

19 they did pervert the ways of YHVH

20 in very many instances

21 therefore for this cause Almah

22 and his brothers went into the land

23 to preach the word unto them

24 now when they had come into the land

25 behold to their astonishment

26 they found that the Zoramiy had built synagogues

27 and that they did gather themselves together

28 on one day of the week

29 which day they did call the day of Adonai

30 and they did worship after a manner

31 which Almah and his brothers had never beheld

32 for they had a place built up

33 in the center of their synagogue

1 a place for standing
2 which was high above the head
3 and the top thereof would only admit one person
4 therefore whoever desired to worship
5 must go forth and stand upon the top thereof
6 and stretch forth his hands towards heaven
7 and cry with a loud voice saying
8
9 " Kadosh Kadosh Adonai
10 we believe that you are Elohiym
11 and we believe that you art holy
12 and that you were ruach
13 and that you are ruach
14 and that you will be ruach forever
15
16 Kadosh Adonai
17 we believe that you hast separated us from our brothers
18 and we do not believe in the tradition of our brothers
19 which were handed down to them
20 by the childishness of their fathers
21 but we believe that you hast chosen us
22 to be your holy children
23 and also you have made it known unto us
24 that there shall be no Mashiach
25 but you are the same
26 yesterday today and forever
27 and you hast chosen us
28 that we shall be saved
29 while all around us are chosen to be cast
30 by your anger down to Sheol
31 for the which holiness O Elohiym we thank you
32 and we also thank you
33 that you hast chosen us

1 that we may not be led away

2 after the foolish traditions of our brothers

3 which does bind them down to a belief of Mashiach

4 which does lead their hearts to wander far from you our Elohiym

5 and again we thank you O Adonai

6 that we are a chosen and a holy people

7 Amein"

8

9 Now it came to pass

10 that after Almah and his brothers

11 and his sons had heard these prayers

12 they were astonished beyond all measure

13 For behold every man did go forth

14 and offer up these same prayers

15 now the place was called by them Rameumptom

16 which being interpreted is the holy stand

17 now from this stand

18 they did offer up every man the selfsame prayer unto Elohiym

19 thanking their Elohiym

20 that they were chosen of him

21 and that he did not lead them away

22 after the tradition of their brothers

23 and that their hearts were not stolen away

24 to believe in things to come

25 which they knew nothing about

26 now after the people had all offered up thanks

27 after this manner

28 they returned to their homes

29 never speaking of their Elohiym again

30 until they had assembled themselves together again

31 to the holy stand to offer up thanks

32 after their manner

33 now when Almah saw this his heart was grieved

1   for he saw

2   that they were a twisted and a perverse people

3   yes he saw

4   that their hearts were set upon gold and upon silver

5   and upon all manner of fine goods

6   Yes and he also saw

7   that their hearts were lifted up

8   unto great boasting in their pride

9   and he lifted up his voice to heaven

10 and cried saying

11

12 "O how long O YHVH will you allow

13 that your servants shall dwell here below in the flesh

14 to behold such gross wickedness

15 among the children of men

16

17 Behold O Elohiym

18 they cry unto you

19 and yet their hearts are swallowed up in their pride

20 behold O Elohiym

21 they cry unto you with their mouths

22 while they are puffed up even to greatness

23 with the vain things of the world

24 behold O my Elohiym

25 their costly apparel and their ringlets

26 and their bracelets and their ornaments of gold

27 and all their precious things which they are ornamented with

28 and behold their hearts are set upon them

29 and yet they cry unto you and say

30

31 'We thank you O Adonai

32 for we are a chosen people unto you

33 while others shall perish'

1 Yes and they say
2 that you have made it known unto them
3 that there shall be no Mashiach
4
5 O YHVH Elohiym
6 how long will you allow
7 that such wickedness and infidelity
8 shall be among this people
9
10 O Adonai will you give me strength
11 that I may bear with mine infirmities
12 for I am infirm
13 and such wickedness among this people
14 does pain my soul
15 O Adonai my heart is exceedingly sorrowful
16 will you comfort my soul in Mashiach
17 O Adonai will you grant unto me
18 that I may have strength
19 that I may endure with patience these afflictions
20 which shall come upon me
21 because of the lawlessness of this people
22
23 O Adonai will you comfort my soul
24 and give unto me success
25 and also my fellow laborers who are with me
26 yes Ammon and Aharon
27 and Omner and also Amulek
28 and Zeezrom and also my two sons
29 yes even all these will you comfort
30 O Adonai
31 yes will you comfort their souls in Mashiach
32 will you grant unto them
33 that they may have strength

1 that they may bear their afflictions
2 which shall come upon them
3 because of the lawlessness of this people
4 O Adonai will you grant unto us
5 that we may have success
6 in bringing them again unto you in Mashiach
7
8 Behold O Adonai their souls are precious
9 and many of them are our brothers
10 therefore give unto us O Adonai power and wisdom
11 that we may bring these our brothers again unto you"
12
13 Now it came to pass
14 that when Almah had said these words
15 that he clapped his hands upon all them
16 who were with him
17 and behold as he clapped his hands upon them
18 they were filled with the Ruach Elohiym
19 and after that they did separate themselves
20 one from another taking no thought for themselves
21 what they should eat
22 or what they should drink
23 or what they should put on
24 and YHVH provided for them
25 that they should hunger not
26 neither should they thirst
27 yes and he also gave them strength
28 that they should endure no manner of afflictions
29 except it were swallowed up in the joy of Mashiach
30 now this was according to the prayer of Almah
31 and this because he prayed in emunah
32
33 And it came to pass

1 that they did go forth

2 and began to preach the word of Elohiym unto the people

3 entering into their synagogues and into their houses

4 yes and even they did preach the word in their streets

5

6 And it came to pass

7 that after much labor among them

8 they began to have success among the poor class of people

9 for behold they were cast out of the synagogues

10 because of the coarseness of their apparel

11 therefore they were not permitted

12 to enter into their synagogues to worship Elohiym

13 being esteemed as filthiness

14 therefore they were poor

15 yes they were esteemed by their brothers as dross

16 therefore they were poor as to things of the world

17 and also they were poor in heart

18 now as Almah was teaching and speaking

19 unto the people upon the hill Onidah

20 there came a great multitude unto him

21 who were those of whom we have been speaking

22 of whom were poor in heart

23 because of their poverty

24 as to the things of the world

25 and they came unto Almah

26 and the one who was the foremost

27 among them said unto him

28

29 "behold what shall these my brothers do

30 for they are despised of all men

31 because of their poverty

32 yes and more especially by our kohanim

33 for they have cast us out of our synagogues

1   which we have labored abundantly

2   to build with our own hands

3   and they have cast us out

4   because of our exceeding poverty

5   and we have no place to worship our Elohiym

6   and behold what shall we do"

7

8   and now when Almah heard this he turned him

9   about his face immediately towards him

10 and he beheld with great joy

11 for he beheld

12 that their afflictions had truly humbled them

13 and that they were in prepared to hear the word

14 therefore he did say no more to the other multitude

15 but he stretched forth his hand

16 and exclaimed unto those whom he beheld

17 who were truly repentant

18 and said unto them

19

20 "I behold that you are lowly in heart

21 and if so blessed are you

22 behold your brother has said

23 'What shall we do

24 for we are cast out of our synagogues

25 that we cannot worship our Elohiym'

26

27 Behold I say unto you do you suppose

28 that you cannot worship Elohiym

29 except it be in your synagogues only

30 and furthermore I would ask do you suppose

31 that you must not worship Elohiym only once in a week

32 I say unto you it is good

33 that you are cast out of your synagogues

1　that you may be humble
2　and that you may learn wisdom
3　for it is necessary that you should learn wisdom
4　for it is because that you are cast out
5　that you are despised of your brothers
6　because of your exceeding poverty
7　that you are brought to a lowliness of heart
8　for you are necessarily brought to be humble
9
10　And now because you are compelled to be humble
11　blessed are you
12　for a man sometimes
13　if he is compelled to be humble seeks repentance
14　and now certainly whoever repents
15　shall find mercy
16　and he that finds mercy
17　and walks forward in the path to the end
18　the same shall be saved
19　and now as I said unto you
20　that because you were compelled to be humble
21　you were blessed
22　do you not suppose that they are more blessed
23　who truly humble themselves because of the word
24　Yes he that truly humbles himself
25　and repents of his sins
26　and walks forward in the path to the end
27　the same shall be blessed
28　yes much more blessed
29　than they who are compelled to be humble
30　because of their exceeding poverty
31　therefore blessed are they who humble themselves
32　without being compelled to be humble
33　or rather in other words blessed is he

1 that believes in the word of Elohiym

2 and is immersed without stubbornness of heart

3 yes without being brought to know the word

4 or even compelled to know before they will believe

5

6 Yes there are many who do say

7 'If you will show unto us a sign from heaven

8 then we shall know of a certainty

9 then we shall believe'

10

11 Now I ask is this emunah

12 behold I say unto you No

13 for if a man knows a thing he has

14 no reason to believe for he knows it

15 and now

16 how much more set apart to destruction is he

17 that knows the will of Elohiym

18 and does it not

19 than he that only believes

20 or only has reason to believe

21 and falls into rebellion

22 now of this thing you must judge

23

24 Behold I say unto you

25 that it is on the one hand

26 even as it is on the other

27 nd it shall be unto every man

28 according to his work

29 and now as I said concerning emunah

30 emunah is not to have a perfect knowledge of things

31 therefore if you walk in emunah

32 you hope[14] for things

---

[14] Tikvah- hope- an expectation based on a promise

1 which are not seen

2 which are true

3

4 And now behold I say unto you

5 and I would that you should remember

6 that Elohiym is merciful unto all who believe on his name

7 therefore he desires in the first place

8 that you should believe

9 yes even on his word

10 and now he imparts his word by angels unto men

11 yes not only men but women also

12 now this is not all

13 little children do have words given unto them many times

14 which confound the wise and the learned

15 and now my beloved brothers

16 as you have desired to know of me

17 what you shall do

18 because you are afflicted and cast out

19 now I do not desire that you should suppose

20 that I mean to judge you

21 only according to that which is true

22 for I do not mean

23 that you all of you have been compelled to humble yourselves

24 for I truthfully believe

25 that there are some among you who would humble themselves

26 let them be in whatever circumstances they might

27 now as I said concerning emunah

28 that it was not a perfect knowledge

29 even so it is with my words

30 you cannot know of their certainty at first unto perfection

31 any more than emunah is a perfect knowledge

32 but behold

33 if you will awake and arouse your mind

1   even to test my words

2   and exercise a particle of emunah

3   yes even if you can no more than desire to believe

4   let this desire work in you

5   even until you believe in a manner

6   that you can give place for a portion of my words

7

8   Now we will compare the word unto a seed

9   now if you give place

10 that a seed may be planted in your heart

11 behold if it be a true seed or a good seed

12 if you do not cast it out by your unbelief

13 that you will resist the Ruach YHVH

14 behold it will begin to swell within your breasts[15]

15 and when you feel these swelling motions

16 you will begin to say within yourselves

17 it must needs be that this is a good seed

18 or that the word is good

19 for it begins to enlarge my soul

20 yes it begins to enlighten my understanding

21 yes it begins to be delicious to me

22 now behold would not this increase your emunah

23 I say unto you Yes

24 nevertheless it has not grown up to a perfect knowledge

25

26 But behold

27 as the seed swells and sprouts and beginns to grow

28 then you must needs say

29 that the seed is good

30 for behold it swells and sprouts and begins to grow

31 and now behold will not this strengthen your emunah

32 Yes it will strengthen your emunah

---

[15] Expansion of thoughts

1 for you will say

2 I know that this is a good seed

3 for behold it sprouts and beginns to grow

4

5 And now behold are you sure

6 that this is a good seed

7 I say unto you Yes

8 for every seed brings forth

9 unto its own likeness

10 therefore if a seed grows it is good

11 but if it grows not

12 behold it is not good

13 therefore it is cast away

14 and now behold

15 because you have tried the test

16 and planted the seed

17 and it swells and sprouts and begins to grow

18 you must necessarily know that the seed is good

19

20 and now behold is your knowledge perfect

21 Yes your knowledge is perfect in that thing

22 and your emunah is dormant

23 and this because you know

24 for you know that the word has swelled your souls

25 and you also know that it has sprouted up

26 that your understanding does begin to be enlightened

27 and your mind does begin to expand

28

29 O then is not this real

30 I say unto you Yes

31 because it is light

32 and whatever is light is good

33 because it is discernible

1   therefore you must know that it is good

2   and now behold after you have tasted this light

3   is your knowledge perfect

4   behold I say unto you No

5   neither must you lay aside your emunah

6   for you have only exercised your emunah

7   to plant the seed

8   that you might try the test

9   to know if the seed was good

10

11   And behold as the tree begins to grow

12   you will say

13   'Let us nourish it with great care

14   that it may get root

15   that it may grow up

16   and bring forth fruit unto us'

17   and now behold if you nourish it with much care

18   it will get root

19   and grow up

20   and bring forth fruit

21   but if you neglect the tree

22   and take no thought for its nourishment

23   behold it will not get any root

24   and when the heat of the sun comes and scorches it

25   because it has no root it withers away

26   and you pluck it up and cast it out

27   now this is not because the seed was not good

28   neither is it because the fruit thereof would not be desirable

29   but it is because your ground is barren

30   and you will not nourish the tree

31   therefore you cannot have the fruit thereof

32

33   And thus

1　if you will not nourish the word looking forward
2　with an eye of faith to the fruit thereof
3　you can never pluck of the fruit of the tree of life
4　but if you will nourish the word
5　yes nourish the tree
6　as it begins to grow by your faith
7　with great diligence and with patience
8　looking forward to the fruit thereof
9　it shall take root
10　and behold it shall be a tree springing up unto everlasting life
11　and because of your diligence and your faith and your patience
12　with the word in nourishing it
13　that it may take root in you
14　behold by and by you shall pluck the fruit thereof
15　which is most precious
16　which is sweet above all that is sweet
17　and which is white above all that is white
18　yes and pure above all that is pure
19　and you shall feast upon this fruit
20　even until you are filled
21　that you hunger not neither shall you thirst
22　then my brothers you shall reap the rewards
23　of your emunah and your diligence
24　and patience and long suffering waiting
25　for the tree to bring forth fruit unto you"
26
27　Now after Almah had spoken these words
28　they sent forth unto him desiring to know
29　whether they should believe in one Elohiym
30　that they might obtain this fruit of which he had spoken
31　or how they should plant the seed
32　or the word of which he had spoken
33　which he said must be planted in their hearts

1   or in what manner they should begin to exercise their emunah

2

3   and Almah said unto them

4

5   "Behold you have said

6   that you could not worship your Elohiym

7   because you are cast out of your synagogues

8   but behold I say unto you

9   if you suppose that you cannot worship Elohiym

10   you do greatly wander from the right path

11   and you ought to search the scriptures

12   if you suppose that they have taught you this

13   you do not understand them

14

15   Do you remember to have read

16   what Zenos the prophet of old has said

17   concerning prayer or worship

18   For he said

19

20   'You are merciful O Elohiym

21   for you hast heard my prayer

22   even when I was in the wilderness

23   yes you were merciful

24   when I prayed concerning those

25   who were my enemies

26   and you did turn them to me

27

28   Yes O Elohiym

29   and you were merciful unto me

30   when I did cry unto you in my field

31   when I did cry unto you in my prayer

32   and you did hear me

33   and again O Elohiym

1   when I did turn to my house

2   you did hear me in my prayer

3   and when I did turn unto my closet

4   O YHVH and prayed unto you

5   you did hear me

6

7   Yes you are merciful unto your children

8   when they cry unto you

9   to be heard of you

10 and not of men

11 and you will hear them

12 Yes O Elohiym

13 you have been merciful unto me

14 and heard my cries

15 in the midst of your congregations

16

17 Yes and you have also heard me

18 when I have been cast out

19 and have been despised by mine enemies

20 yes you did hear my cries

21 and was angry with my enemies

22 and you did visit them in your anger

23 with speedy destruction

24 and you didst hear me

25 because of mine afflictions

26 and my sincerity

27 and it is because of your Son

28 that you have been thus merciful unto me

29 therefore I will cry unto you in all mine afflictions

30 for in you is my joy

31 for you have turned your judgments away from me

32 because of your Son'

33

1   and now Almah said unto them

2

3   "Do you believe those scriptures

4   which have been written by them of old

5   behold if you do

6   you must believe what Zenos said

7   for behold he said

8

9   'You hast turned away your judgments

10   because of your Son'

11

12   Now behold my brothers I would ask

13   if you have read the scriptures

14   if you have

15   how can you disbelieve

16   on the Son of Elohiym

17   for it is not written

18   that Zenos alone spoke of these things

19   but Zenock also spoke of these things

20   For behold he said

21

22   'You are angry O YHVH with this people

23   because they will not understand your mercies

24   which you hast bestowed upon them

25   because of your Son'

26

27   And now my brothers you see

28   that a second prophet of old has testified

29   of the Son of Elohiym

30   and because the people would not understand his words

31   they stoned him to death

32   but behold this is not all

33   these are not the only ones

1   who have spoken concerning the Son of Elohiym
2   behold he was spoken of by Moshe
3   yes and behold a type was raised up in the wilderness
4   that whoever would look upon it might live
5   and many did look and live
6   but few understood the meaning of those things
7   and this because of the hardness of their hearts
8   but there were many who were so hardened
9   that they would not look
10 therefore they perished
11 now the reason they would not look is because
12 they did not believe that it would heal them
13
14 O my brothers
15 if you could be healed by merely casting about your eyes
16 that you might be healed would you not behold quickly
17 or would you rather harden your hearts in unbelief
18 and be lazy that you would not cast about your eyes
19 that you might perish
20 if so OY shall come upon you
21 but if not so then cast about your eyes
22 and begin to believe in the Son of Elohiym
23 that he will come to redeem his people
24 and that he shall suffer and die
25 to atone for their sins
26 and that he shall rise again from the dead
27 which shall bring to pass the resurrection
28 that all men shall stand before him to be judged
29 at the last and judgment day
30 according to their works
31
32 And now my brothers I desire
33 that you shall plant this word in your hearts

1   and as it begins to swell
2   even so nourish it by your emunah
3   and behold it will become a tree
4   springing up in you unto everlasting life
5   and then may Elohiym grant unto you
6   that your burdens may be light
7   through the joy of his Son
8   and even all this can you do
9   if you will
10 Amein"
11
12 And now it came to pass
13 that after Almah had spoken these words unto them
14 he sat down upon the ground
15 and Amulek arose
16 and began to teach them saying
17
18 "My brothers I think that it is impossible
19 that you should be ignorant of the things
20 which have been spoken
21 concerning the coming of Mashiach
22 who is taught by us to be the Son of Elohiym
23 yes I know that these things were taught
24 unto you bountifully
25 before your dissension from among us
26 and as you have desired of my beloved brother
27 that he should make known unto you
28 what you should do because of your afflictions
29 and he hath spoken somewhat unto you
30 to prepare your minds
31 yes and he has exhorted you
32 unto faith and to patience
33 Yes even that you would have so much emunah

1   as even to plant the word in your hearts

2   that you may try the test of its goodness

3

4   And we have beheld

5   that the great question which is in your minds is

6   whether the word be in the Son of Elohiym

7   or whether there shall be no Mashiach

8   and you also beheld

9   that my brother has proved unto you

10   in many instances

11   that the word is in Mashiach unto salvation

12   my brother has called upon the words of Zenos

13   that redemption comes through the Son of Elohiym

14   and also upon the words of Zenock

15   and also he has appealed unto Moshe

16   to prove that these things are true

17   and now behold I will testify unto you of myself

18   that these things are true

19   behold I say unto you that I do know

20   that Mashiach shall come among the children of men

21   to take upon him the rebellion of his people

22   and that he shall atone for the sins of the world

23   for YHVH Elohiym has spoken it

24

25   For it is necessary

26   that an atonement should be made

27   for according to the great plan of the Eternal Elohiym

28   there must be an atonement made

29   or else all mankind must unavoidably perish

30   yes all are hardened

31   yes all are fallen

32   and are lost and must perish

33   except it be through the atonement

1 which it is necessary should be made

2 for it is necessary

3 that there should be a great and last sacrifice

4 yes not a sacrifice of man

5 neither of beast

6 neither of any manner of fowl

7 for it shall not be a human sacrifice

8 but it must be an infinite and eternal sacrifice

9 now there is not any man that can sacrifice his own blood

10 which will atone for the sins of another

11 now if a man murders

12 behold will our mishpatim which are just

13 take the life of his brother

14 I say unto you No

15 but the Torah requires the life of him who has murdered

16 therefore there can be nothing

17 which is short of an infinite atonement

18 which will suffice for the sins of the world

19 therefore it is necessary

20 that there should be a great and last sacrifice

21 and then shall there be

22 or it is necessary there should be a stop

23 to the shedding of blood

24 then shall the Torah of Moshe be fully established

25 yes it shall be all established

26 every Yod and stroke of a brush

27 and none shall have passed away

28

29 And behold this is the whole meaning of the Torah

30 every yod pointing

31 to that great and last sacrifice

32 and that great and last sacrifice will be the Son of Elohiym

33 yes infinite and eternal

1 and thus he shall bring salvation

2 to all those who shall believe on his name

3 this being the intent of this last sacrifice

4 to bring about the bowels of mercy

5 which overpowers justice

6 and brings about means unto men

7 that they may have faith unto repentance

8 and thus mercy can satisfy the demands of justice

9 and encircles them in the arms of safety

10 while he that exercises no emunah unto repentance is exposed

11 to the whole mishpat of the demands of justice

12 therefore only unto him

13 that has emunah unto repentance is brought

14 about the great and eternal plan of redemption

15 therefore may Elohiym grant unto you my brothers

16 that you may begin to exercise your faith unto repentance

17 that you begin to call upon his holy name

18 that he would have mercy upon you

19

20 Yes cry unto him for mercy

21 for he is mighty to save

22 Yes humble yourselves

23 and continue in prayer unto him

24

25 Cry unto him

26 when you are in your fields

27 yes over all your flocks

28

29 Cry unto him

30 in your houses

31 yes over all your household

32 both morning midday and evening

33

1   Yes cry unto him
2   against the power of your enemies
3   Yes cry unto him against the evil one
4   who is an enemy to all righteousness
5
6   Cry unto him
7   over the crops of your fields
8   that you may prosper in them
9   Cry over the flocks of your fields
10   that they may increase
11
12   But this is not all
13   you must pour out your souls
14   in your closets and your secret places
15   and in your wilderness
16   yes and when you do not cry unto YHVH
17   let your hearts be full drawn out
18   in prayer unto him continually
19   for your welfare
20   and also for the welfare of those
21   who are around you
22
23   And now behold
24   my beloved brothers
25   I say unto you
26   do not suppose that this is all
27   for after you have done all these things
28   if you turn away the needy and the naked
29   and visit not the sick and afflicted
30   and impart of your substance
31   if you have
32   to those who stand in need
33   I say unto you

1   if you do not any of these things

2   behold your prayer is vain

3   and avails you nothing

4   and you are as hypocrites

5   who do deny Elohiym

6   therefore if you do not remember tzedekah

7   you are as dross

8   which the refiners do cast out

9   it being of no worth

10   and is trodden under foot of men

11

12   And now my brothers

13   I would that after you have received so many witnesses seeing

14   that the holy scriptures testify of these things

15   you come forth and bring fruit unto repentance

16   Yes I would

17   that you would come forth

18   and harden not your hearts any longer

19   for behold

20   now is the time and the day of your salvation

21   and therefore if you will repent

22   and harden not your hearts immediately

23   shall the great plan of redemption be brought about unto you

24   For behold

25   this life is the time

26   for men to prepare to meet Elohiym

27   yes behold the day of this life is the day

28   for men to perform their labors

29

30   And now as I said unto you before

31   as you have had so many witnesses

32   therefore I implore of you

33   that you do not procrastinate the day

1   of your repentance until the end
2   for after this day of life
3   which is given us to prepare for eternity
4   behold if we do not improve our time
5   while in this life
6   then comes the night of darkness
7   wherein there can be no labor performed
8   you cannot say
9   when you are brought to that awful crisis
10 that I will repent that I will return to my Elohiym
11 No you cannot say this
12 for that same ruach
13 which does possess your bodies
14 at the time that you go out of this life
15 that same ruach will have power
16 to possess your body
17 in that eternal world
18
19 For behold
20 if you have procrastinated the day of your repentance
21 even until death
22 behold you have become subjected to the ruach of the evil one
23 and he does seal you his
24 therefore the Ruach YHVH has withdrawn from you
25 and has no place in you
26 and the evil one has all power over you
27 and this is the final state of the wicked
28 and this I know
29 because YHVH has said
30 he dwells not in unholy temples
31 but in the hearts of the righteous does he dwell
32 yes and he has also said
33 that the righteous shall sit down in his kingdom

1   to go no more out
2   but their garments should be made white
3   through the blood of the Lamb
4
5   And now my beloved brothers I desire
6   that you should remember these things
7   and that you should work out your salvation
8   with wisdom before Elohiym
9   and that you should no more deny the coming of Mashiach
10   that you contend no more against the Ruach Elohiym
11   but that you receive it
12   and take upon you the name of Mashiach
13   that you humble yourselves even to the dust
14   and worship Elohiym in whatever place you may be in
15   in ruach and in truth
16   and that you live in thanksgiving daily
17   for the many mercies and blessings
18   which he does bestow upon you
19   yes and I also exhort you my brothers
20   that you be watchful unto prayer continually
21   that you may not be led away
22   by the temptations of the evil one
23   that he may not overpower you
24   that you may not become his subjects at the last day
25   for behold he rewards you no good thing
26
27   And now my beloved brothers
28   I would implore you to have patience
29   and that you bear with all manner of afflictions
30   that you do not revile against those
31   who do cast you out
32   because of your exceeding poverty
33   for fear that you become sinners like unto them

1 but that you have patience
2 and bear with those afflictions
3 with a firm hope
4 that you shall one day rest
5 from all your afflictions"
6
7 Now it came to pass
8 that after Amulek had made an end of these words
9 they withdrew themselves from the multitude
10 and came over into the land of Yershon
11 Yes and the rest of the brothers
12 after they had preached the word unto the Zoramiy
13 also came over into the land of Yershon
14
15 And it came to pass
16 that after the more popular part
17 of the Zoramiy had consulted together
18 concerning the words
19 which had been preached unto them
20 they were angry because of the word
21 for it did destroy their craft
22 therefore they would not hearken unto the words
23 and they sent and gathered together
24 throughout all the land all the people
25 and consulted with them concerning the words
26 which had been spoken
27 now their rulers and their kohanim
28 and their morim did not let the people know
29 concerning their desires
30 therefore they found out secretly the minds
31 of all the people
32
33 And it came to pass

1 that after they had found out the minds
2 of all the people
3 those who were in favor of the words
4 which had been spoken
5 by Almah and his brothers were cast out of the land
6 and they were many
7 and they came over also into the land of Yershon
8
9 And it came to pass
10 that Almah and his brothers
11 did minister unto them
12 now the people of the Zoramiy were angry
13 with the people of Ammon
14 who were in Yershon
15 and the chief ruler of the Zoramiy
16 being a very wicked man sent over
17 unto the people of Ammon desiring them
18 that they should cast out of their land
19 all those who came over from them into their land
20 and he breathed out many threats against them
21 and now the people of Ammon did not fear their words
22 therefore they did not cast them out
23 but they did receive all the poor of the Zoramiy
24 that came over unto them
25 and they did nourish them
26 and did clothe them
27 and did give unto them lands for their inheritance
28 and they did administer unto them
29 according to their wants
30 now this did stir up the Zoramiy
31 to anger against the people of Ammon
32 and they began to mix with the Lamaniy
33 and to stir them up also to anger against them

1 and thus the Zoramiy and the Lamaniy
2 began to make preparations for war
3 against the people of Ammon
4 and also against the Nephiy
5 and thus ended the seventeenth year
6 of the reign of the judges
7 over the people of Nephi
8
9 And the people of Ammon departed
10 out of the land of Yershon
11 and came over into the land of Melek
12 and gave place in the land of Yershon
13 for the armies of the Nephiy
14 that they might contend
15 with the armies of the Lamaniy
16 and the armies of the Zoramiy
17 and thus commenced a war
18 between the Lamaniy and the Nephiy
19 in the eighteenth year of the reign of the judges
20 and an account shall be given of their wars hereafter
21 and Almah and Ammon
22 and their brothers
23 and also the two sons of Almah returned
24 to the land of Zarahemla
25 after having been instruments
26 in the hands of Elohiym
27 of bringing many of the Zoramiy to repentance
28 and as many as were brought to repentance
29 were driven out of their land
30 but they have lands for their inheritance
31 in the land of Yershon
32 and they have taken up arms
33 to defend themselves

1 and their wives and children and their lands

2

3 Now Almah being grieved

4 for the lawlessness of his people

5 yes for the wars and the bloodsheds

6 and the contentions which were among them

7 and having been to declare the word

8 or sent to declare the word

9 among all the people in every city

10 and seeing that the hearts of the people

11 began to wax hard

12 and that they began to be offended

13 because of the strictness of the word

14 his heart was exceedingly sorrowful

15 therefore he caused that his sons

16 should be gathered together

17 that he might give unto them

18 every one his charge separately

19 concerning the things pertaining unto righteousness

20 and we have an account of his mitzvot

21 which he gave unto them

22 according to his own record

23

24

25

26

27

28

29

30

31

32

33

7-COMMANDMENTS TO MY SONS

The mitzvot of Almah
to his son Helaman

1
2
3
4
5
6
7 My son give ear to my words
8 for I swear unto you
9 that inasmuch as you
10 shall keep the mitzvot of Elohiym
11 you shall prosper in the land
12
13 I would that you should do as I have done
14 in remembering the captivity of our fathers
15 for they were in bondage
16 and none could deliver them
17 except it was the Elohiym of Avraham
18 and the Elohiym of Yitzchak
19 and the Elohiym of Yacov
20 and he surely did deliver them
21 in their afflictions
22
23 And now O my son Helaman
24 behold you are in your youth
25 and therefore I implore of you
26 that you will hear my words
27 and learn of me for I do know
28 that whoever shall put their trust in Elohiym
29 shall be supported
30 in their trials and their troubles
31 and their afflictions
32 and shall be lifted up at the last day
33 and I would not that you think

1   that I know of myself
2   not of the temporal
3   but of the spiritual
4   not of the carnal mind
5   but of Elohiym
6
7   Now behold I say unto you
8   if I had not been born of Elohiym
9   I should not have known these things
10 but Elohiym has
11 by the mouth of his holy angel made
12 these things known unto me
13 not of any worthiness of myself
14 For I went about with the sons of Mosheyahu seeking
15 to destroy the assembly of Elohiym
16 but behold Elohiym sent his holy angel
17 to stop us by the way
18
19 And behold he spoke unto us
20 as it were the voice of thunder
21 and the whole earth did tremble beneath our feet
22 and we all fell to the earth
23 for the fear of YHVH came upon us
24 but behold the voice said unto me
25
26 "Arise "
27
28 And I arose and stood up
29 and beheld the angel
30 and he said unto me
31
32 "If you will of yourself be destroyed
33 seek no more to destroy the assembly of Elohiym"

1

2　And it came to pass

3　that I fell to the earth

4　and it was for the space

5　of three days and three nights

6　that I could not open my mouth

7　neither had I the use of my limbs

8　And the angel spoke more things unto me

9　which were heard by my brothers

10　but I did not hear them

11　for when I heard the words

12　'If you will be destroyed of yourself

13　seek no more to destroy the assembly of Elohiym'

14　I was struck with such great fear and amazement

15　for fear that perhaps I should be destroyed

16　that I fell to the earth

17　and I did hear no more

18　but I was racked with eternal torment

19　for my soul was broken up

20　to the greatest degree

21　and racked with all my sins

22　Yes I did remember

23　all my sins and lawlessness

24　for which I was tormented

25　with the pains of Sheol

26　yes I saw

27　that I had rebelled against my Elohiym

28　and that I had not kept his holy mitzvot

29　yes and I had murdered many of his children

30　or rather led them away unto destruction

31　yes and in sum so great had been my lawlessness

32　that the very thought of coming into the presence of my Elohiym

33　did rack my soul with inexpressible horror

1 Oh thought I
2 that I could be banished and become extinct
3 both soul and body
4 that I might not be brought to stand
5 in the presence of my Elohiym
6 to be judged of my deeds
7 And now
8 for three days and for three nights was I racked
9 even with the pains of a condemned soul
10
11 And it came to pass
12 that as I was thus racked with torment
13 while I was broken up
14 by the memory of my many sins
15 behold I remembered also to have heard
16 my father prophesy unto the people
17 concerning the coming of one Yehoshua Mashiach
18 a Son of Elohiym to atone for the sins of the world
19
20 Now as my mind caught hold
21 upon this thought
22 I cried within my heart
23 'O Yehoshua you Son of Elohiym have mercy on me
24 who am in a malignant mind
25 and am encircled about
26 by the everlasting chains of death
27 and now behold when I thought this
28 I could remember my pains no more
29 yes I was broken up by the memory of my sins no more
30 and oh what joy
31 and what marvelous light I did behold
32 yes my soul was filled with joy
33 as exceeding as was my pain

1 Yes I say unto you my son
2 that there could be nothing
3 so exquisite and so bitter as were my pains
4 Yes and again I say unto you my son
5 that on the other hand
6 there can be nothing s
7 o exquisite and sweet as was my joy
8 Yes in my thoughts I saw
9 even as our father Lechi saw Elohiym sitting
10 upon his throne surrounded
11 with numberless concourses of angels
12 in the attitude of singing and praising their Elohiym
13 yes and my soul did long to be there
14
15 But behold my limbs did receive their strength again
16 and I stood upon my feet
17 and did manifest unto the people
18 that I had been born of Elohiym
19 Yes and from that time
20 even until now I have labored without ceasing
21 that I might bring souls unto repentance
22 that I might bring them to taste
23 of the exceeding joy of which I did taste
24 that they might also be born of Elohiym
25 and be filled with the Ruach Elohiym
26
27 Yes and now behold
28 O my son YHVH does give me exceedingly great joy
29 in the fruit of my labors
30 For because of the word
31 which he has imparted unto me
32 behold many have been born of Elohiym
33 and have tasted as I have tasted

1 and have seen eye to eye

2 as I have seen

3 therefore they do know of these things

4 of which I have spoken

5 as I do know

6 and the knowledge which I have is of Elohiym

7

8 And I have been supported

9 under trials and troubles of every kind

10 yes and in all manner of afflictions

11 yes Elohiym has delivered me from prison

12 and from bonds and from death

13 yes and I do put my trust in him

14 and he will still deliver me

15 and I know that he will raise me up

16 at the last day

17 to dwell with him in glory

18 yes and I will praise him forever

19 for he has brought our fathers out of Egypt

20 and he has swallowed up the Egyptians

21 in the Red Sea

22 and he led them by his power

23 into the promised land

24 yes and he has delivered them out

25 of bondage and captivity

26 from time to time

27 Yes and he has also brought our fathers

28 out of the land of Yerushalayim

29 and he has also by his everlasting power delivered them

30 out of bondage and captivity

31 from time to time even

32 down to the present day

33 and I have always retained in remembrance

1   their captivity
2   yes and you also ought to retain in remembrance
3   as I have done
4   their captivity
5
6   But behold my son
7   this is not all
8   for you ought to know as I do know
9   that inasmuch as you shall keep the mitzvot of Elohiym
10   you shall prosper in the land
11   and you ought to know also
12   that inasmuch as you will not keep the mitzvot of Elohiym
13   you shall be cut off from his presence
14   Now this is according to his word
15
16   And now my son Helaman
17   I command you
18   that you take the records
19   which have been entrusted with me
20   and I also command you
21   that you keep a record of this people
22   according as I have done upon the plates of Nephi
23   and keep all these things sacred
24   which I have kept even as I have kept them
25   for it is for a wise purpose that they are kept
26   And these plates of brass
27   which contain these engravings
28   which have the records of the holy scriptures upon them
29   which have the genealogy of our forefathers
30   even from the beginning
31   behold it has been prophesied by our fathers
32   that they should be kept and handed down
33   from one generation to another

1 and be kept and preserved by the hand of YHVH
2 until they should go forth
3 unto every nation tribe language and people
4 that they shall know of the mysteries contained thereon
5
6 And now behold
7 if they are kept they must retain their brightness
8 yes and they will retain their brightness
9 yes and also shall all the plates
10 which do contain that which is holy writ
11 now you may suppose that this is foolishness in me
12 but behold I say unto you
13 that by small and simple things
14 are great things brought to pass
15 and small means in many instances
16 does confound the wise
17 and YHVH Elohiym does work by means
18 to bring about his great and eternal purposes
19 and by very small means YHVH does confound the wise
20 and brings about the salvation of many souls
21 And now it has to this time been wisdom in Elohiym
22 that these things should be preserved
23 for behold they have enlarged the memory of this people
24 yes and convinced many of the error of their ways
25 and brought them to the knowledge of their Elohiym
26 unto the salvation of their souls
27 Yes I say unto you were it not for these things
28 that these records do contain
29 which are on these plates
30 Ammon and his brothers could not have convinced
31 so many thousands of the Lamaniy
32 of the incorrect tradition of their fathers
33 yes these records and their words brought them unto repentance

1 that is they brought them to the knowledge of YHVH their Elohiym

2 and to rejoice in Yehoshua Mashiach their Redeemer

3

4 And who knows but what they will be the means

5 of bringing many thousands of them

6 yes and also many thousands of our stubborn brothers the Nephiy

7 who are now hardening their hearts

8 in sin and lawlessness

9 to the knowledge of their Redeemer

10

11 Now these mysteries are not yet

12 fully made known unto me

13 therefore I shall forbear

14 and it may suffice if I only say

15 they are preserved for a wise purpose

16 which purpose is known unto Elohiym

17 for he does counsel in wisdom over all his works

18 and his paths are straight

19 and his course is one eternal round

20

21 O remember remember my son Helaman

22 how strict are the mitzvot of Elohiym

23 And he said

24 If you will keep my mitzvot

25 you shall prosper in the land

26 but if you keep not his mitzvot

27 you shall be cut off from his presence

28 and now remember my son

29 that Elohiym has entrusted you with these things

30 which are sacred

31 which he has kept sacred

32 and also which he will keep and preserve

33 for a wise purpose in him

1   that he may show forth his power
2   unto future generations
3   and now behold I tell you by the ruach of prophecy
4   that if you rebel against the mitzvot of Elohiym
5   behold these things which are sacred
6   shall be taken away from you by the power of Elohiym
7   and you shall be delivered up unto the evil one
8   that he may sift you as chaff before the wind
9   but if you keep the mitzvot of Elohiym
10 and do with these things which are sacred
11 according to that which YHVH does command you
12 for you must appeal unto YHVH for all things
13 whatever you must do with them
14 behold no power of earth or sheol can take them from you
15 for Elohiym is powerful
16 to the fulfilling of all his words
17 for he will fulfil all his promises
18 which he shall make unto you
19 for he has fulfilled his promises
20 which he has made unto our fathers
21 for he promised unto them
22 that he would preserve these things
23 for a wise purpose in him
24 that he might show forth his power
25 unto future generations
26
27 And now behold one purpose has he fulfilled
28 even to the restoration of many thousands of the Lamaniy
29 to the knowledge of the truth
30 and he has shown forth his power in them
31 and he will also still show forth his power in them
32 unto future generations
33 therefore they shall be preserved

1 therefore I command you my son Helaman

2 that you be diligent in fulfilling all my words

3 and that you be diligent in keeping the mitzvot of Elohiym

4 as they are written

5

6 And now I will speak unto you

7 concerning those twenty four plates

8 that you guard them

9 that the mysteries and the works of darkness

10 and their secret works or the secret works of those people

11 who have been destroyed

12 may be made manifest unto this people

13 yes all their murders and robbings

14 and their plunderings and all their wickedness

15 and abominations may be made manifest unto this people

16 yes and that you preserve these interpreters

17

18 For behold YHVH saw that his people began to work in darkness

19 yes work secret murders and abominations

20 therefore YHVH said

21

22 "if they did not repent

23 they should be destroyed

24 from off the face of the land"

25

26 And YHVH said

27

28 "I will prepare unto my servant Gazelem a stone

29 which shall shine forth in darkness unto light

30 that I may discover unto my people who serve me

31 that I may discover unto them the works of their brothers

32 yes their secret works their works of darkness

33 and their wickedness and abominations"

1
2 And now my son these interpreters were prepared
3 that the word of Elohiym might be fulfilled
4 which he spoke saying
5
6 " I will bring forth out of darkness unto light
7 all their secret works and their abominations
8 and except they repent I will destroy them
9 from off the face of the land
10 and I will bring to light
11 all their secrets and abominations unto every nation
12 that shall hereafter possess the land"
13
14 And now my son we see that they did not repent
15 therefore they have been destroyed
16 and thus far the word of Elohiym has been fulfilled
17 yes their secret abominations have been brought out of darkness
18 and made known unto us
19
20 And now my son I command you
21 that you retain all their oaths and their covenants
22 and their agreements in their secret abominations
23 yes and all their signs and their wonders
24 you shall keep from this people
25 that they know them not
26 for fear that it may be they should fall into darkness also
27 and be destroyed
28 for behold there is a curse upon all this land
29 that destruction shall come
30 upon all those workers of darkness
31 according to the power of Elohiym
32 when they are fully ripe
33 therefore I desire that this people

1 might not be destroyed
2 therefore you shall keep these secret plans
3 of their oaths and their covenants from this people
4 and only their wickedness and their murders and their abominations
5 shall you make known unto them
6 and you shall teach them to abhor
7 such wickedness and abominations and murders
8 and you shall also teach them
9 that these people were destroyed on account
10 of their wickedness and abominations and their murders
11 for behold they murdered all the prophets of YHVH
12 who came among them to declare unto them
13 concerning their lawlessness
14 and the blood of those whom they murdered
15 did cry unto the Lord their Elohiym for vengeance
16 upon those who were their murderers
17 and thus the judgments of Elohiym
18 did come upon these workers
19 of darkness and secret conspiracies
20 Yes and cursed be the land forever and ever
21 unto those workers of darkness and secret conspiracies
22 even unto destruction
23 except they repent
24 before they are fully ripe
25
26 And now my son remember the words
27 which I have spoken unto you
28 trust not those secret plans unto this people
29 but teach them an everlasting hatred
30 against sin and lawlessness
31 preach unto them repentance and faith
32 on Adon Yehoshua Mashiach
33 teach them to humble themselves

1 and to be meek and lowly in heart
2 teach them to withstand every temptation of the devil
3 with their faith on Adon Yehoshua Mashiach
4 teach them to never be weary of good works
5 but to be meek and lowly in heart
6 for such shall find rest to their souls
7
8 O remember my son
9 and learn wisdom in your youth
10 yes learn in your youth
11 to keep the mitzvot of Elohiym
12 Yes and cry unto Elohiym for all your support
13 yes let all your doings be unto YHVH
14 and wherever you go let it be in YHVH
15 yes let all your thoughts be directed unto YHVH
16 yes let the affections of your heart be placed upon YHVH forever
17 counsel with YHVH in all your doings
18 and he will direct you for good
19 yes when you lie down at night lie down unto YHVH
20 that he may watch over you in your sleep
21 and when you rise in the morning
22 let your heart be full of thanks unto Elohiym
23 and if you do these things you
24 shall be lifted up at the last day
25
26 And now my son
27 I have something to say concerning the thing
28 which our fathers call a ball or director
29 or our fathers called it Liahona
30 which is being interpreted a compass
31 and YHVH prepared it
32 and behold there cannot any man work
33 after the manner of so curious a workmanship

1 and behold it was prepared
2 to show unto our fathers the course
3 which they should travel in the wilderness
4 and it did work for them
5 according to their faith in Elohiym
6 therefore if they had faith to believe
7 that Elohiym could cause that those spindles
8 should point the way they should go
9 behold it was done
10 therefore they had this miracle
11 and also many other miracles performed
12 by the power of Elohiym day by day
13 nevertheless because those miracles were worked by small means
14 it did show unto them marvelous works
15 they were lazy and forgot to exercise
16 their faith and diligence
17 and then those marvelous works ceased
18 and they did not progress in their journey
19 therefore they tarried in the wilderness
20 or did not travel a direct course
21 and were afflicted with hunger and thirst
22 because of their rebellion
23
24 And now my son I desire that you should understand
25 that these things are not without a shadow
26 for as our fathers were slow to give heed to this compass
27 now these things were temporal
28 they did not prosper
29 even so it is with things which are spiritual
30 for behold it is as easy to give heed to the word of Mashiach
31 which will point to you a straight course to eternal bliss
32 as it was for our fathers to give heed to this compass
33 which would point unto them a straight course to the promised land

1 and now I say is there not a type in this thing
2 for just as surely as this director did bring our fathers
3 by following its course to the promised land
4 shall the words of Mashiach
5 if we follow their course carry us
6 beyond this valley of sorrow
7 into a far better land of promise
8
9 O my son do not let us be idle
10 because of the easiness of the way
11 for so was it with our fathers
12 for so was it prepared for them
13 that if they would look
14 they might live
15 even so it is with us the way is prepared
16 and if we will look we may live forever
17
18 And now my son see that you take care of these sacred things
19 yes see that you look to Elohiym and live
20 go unto this people and declare the word
21 and be sober my son
22 Shalom
23
24 **The mitzvot of Almah to his son Shiblon**
25
26 My son give ear to my words
27 for I say unto you even as I said unto Helaman
28 that inasmuch as you shall keep the mitzvot of Elohiym you
29 shall prosper in the land
30 and inasmuch as you will not keep the mitzvot of Elohiym you
31 shall be cut off from his presence
32 And now my son
33 I trust that I shall have great joy in you

1 because of your steadiness and your faithfulness unto Elohiym
2 for as you have commenced in your youth
3 to look to YHVH your Elohiym
4 even so I hope that you will continue
5 in keeping his mitzvot
6 for blessed is he that walks forward in them to the end
7
8 I say unto you my son
9 that I have had great joy in you already
10 because of your faithfulness and your diligence
11 and your patience and your longsuffering
12 among the people of the Zoramiy
13 for I know that you were in bonds
14 yes and I also know that you were stoned for the word's sake
15 and you didst bear all these things with patience
16 because YHVH was with you
17 and now you know
18 that YHVH did deliver you
19 and now my son Shiblon
20 I would that you should remember
21 that as much as you shall put your trust in Elohiym
22 even so much you shall be delivered out of your trials
23 and your troubles and your afflictions
24 and you shall be lifted up at the last day
25
26 Now my son I would not
27 that you should think that I know these things of myself
28 but it is the Ruach of Elohiym which is in me
29 which makes these things known unto me
30 for if I had not been born of Elohiym
31 I should not have known these things
32 but behold YHVH in his great mercy sent his angel
33 to declare unto me

1   that I must stop the work of destruction

2   among his people

3   yes and I have seen an angel face to face

4   and he spoke with me

5   and his voice was as thunder

6   and it shook the whole earth

7

8   And it came to pass

9   that I was three days and three nights

10   in the most bitter pain

11   and anguish of soul

12   and never until I did cry out

13   unto Adon Yehoshua Mashiach for mercy

14   did I receive a remission of my sins

15   but behold I did cry unto him

16   and I did find peace to my soul

17

18   And now my son I have told you this

19   that you may learn wisdom

20   that you may learn of me

21   that there is no other way or means

22   whereby man can be saved

23   only in and through Mashiach

24   behold he is the life and the light of the world

25   behold he is the word of truth and righteousness

26

27   And now as you have begun to teach the word

28   even so I would that you should continue to teach

29   and I would that you would be diligent

30   and temperate in all things

31   see that you are not lifted up unto pride

32   yes see that you do not boast

33   in your own wisdom

1 nor of your much strength
2 use boldness but not overbearance
3 and also see that you bridle all your passions
4 that you may be filled with love
5 see that you refrain from idleness
6
7 Do not pray as the Zoramiy do
8 for you have seen that they pray to be heard of men
9 and to be praised for their wisdom
10
11 Do not say O Elohiym
12 I thank you that we are better than our brothers
13 but rather say
14
15 O Adonai forgive my uncleanliness
16 and remember my brothers in mercy
17 yes acknowledge your uncleanliness before Elohiym at all times
18
19 And may YHVH bless your soul
20 and receive you at the last day into his kingdom
21 to sit down in peace
22 now go my son
23 and teach the word unto this people
24 be sober my son
25
26 Shalom
27
28 **The mitzvot of Almah to his son Corianton**
29
30 And now my son
31 I have somewhat more to say unto you
32 than what I said unto your brother
33 for behold have you not observed the steadiness of your brother

1 his faithfulness and his diligence

2 in keeping the mitzvot of Elohiym

3 behold has he not set a good example for you

4 For you did not give so much heed unto my words

5 as did your brother among the people of the Zoramiy

6 Now this is what I have against you

7 you did go on unto boasting

8 in your strength and your wisdom

9

10 And this is not all my son

11 you did do that which was grievous unto me

12 or you did forsake your service

13 and did go over into the land of Siron

14 among the borders of the Lamaniy

15 after the harlot Elisheva

16 Yes she did steal away the hearts of many

17 but this was no excuse for you my son

18 you should have tended to the service

19 wherein you were entrusted

20

21 Know you not my son

22 that these things are an abomination in the sight of YHVH

23 yes most abominable above all sins

24 except it be the shedding of innocent blood

25 or disavow the Ruach Elohiym

26 for behold if you disavor the Ruach Elohiym

27 when it once has had place in you

28 and you know that you disavow it

29 behold this is a sin which is unpardonable

30 yes and whoever murders

31 against the light and knowledge of Elohiym

32 it is not easy for him to obtain forgiveness

33 yes I say unto you my son

1 that it is not easy for him to obtain a forgiveness

2 and now my son

3 I would to Elohiym

4 that you had not been guilty of so great a crime

5 I would not dwell upon your crimes

6 to harrow up your soul

7 if it were not for your good

8 but behold you cannot hide your crimes from Elohiym

9 and except you repent

10 they will stand as a testimony against you

11 at the last day

12

13 Now my son I would that you should repent

14 and forsake your sins

15 and go no more after the lusts of your eyes

16 but stop yourself in all these things

17 for except you do this

18 you can in nowise inherit the kingdom of Elohiym

19 Oh remember and take it upon you

20 and stop yourself in these things

21 and I command you to take it upon you

22 to counsel with your elder brothers in your undertakings

23 for behold you are in your youth

24 and you stand in need to be nourished by your brothers

25 and give heed to their counsel

26 allow not yourself to be led away

27 by any vain or foolish thing

28 allow not the evil one to lead away your heart again

29 after those wicked harlots

30 behold O my son how great lawlessness

31 you brought upon the Zoramiy

32 for when they saw your conduct

33 they would not believe in my words

1 and now the Ruach of YHVH does say unto me

2

3 'Command your children to do good

4 for fear that they lead away the hearts

5 of many people to destruction'

6

7 Therefore I command you my son

8 in the fear of Elohiym

9 that you refrain from your lawlessness

10 that you turn to YHVH

11 with all your mind might and strength

12 that you lead away the hearts of no more

13 to do depart from the mitvot

14 but rather return unto them

15 and acknowledge your faults

16 and that wrong which you have done

17 seek not after riches

18 nor the vain things of this world

19 for behold you cannot carry them with you

20

21 And now my son

22 I would say somewhat unto you

23 concerning the coming of Mashiach

24 behold I say unto you

25 that it is he that certainly shall come

26 to take away the sins of the world

27 yes he comes

28 to declare glad tidings of salvation

29 unto his people

30 and now my son

31 this was the ministry unto which you were called

32 to declare these glad tidings unto this people

33 to prepare their minds

1   or rather that salvation might come unto them

2   that they may prepare the minds of their children

3   to hear the word at the time of his coming

4

5   And now I will ease your mind

6   somewhat on this subject

7   behold you marvel

8   why these things should be known

9   so long beforehand

10   behold I say unto you

11   is not a soul at this time as precious unto Elohiym

12   as a soul will be at the time of his coming

13   is it not as necessary

14   that the plan of redemption

15   should be made known unto this people

16   as well as unto their children

17   is it not as easy at this time

18   for YHVH to send his angel

19   to declare these glad tidings unto us

20   as unto our children

21   or as after the time of his coming

22

23   Now my son here is somewhat more

24   I would say unto you

25   for I perceive that your mind is worried

26   concerning the resurrection of the dead

27   behold I say unto you

28   that there is no resurrection

29   or I would say in other words

30   that this mortal does not put on immortality

31   this corruption does not put on incorruption

32   until after the coming of Mashiach

33   behold he brings to pass the resurrection of the dead

1 but behold my son the resurrection is not yet
2 now I unfold unto you a mystery
3 nevertheless there are many mysteries
4 which are kept
5 that no one knows them
6 except Elohiym himself
7 but I show unto you one thing
8 which I have inquired diligently of Elohiym
9 that I might know
10 that is concerning the resurrection
11
12 Behold there is a time appointed
13 that all shall come forth from the dead
14 now when this time comes
15 no one knows
16 but Elohiym knows
17 the time which is appointed
18 now whether there shall be one time
19 or a second time
20 or a third time
21 that men shall come forth from the dead
22 it matters not
23 for Elohiym knows all these things
24 and it sufficient for me to know that this is the case
25 that there is a time appointed
26 that all shall rise from the dead
27 now there must needs be a space between the time of death
28 and the time of the resurrection
29 and now I would inquire
30 what becomes of the souls of men
31 from this time of death
32 to the time appointed for the resurrection
33

1 Now whether there is more than one time appointed

2 for men to rise

3 it matters not

4 for all do not die at once

5 and this matters not

6 all is as one day with Elohiym

7 and time only is measured unto men

8 therefore there is a time appointed unto men

9 that they shall rise from the dead

10 and there is a space between the time of death

11 and the resurrection

12 and now concerning this space of time

13 what becomes of the souls of men

14 is the thing which I have inquired diligently

15 of YHVH to know

16 and this is the thing of which I do know

17 and when the time comes

18 when all shall rise

19 then shall they know that Elohiym knows all the times

20 which are appointed unto man

21 now concerning the state of the soul

22 between death and the resurrection

23 behold it has been made known unto me by an angel

24 that the ruach of all men

25 as soon as they are departed from this mortal body

26 yes the ruach of all men

27 whether they be good or evil are taken home

28 to that Elohiym who gave them life

29

30 And then shall it come to pass

31 that the spirits of those who are righteous are received

32 into a state of happiness

33 which is called paradise

1   a state of rest
2   a state of peace
3   where they shall rest from all their troubles
4   and from all care and sorrow
5
6   And then shall it come to pass
7   that the spirits of the wicked
8   yes who are evil
9   for behold they have no part nor portion of the Ruach of YHVH
10 for behold they chose evil works
11 rather than good
12 therefore the ruach of the evil one did enter into them
13 and take possession of their house
14 and these shall be cast out into outer darkness
15 there shall be weeping and wailing and gnashing of teeth
16 and this because of their own lawlessness
17 being led captive by the will of the evil one
18 now this is the state of the souls of the wicked
19 yes in darkness
20 and a state of awful fearful looking
21 for the fiery indignation of the wrath of Elohiym upon them
22 thus they remain in this state
23 as well as the righteous in paradise
24 until the time of their resurrection
25 now there are some that have understood
26 that this state of happiness
27 and this state of misery of the soul
28 before the resurrection was a first resurrection
29 Yes I admit it may be termed a resurrection
30 the raising of the Ruach or the soul
31 and their setting apart to happiness or misery
32 according to the words which have been spoken
33 and behold again it has been spoken

1   that there is a first resurrection

2   a resurrection of all those who have been

3   or who are

4   or who shall be

5   down to the resurrection of Mashiach

6   from the dead

7

8   Now we do not suppose that this first resurrection

9   which is spoken of in this manner

10 can be the resurrection of the souls

11 and their setting apart to happiness or misery

12 you cannot suppose that this is what it means

13 behold I say unto you No

14 but it means the reuniting

15 of the soul with the body

16 of those from the days of Adam

17 down to the resurrection of Mashiach

18 now whether the souls and the bodies of those

19 of whom has been spoken shall all be reunited at once

20 the wicked as well as the righteous

21 I do not say

22 let it be enough that I say that they all come forth

23 or in other words their resurrection comes to pass

24 before the resurrection of those who die

25 after the resurrection of Mashiach

26

27 Now my son I do not say that their resurrection comes

28 at the resurrection of Mashiach

29 but behold I give it as my opinion

30 that the souls and the bodies are reunited of the righteous

31 at the resurrection of Mashiach

32 and his ascension into heaven

33 but whether it be at his resurrection

1   or after I do not say
2   but this much I say
3   that there is a space
4   between death and the resurrection of the body
5   and a state of the soul
6   in happiness or in misery
7   until the time which is appointed of Elohiym
8   that the dead shall come forth
9   and be reunited both soul and body
10 and be brought to stand before Elohiym
11 and be judged according to their works
12 Yes this brings about the restoration of those things
13 of which has been spoken
14 by the mouths of the prophets
15 the soul shall be restored to the body
16 and the body to the soul
17 yes and every limb and joint shall be restored to its body
18 yes even a hair of the head shall not be lost
19 but all things shall be restored
20 to their proper and perfect frame
21 and now my son this is the restoration
22 of which has been spoken
23 by the mouths of the prophets
24 and then shall the righteous shine forth
25 in the kingdom of Elohiym
26 but behold an awful death comes upon the wicked
27 for they die as to things pertaining to things of righteousness
28 for they are unclean
29 and no unclean thing can inherit the kingdom of Elohiym
30 but they are cast out and consigned
31 to partake of the fruits
32 of their labors or their works
33 which have been evil

1 and they drink the dregs of a bitter cup

2

3 And now my son I have somewhat to say

4 concerning the restoration of which has been spoken

5 for behold some have distorted the scriptures

6 and have gone far astray because of this thing

7 and I perceive that your mind has been worried also

8 concerning this thing

9 but behold I will explain it unto you

10 I say unto you my son

11 that the plan of restoration is necessary

12 with the justice of Elohiym

13 for it is necessary

14 that all things should be restored to their proper order

15 behold it is necessary and just

16 according to the power and resurrection of Mashiach

17 that the soul of man should be restored to its body

18 and that every part of the body

19 should be restored to itself

20 and it is necessary

21 with the justice of Elohiym

22 that men should be judged according to their works

23 and if their works were good in this life

24 and the desires of their hearts were good

25 that they should also at the last day be restored

26 unto that which is good

27 and if their works are evil

28 they shall be restored unto them for evil

29 therefore all things shall be restored to their proper order

30 everything to its natural frame

31 mortality raised to immortality

32 corruption to incorruption

33 raised to endless happiness

1   to inherit the kingdom of Elohiym
2   or to endless misery
3   to inherit the kingdom of the evil one
4   the one on one hand the other on the other
5   the one raised to happiness
6   according to his desires of happiness
7   or good according to his desires of good
8   and the other to evil according to his desires of evil
9   for as he has desired to do evil all the day long
10 even so shall he have his reward of evil
11 when the night comes
12
13 And so it is on the other hand
14 if he has repented of his sins
15 and desired righteousness until the end of his days
16 even so he shall be rewarded unto righteousness
17 these are they that are redeemed of YHVH
18 yes these are they that are taken out
19 that are delivered from that endless night of darkness
20 and thus they stand or fall
21 for behold they are their own judges
22 whether to do good or do evil
23
24 Now the decrees of Elohiym are unalterable
25 therefore the way is prepared
26 that whoever will
27 may walk therein and be saved
28 and now behold my son
29 do not risk one more offense against your Elohiym
30 upon those points of teaching
31 which you have previously risked to commit sin
32 do not suppose
33 because it has been spoken concerning restoration

1   that you shall be restored from sin to happiness

2   behold I say unto you wickedness never was happiness

3   and now my son all men

4   that are in a state of nature

5   or I would say in a carnal state

6   are in the gall of bitterness

7   and in the slavery of lawlessness

8   they are without Elohiym in the world

9   and they have gone contrary to the nature of Elohiym

10   therefore they are in a state contrary to the nature of happiness

11

12   And now behold is the meaning of the word restoration

13   to take a thing of a natural state

14   and place it in an unnatural state

15   or to place it in a state opposite to its nature

16   O my son

17   this is not the case

18   but the meaning of the word restoration is

19   to bring back again evil for evil

20   or carnal for carnal

21   or lawless for lawless

22   good for that which is good

23   righteous for that which is righteous

24   just for that which is just

25   merciful for that which is merciful

26   therefore my son see that you are merciful

27   unto your brothers

28   deal justly

29   judge righteously

30   and do good continually

31   and if you do all these things

32   then shall you receive your reward

33   yes you shall have mercy restored unto you again

1 you shall have justice restored unto you again

2 you shall have a righteous judgment restored unto you again

3 and you shall have good rewarded unto you again

4 for that which you do send out

5 shall return unto you again and be restored

6 therefore the word restoration

7 more fully condemns the sinner

8 and justifies him not at all

9

10 And now my son

11 I perceive there is somewhat more

12 which does worry your mind

13 which you cannot understand

14 which is concerning the justice of Elohiym

15 in the punishment of the sinner

16 for you do try to suppose that it is injustice

17 that the sinner should be delivered to a state of misery

18 now behold my son

19 I will explain this thing unto you

20 for behold after YHVH Elohiym sent our first parents forth

21 from the Gan Eden to till the ground

22 from where they were taken

23 yes he drew out the man

24 and he placed at the east end of the Gan Eden

25 keruvim and a flaming sword

26 which turned every way to keep Etz Chaim

27 now we see that the man had become as Elohiym

28 knowing good and evil

29 and for fear that he should put forth his hand

30 and take also of Etz Chaim

31 and eat and live forever

32 YHVH Elohiym placed Keruvim and the flaming sword

33 that he should not partake of the fruit

1 and thus we see that there was a time granted unto man to repent

2 yes a probationary time a time to repent and serve Elohiym

3

4 For behold if Adam had put forth his hand immediately

5 and partaken of the Etz Chaim

6 he would have lived forever

7 according to the word of Elohiym

8 having no space for repentance

9 yes and also the word of Elohiym would have been void

10 and the great plan of salvation would have been frustrated

11 but behold it was appointed unto man to die

12 therefore as they were cut off from the Etz Chaim

13 they should be cut off from the face of the earth

14 and man became lost forever

15 yes they became fallen man

16 and now you see by this

17 that our first parents were cut off

18 both temporally and spiritually

19 from the presence of YHVH

20 and thus we see they became subjects

21 to follow after their own will

22

23 Now behold it was not necessary

24 that man should be reclaimed from this temporal death

25 for that would destroy the great plan of happiness

26 therefore as the soul could never die

27 and the fall had brought upon all mankind

28 a spiritual death as well as a temporal

29 that is they were cut off

30 from the presence of YHVH

31 it was necessary that mankind should be reclaimed

32 from this spiritual death

33 therefore as they had become carnal sensual and fallen by nature

1   this probationary state
2   became a state for them to prepare
3   it became a preparatory state
4   and now remember my son
5   if it were not for the plan of redemption
6   laying it aside
7   as soon as they were dead
8   their souls were miserable being cut off
9   from the presence of YHVH
10 and now there was no means to reclaim men
11 from this fallen state
12 which man had brought upon himself
13 because of his own disobedience
14 therefore according to justice
15 the plan of redemption could not be brought about
16 only on conditions of repentance of men in this probationary state
17 yes this preparatory state
18 for except it were for these conditions mercy could not take effect
19 except it should destroy the work of justice
20 now the work of justice could not be destroyed
21 if so Elohiym would cease to be Elohiym
22 and thus we see that all mankind were fallen
23 and they were in the grasp of justice
24 yes the justice of Elohiym
25 which delivered them forever
26 to be cut off from his presence
27
28 And now the plan of mercy could not be brought about
29 except an atonement should be made
30 therefore Elohiym himself atones for the sins of the world
31 to bring about the plan of mercy
32 to appease the demands of justice
33 that Elohiym might be a perfect just Elohiym

1 and a merciful Elohiym also
2 now repentance could not come unto men
3 except there were a punishment
4 which also was eternal as the life of the soul should be
5 affixed opposite to the plan of happiness
6 which was as eternal also as the life of the soul
7 now how could a man repent
8 except he should sin
9 how could he sin
10 if there was no Torah
11 how could there be a Torah
12 except there was a punishment
13 now there was a punishment affixed
14 and a just Torah given
15 which brought remorse of conscience unto man
16 now if there was no Torah given
17 if a man murdered he should die
18 would he be afraid he would die
19 if he should murder
20 and also if there was no Torah given against sin
21 men would not be afraid to sin
22 and if there was no Torah given
23 if men sinned
24 what could justice do
25 or mercy either
26 for they would have no claim upon the creature
27 but there is a Torah given
28 and a punishment affixed
29 and a repentance granted
30 which repentance mercy claims
31 otherwise justice claims the creature
32 and executes the Torah
33 and the Torah inflicts the punishment

1   if not so the works of justice would be destroyed
2   and Elohiym would cease to be Elohiym
3   but Elohiym ceases not to be Elohiym
4   and mercy claimes the repentant
5   and mercy comes because of the atonement
6   and the atonement brings to pass the resurrection of the dead
7   and the resurrection of the dead brings back men into the presence of Elohiym
8   and thus they are restored into his presence
9   to be judged according to their works
10 according to the Torah and justice
11 for behold justice exercises all his demands
12 and also mercy claims all which is her own
13 and thus none but the truly repentant are saved
14
15 What do you suppose that mercy can rob justice
16 I say unto you
17 No not at all
18 if so Elohiym would cease to be Elohiym
19 and thus Elohiym brings about his great and eternal purposes
20 which were prepared from the foundation of the world
21 and thus comes about the salvation and the redemption of men
22 and also their destruction and misery
23 therefore O my son
24 whoever will come may come
25 and partake of the waters of life freely
26 and whoever will not come
27 the same is not compelled to come
28 but in the last day it shall be restored unto him
29 according to his deeds
30 if he has desired to do evil
31 and has not repented in his days
32 behold evil shall be done unto him
33 according to the restoration of Elohiym

1
2 And now my son
3 I desire that you should let these things trouble you no more
4 and only let your sins trouble you with that trouble
5 which shall bring you down unto repentance
6 O my son
7 I desire that you should deny the justice of Elohiym no more
8 do not endeavor to excuse yourself in the least point
9 because of your sins by denying the justice of Elohiym
10 but do you let the justice of Elohiym
11 and his mercy and his long suffering have
12 full sway in your heart
13 and let it bring you down to the dust in humility
14 and now O my son
15 you are called of Elohiym to preach the word unto this people
16 and now my son go your way
17 declare the word
18 with truth and soundness of mind
19 that you may bring souls unto repentance
20 that the great plan of mercy may have claim upon them
21 and may Elohiym grant unto you
22 even according to my words
23 Amein
24
25 And now it came to pass
26 that the sons of Almah did go forth among the people
27 to declare the word unto them
28 and Almah also himself could not rest
29 and he also went forth
30 now we shall say no more concerning their preaching
31 except that they preached the word and the truth
32 according to the Ruach of prophecy and revelation
33 and they preached after the holy manner of Elohiym

1   by which they were called
2
3
4
5
6
7
8
9
10
11
12
13
14
15
16
17
18
19
20
21
22
23
24
25
26
27
28
29
30
31
32
33

1
2
8-WARS OF THE NEPHIY AND THE LAMANIY
4
5 And now I return to an account of the wars
6 between the Nephiy and the Lamaniy
7 in the eighteenth year of the reign of the judges
8
9 For behold it came to pass
10 that the Zoramiy became Lamaniy
11 therefore in the commencement of the eighteenth year
12 the people of the Nephiy saw
13 that the Lamaniy were coming upon them
14 therefore they made preparations for war
15 yes they gathered together their armies in the land of Yershon
16
17 And it came to pass
18 that the Lamaniy came with their thousands
19 and they came into the land of Antionum
20 which is the land of the Zoramiy
21 and a man by the name of Zerahemnah was their leader
22 and now as the Amalekiy were
23 of a more wicked and murderous disposition
24 than the Lamaniy were
25 in and of themselves
26 therefore Zerahemnah appointed sarim over the Lamaniy
27 and they were all Amalekiy and Zoramiy
28 now this he did
29 that he might preserve their hatred towards the Nephiy
30 that he might bring them into subjection
31 to the accomplishment of his designs
32 for behold his designs were to stir up the Lamaniy
33 to anger against the Nephiy

1 this he did that he might usurp great power over them

2 and also that he might gain power over the Nephiy

3 by bringing them into bondage

4

5 And now the design of the Nephiy was to support

6 their lands and their houses

7 and their wives and their children

8 that they might preserve them

9 from the hands of their enemies

10 and also that they might preserve

11 their rights and their privileges

12 yes and also their liberty

13 that they might worship Elohiym

14 according to their desires

15 for they knew

16 that if they should fall into the hands of the Lamaniy

17 that whoever should worship Elohiym

18 in ruach and in truth

19 the true and the living Elohiym

20 the Lamaniy would destroy

21 Yes and they also knew the extreme hatred of the Lamaniy

22 towards their brothers

23 who were the people of Paniym Nephi Lechi

24 who were called the people of Ammon

25 and they would not take up arms

26 yes they had entered into a covenant

27 and they would not break it

28 therefore if they should fall into the hands of the Lamaniy

29 they would be destroyed

30 and the Nephiy would not allow that they should be destroyed

31 therefore they gave them lands for their inheritance

32 and the people of Ammon did give unto the Nephiy

33 a large portion of their substance to support their armies

1   and thus the Nephiy were compelled alone
2   to withstand against the Lamaniy
3   who were a mixture of Laman and L'muel
4   and the sons of Yishma'el
5   and all those who had deserted from the Nephiy
6   who were Amalekiy and Zoramiy
7   and the descendants of the kohanim of Noach
8   now those descendants were as numerous
9   nearly as were the Nephiy
10   and thus the Nephiy were required to contend with their brothers
11   even unto bloodshed
12

13   And it came to pass
14   as the armies of the Lamaniy had gathered together
15   in the land of Antionum
16   behold the armies of the Nephiy were prepared
17   to meet them in the land of Yershon
18   now the leader of the Nephiy
19   or the man who had been appointed
20   to be the sar over the Nephiy
21   now the sar took the command
22   of all the armies of the Nephiy
23   and his name was M'runi
24   and M'runi took all the command and the government of their wars
25   and he was only twenty and five years old
26   when he was appointed sar
27   over the armies of the Nephiy
28

29   And it came to pass
30   that he met the Lamaniy in the borders of Yershon
31   and his people were armed
32   with swords and with cimeters
33   and all manner of weapons of war

1   and when the armies of the Lamaniy saw
2   that the people of Nephi
3   or that M'runi had prepared his people
4   with breastplates and with arm-shields
5   yes and also shields to defend their heads
6   and also they were dressed with thick clothing
7   now the army of Zerahemnah was not prepared
8   with any such thing
9   they had only their swords and their cimeters
10 their bows and their arrows
11 their stones and their slings
12 and they were naked
13 except it were a skin
14 which was belted about their waist
15 yes all were naked
16 except it were the Zoramiy and the Amalekiy
17 but they were not armed
18 with breastplates nor shields
19 therefore they were exceedingly afraid
20 of the armies of the Nephiy
21 because of their armor
22 despite their number
23 being so much greater than the Nephiy
24
25 Behold now it came to pass
26 that they did not come against the Nephiy
27 in the borders of Yershon
28 therefore they departed out of the land of Antionum
29 into the wilderness
30 and took their journey round about in the wilderness
31 away by the head of the river Tzidon
32 that they might come into the land of Manti
33 and take possession of the land

1   for they did not suppose that the armies of M'runi would know

2   where they had gone

3   But it came to pass

4   as soon as they had departed into the wilderness

5   M'runi sent spies into the wilderness to watch their camp

6   and M'runi also knowing of the prophecies of Almah

7   sent certain men unto him desiring him

8   that he should inquire of YHVH

9   where the armies of the Nephiy should go

10 to defend themselves against the Lamaniy

11

12 And it came to pass

13 that the word of YHVH came unto Almah

14 and Almah informed the messengers of M'runi

15 that the armies of the Lamaniy were marching

16 round about in the wilderness

17 that they might come over into the land of Manti

18 that they might commence an attack

19 upon the weaker part of the people

20 and those messengers went

21 and delivered the message unto M'runi

22 now M'runi leaving a part of his army in the land of Yershon

23 for fear that by any means a part of the Lamaniy

24 should come into that land

25 and take possession of the city

26 took the remaining part of his army

27 and marched over into the land of Manti

28 and he caused that all the people

29 in that quarter of the land

30 should gather themselves together

31 to battle against the Lamaniy

32 to defend their lands and their country

33 their rights and their liberties

1 therefore they were prepared against the time

2 of the coming of the Lamaniy

3 And it came to pass

4 that M'runi caused that his army

5 should be secreted in the valley

6 which was near the bank of the river Tzidon

7 which was on the west of the river Tzidon in the wilderness

8 and M'runi placed spies roundabout

9 that he might know when the camp of the Lamaniy should come

10 and now as M'runi knew the intention of the Lamaniy

11 that it was their intention to destroy their brothers

12 or to subject them

13 and bring them into bondage

14 that they might establish a kingdom unto themselves

15 over all the land

16 and he also knowing

17 that it was the only desire of the Nephiy to preserve

18 their lands and their liberty and their assembly

19 therefore he thought it no sin

20 that he should defend them by stratagem

21 therefore he found by his spies

22 which course the Lamaniy were to take

23 therefore he divided his army

24 and brought a part over into the valley

25 and concealed them on the east

26 and on the south of the hill Riplah

27 and the remainder he concealed in the west valley

28 on the west of the river Tzidon

29 and so down into the borders of the land Manti

30 and thus having placed his army

31 according to his desire he was prepared to meet them

32

33 And it came to pass

1   that the Lamaniy came up on the north of the hill

2   where a part of the army of M'runi was concealed

3   and as the Lamaniy had passed the hill Riplah

4   and came into the valley

5   and began to cross the river Tzidon

6   the army which was concealed on the south of the hill

7   which was led by a man whose name was Lechi

8   and he led his army forth

9   and encircled the Lamaniy about

10 on the east in their rear

11

12 And it came to pass

13 that the Lamaniy

14 when they saw the Nephiy coming

15 upon them in their rear turned them about

16 and began to contend with the army of Lechi

17 and the work of death commenced on both sides

18 but it was more dreadful on the part of the Lamaniy

19 for their nakedness was exposed to the heavy blows of the Nephiy

20 with their swords and their cimeters

21 which brought death almost at every stroke

22 while on the other hand

23 there was now and then a man fell among the Nephiy

24 by their swords and the loss of blood

25 they being shielded from the more vital parts of the body

26 or the more vital parts of the body being shielded

27 from the strokes of the Lamaniy

28 by their breastplates and their armshields and their head plates

29 and thus the Nephiy did carry on the work of death among the Lamaniy

30

31 And it came to pass

32 that the Lamaniy became frightened

33 because of the great destruction among them

1 even until they began to flee towards the river Tzidon
2 and they were pursued by Lechi and his men
3 and they were driven by Lechi into the waters of Tzidon
4 and they crossed the waters of Tzidon
5 and Lechi retained his armies upon the bank of the river Tzidon
6 that they should not cross
7
8 And it came to pass
9 that M'runi and his army met the Lamaniy
10 in the valley on the other side of the river Tzidon
11 and began to fall upon them and to kill them
12 and the Lamaniy did flee again before them
13 towards the land of Manti
14 and they were met again by the armies of M'runi
15 now in this case the Lamaniy did fight exceedingly
16 yes never had the Lamaniy been known to fight
17 with such exceedingly great strength and courage
18 no not even from the beginning
19 and they were inspired by the Zoramiy and the Amalekiy
20 who were their sarim and leaders
21 and by Zerahemnah who was their sar or their chief leader and commander
22 yes they did fight like dragons
23 and many of the Nephiy were killed by their hands
24 yes for they did strike in two many of their head-plates
25 and they did pierce many of their breastplates
26 and they did strike off many of their arms
27 and thus the Lamaniy did strike in their fierce anger
28 nevertheless the Nephiy were inspired by a better cause
29 for they were not fighting for their king nor power
30 but they were fighting for their homes and their liberties
31 their wives and their children and their all
32 yes for their rites of worship and their assembly
33

1   and they were doing that which they felt was the duty
2   which they owed to their Elohiym
3   for YHVH had said unto them
4   and also unto their fathers
5   that 'Inasmuch as you are not guilty of the first offense
6   neither the second
7   you shall not allow yourselves to be killed
8   by the hands of your enemies'
9   and again YHVH has said that
10 'You shall defend your families even unto bloodshed'
11 therefore for this cause were the Nephiy contending with the Lamaniy
12 to defend themselves and their families and their lands
13 their country and their rights and their religion
14
15 And it came to pass
16 that when the men of M'runi saw
17 the fierceness and the anger of the Lamaniy
18 they were about to shrink and flee from them
19 and M'runi perceiving their intent
20 sent forth and inspired their hearts with these thoughts
21 yes the thoughts of their lands
22 their liberty
23 yes their freedom from bondage
24
25 And it came to pass
26 that they turned upon the Lamaniy
27 and they cried with one voice unto YHVH their Elohiym
28 for their liberty and their freedom from bondage
29 and they began to stand against the Lamaniy with power
30 and in that selfsame hour that they cried unto YHVH
31 for their freedom the Lamaniy began to flee before them
32 and they fled even to the waters of Tzidon
33 now the Lamaniy were more numerous

1 yes by more than double the number of the Nephiy

2 nevertheless they were driven insomuch

3 that they were gathered together in one body

4 in the valley upon the bank by the river Tzidon

5 therefore the armies of M'runi encircled them about

6 yes even on both sides of the river

7 for behold on the east were the men of Lechi

8 therefore when Zerahemnah saw the men of Lechi

9 on the east of the river Tzidon

10 and the armies of M'runi

11 on the west of the river Tzidon

12 that they were encircled about by the Nephiy

13 they were struck with terror

14 now M'runi when he saw their terror commanded his men

15 that they should stop shedding their blood

16

17 And it came to pass

18 that they did stop

19 and withdrew a degree away from them

20 and M'runi said unto Zerahemnah

21

22 "Behold Zerahemnah

23 that we do not desire to be men of blood

24 You know that you are in our hands

25 yet we do not desire to kill you

26 behold we have not come out to battle against you

27 that we might shed your blood for power

28 neither do we desire to bring any one

29 to the yoke of bondage

30 but this is the very cause for which you have come against us

31 yes and you are angry with us because of our religion

32

33 But now you behold

1 that YHVH is with us

2 and you behold that he has delivered you into our hands

3 and now I would that you should understand

4 that this is done unto us

5 because of our religion and our faith in Mashiach

6 and now you see that you cannot destroy this our faith

7 now you see that this is the true faith of Elohiym

8 yes you see that Elohiym will support and keep and preserve us

9 so long as we are faithful unto him

10 and unto our faith and our religion

11 and never will YHVH allow

12 that we shall be destroyed

13 except we should fall into rebellion

14 and deny our faith

15

16 And now Zerahemnah

17 I command you in the name of that all powerful Elohiym

18 who has strengthened our arms

19 that we have gained power over you

20 by our faith by our religion

21 and by our rites of worship and by our assembly

22 and by the sacred support which we owe

23 to our wives and our children

24 by that liberty which binds us

25 to our lands and our country

26 yes and also by the maintenance of the sacred word of Elohiym

27 to which we owe all our happiness

28 and by all that is most dear unto us

29 yes and this is not all

30 I command you by all the desires which you have for life

31 that you deliver up your weapons of war unto us

32 and we will seek not your blood

33 but we will spare your lives

1 if you will go your way
2 and come not again to war against us
3
4 And now if you do not this
5 behold you are in our hands
6 and I will command my men
7 that they shall fall upon you
8 and inflict the wounds of death in your bodies
9 that you may become extinct
10 and then we will see who shall have power over this people
11 yes we will see who shall be brought into bondage"
12
13 And now it came to pass
14 that when Zerahemnah had heard these sayings he came forth
15 and delivered up his sword and his cimeter and his bow
16 into the hands of M'runi
17 and said unto him
18
19 "Behold here are our weapons of war
20 we will deliver them up unto you
21 but we will not allow ourselves to take an oath unto you
22 which we know that we shall break
23 and also our children
24 but take our weapons of war
25 and allow that we may depart into the wilderness
26 otherwise we will retain our swords
27 and we will perish or conquer
28 behold we are not of your faith
29 we do not believe that it is Elohiym
30 that has delivered us into your hands
31 but we believe that it is your cunning
32 that has preserved you from our swords
33 behold it is your breastplates and your shields

1   that have preserved you"

2

3   And now when Zerahemnah had made an end

4   of speaking these words

5   M'runi returned the sword and the weapons of war

6   which he had received unto Zerahemnah saying

7

8   "behold we will end the conflict

9   now I cannot recall the words which I have spoken

10   therefore as YHVH lives you shall not depart

11   except you depart with an oath

12   that you will not return again against us to war

13   now as you are in our hands

14   we will spill your blood upon the ground

15   or you shall submit to the conditions

16   which I have proposed"

17

18   And now when M'runi had said these words

19   Zerahemnah retained his sword

20   and he was angry with M'runi

21   and he rushed forward that he might kill M'runi

22   but as he raised his sword

23   behold one of M'runi's soldiers struck it even to the earth

24   and it broke by the hilt

25   and he also struck Zerahemnah

26   that he took off his scalp

27   and it fell to the earth

28   and Zerahemnah withdrew from before them

29   into the midst of his soldiers

30

31   And it came to pass

32   that the soldier who stood by

33   who struck off the scalp of Zerahemnah

1 took up the scalp from off the ground by the hair
2 and laid it upon the point of his sword
3 and stretched it forth unto them
4 saying unto them with a loud voice
5
6 "Even as this scalp has fallen to the earth
7 which is the scalp of your chief
8 so shall you fall to the earth
9 except you will deliver up your weapons of war
10 and depart with a covenant of peace"
11
12 Now there were many
13 when they heard these words
14 and saw the scalp which was upon the sword
15 that were struck with fear
16 and many came forth
17 and threw down their weapons of war
18 at the feet of M'runi
19 and entered into a covenant of peace
20 and as many as entered into a covenant
21 they allowed to depart into the wilderness
22
23 Now it came to pass
24 that Zerahemnah was exceedingly angry
25 and he did stir up the remainder of his soldiers to anger
26 to contend more powerfully against the Nephiy
27 and now M'runi was angry
28 because of the stubbornness of the Lamaniy
29 therefore he commanded his people
30 that they should fall upon them
31 and kill them
32
33 And it came to pass

1   that they began to kill them

2   yes and the Lamaniy did contend

3   with their swords and their might

4   but behold their naked skins

5   and their bare heads were exposed

6   to the sharp swords of the Nephiy

7   yes behold they were pierced and struck down

8   yes and did fall exceedingly fast

9   before the swords of the Nephiy

10   and they began to be swept down

11   even as the soldier of M'runi had prophesied

12   now Zerahemnah

13   when he saw that they were all about to be destroyed

14   cried mightily unto M'runi promising

15   that he would covenant

16   and also his people with them

17   if they would spare the remainder of their lives

18   that they never would come to war again against them

19

20   And it came to pass

21   that M'runi caused that the work of death

22   should cease again among the people

23   and he took the weapons of war from the Lamaniy

24   and after they had entered into a covenant with him of peace

25   they were allowed to depart into the wilderness

26   now the number of their dead was not numbered

27   because of the greatness of the number

28   yes the number of their dead was exceedingly great

29   both on the Nephiy and on the Lamaniy

30

31   And it came to pass

32   that they did cast their dead into the waters of Tzidon

33   and they have gone forth

1 and are buried in the depths of the sea
2 and the armies of the Nephiy or of M'runi returned
3 and came to their houses and their lands
4 and thus ended the eighteenth year
5 of the reign of the judges over the people of Nephi
6 and thus ended the record of Almah
7 which was written upon the plates of Nephi
8
9 The account of the people of Nephi
10 and their wars and dissensions in the days of Helaman
11 according to the record of Helaman
12 which he kept in his days
13
14 Behold now it came to pass
15 that the people of Nephi were exceedingly joyful
16 because YHVH had again delivered them
17 out of the hands of their enemies
18 therefore they gave thanks unto YHVH their Elohiym
19 yes and they did fast much and pray much
20 and they did worship Elohiym with exceedingly great joy
21
22 And it came to pass
23 in the nineteenth year of the reign of the judges
24 over the people of Nephi
25 that Almah came unto his son Helaman
26 and said unto him
27
28 "Believe you the words which I spoke unto you
29 concerning those records which have been kept"
30
31 and Helaman said unto him
32
33 "Yes I believe"

1
2 and Almah said again
3 "Believe you in Yehoshua Mashiach who shall come"
4
5 and he said
6
7 "Yes I believe all the words which you have spoken"
8
9 and Almah said unto him again
10
11 "Will you keep my mitzvot"
12
13 and he said
14
15 "Yes I will keep your mitzvot with all my heart"
16
17 Then Almah said unto him
18
19 "Blessed are you
20 and YHVH shall prosper you in this land
21 but behold I have somewhat to prophesy unto you
22 but what I prophesy unto you
23 you shall not make known
24 yes what I prophesy unto you
25 shall not be made known
26 even until the prophecy is fulfilled
27 therefore write the words which I shall say
28 and these are the words
29
30 Behold I perceive
31 that this very people the Nephiy
32 according to the Ruach of revelation which is in me
33 in four hundred years from the time

1 that Yehoshua Mashiach shall manifest himself unto them

2 shall fall away in unbelief

3 Yes and then shall they see wars and pestilences

4 yes famines and bloodshed

5 even until the people of Nephi shall become extinct

6 Yes and this because they shall fall away in unbelief

7 and fall into the works of darkness and given to lust

8 and all manner of lawlessness

9 yes I say unto you

10 that because they shall sin against

11 so great light and knowledge

12 yes I say unto you

13 that from that day even the fourth generation

14 shall not all pass away

15 before this great lawlessness shall come

16

17 And when that great day comes

18 behold the time very soon comes

19 that those who are now

20 or the seed of those

21 who are now numbered among the people of Nephi

22 shall no more be numbered among the people of Nephi

23 but whoever remains and is not destroyed

24 in that great and dreadful day

25 shall be numbered among the Lamaniy

26 and shall become like unto them all

27 except it be a few

28 who shall be called the talmidim of YHVH

29 and them shall the Lamaniy pursue

30 even until they shall become extinct

31 and now because of lawlessness

32 this prophecy shall be fulfilled"

33

1 And now it came to pass
2 that after Almah had said these things to Helaman he blessed him
3 and also his other sons
4 and he also blessed the land for the righteous sake
5 and he said
6
7 "Thus says YHVH Elohiym
8 cursed shall be the land
9 yes this land
10 unto every nation tribe tongue and people unto destruction
11 which do lawlessness
12 when they are fully ripe
13 and as I have said so shall it be
14 for this is the cursing
15 and the blessing of Elohiym upon the land
16 for YHVH cannot look upon sin
17 with the least degree of allowance"
18
19 And now when Almah had said these words
20 he blessed the assembly
21 yes all those who should stand fast in the faith
22 from that time forward
23 and when Almah had done this
24 he departed out of the land of Zarahemla
25 as if to go into the land of Melek
26
27 And it came to pass
28 that he was never heard of more
29 as to his death or burial we know not of
30 behold this we know
31 that he was a righteous man
32 and the saying went abroad in the assembly
33 that he was taken up by the Ruach

1   or buried by the hand of YHVH even as Moshe

2   but behold the scriptures say

3   YHVH took Moshe unto himself

4   and we suppose

5   that he has also received Almah

6   in the Ruach unto himself

7   therefore for this cause we know nothing

8   concerning his death and burial

9

10   And now it came to pass

11   in the commencement of the nineteenth year

12   of the reign of the judges over the people of Nephi

13   that Helaman went forth among the people

14   to declare the word unto them

15   for behold because of their wars with the Lamaniy

16   and the many little dissensions and disturbances

17   which had been among the people it became necessary

18   that the word of Elohiym should be declared among them

19   yes and that a regulation should be made throughout the assembly

20   therefore Helaman and his brothers went forth

21   to establish the assembly again in all the land

22   yes in every city throughout all the land

23   which was possessed by the people of Nephi

24

25   And it came to pass

26   that they did appoint kohanim and murim

27   throughout all the land

28   over all the assemblies

29

30   And now it came to pass

31   that after Helaman and his brothers

32   had appointed kohanim and murim over the assemblies

33   that there arose a dissension among them

1   and they would not give heed to the words of Helaman

2   and his brothers

3   but they grew proud

4   being lifted up in their hearts

5   because of their exceedingly great riches

6   therefore they grew rich in their own eyes

7   and would not give heed to their words

8   to walk uprightly before Elohiym

9

10 And it came to pass

11 that as many as would not listen to

12 and obey the words of Helaman and his brothers

13 were gathered together against their brothers

14 and now behold they were exceedingly angry insomuch

15 that they were determined to kill them

16 now the leader of those

17 who were angry against their brothers

18 was a large and a strong man

19 and his name was Amalick'yahu

20 and Amalick'yahu desired to be a king

21 and those people who were angry also desired

22 that he should be their king

23 and they were the greater part of them

24 the lower judges of the land

25 and they were seeking for power

26 and they had been led by the flatteries of Amalick'yahu

27 that if they would support him

28 and establish him to be their king

29 that he would make them rulers over the people

30 thus they were led away by Amalick'yahu to dissensions

31 notwithstanding the preaching of Helaman and his brothers

32 yes notwithstanding their exceedingly great care over the assembly

33 for they were kohanim gadolim over the assembly

1   and there were many in the assembly
2   who believed in the flattering words of Amalick'yahu
3   therefore they dissented even from the assembly
4   and thus were the affairs of the people of Nephi
5   exceedingly precarious and dangerous
6   notwithstanding their great victory
7   which they had had over the Lamaniy
8   and their great rejoicings
9   which they had had because of their deliverance
10 by the hand of YHVH
11 thus we see how quick the children of men
12 do forget YHVH their Elohiym
13 yes how quick to do lawlessness
14 and to be led away by the evil one
15 Yes and we also see the great wickedness
16 one very wicked man can cause
17 to take place among the children of men
18 Yes we see that Amalick'yahu
19 because he was a man of cunning device
20 and a man of many flattering words
21 that he led away the hearts of many people to do wickedly
22 yes and to seek to destroy the assembly of Elohiym
23 and to destroy the foundation of liberty
24 which Elohiym had granted unto them
25 or which blessing Elohiym had sent
26 upon the face of the land for the righteous' sake
27
28 And now it came to pass
29 that when M'runi
30 who was the chief commander of the armies of the Nephiy
31 had heard of these dissensions
32 he was angry with Amalick'yahu
33

1   And it came to pass

2   that he rent[16] his coat

3   and he took a piece thereof

4   and wrote upon it

5

6   'In memory of our Elohiym

7   our religion and freedom

8   and our peace our wives and our children'

9   And he fastened it upon the end of a pole

10 and he fastened on his head plate

11 and his breastplate and his shields

12 and put on his armor about his waist

13 and he took the pole

14 which had on the end thereof his rent coat

15 and he called it the title of liberty

16 and he bowed himself to the earth

17 and he prayed mightily unto his Elohiym

18 for the blessings of liberty to rest upon his brothers

19 so long as there should a band of talmidim of Mashiach remain

20 to possess the land

21 for thus were all the true believers of Mashiach

22 who belonged to the assembly of Elohiym called

23 by those who did not belong to the assembly

24 and those who did belong to the assembly were faithful

25 yes all those who were true believers in Mashiach

26 took upon them gladly the name of Mashiach

27 or talmidim of Mashiach

28 as they were called

29 because of their belief in Mashiach

30 who should come

31 and therefore at this time M'runi prayed

32 that the cause of the talmidim

---

[16] K'riah

1 and the freedom of the land might be favored

2

3 And it came to pass

4 that when he had poured out his soul to Elohiym

5 he named all the land which was south of the land Desolation

6 yes and in sum all the land

7 both on the north and on the south

8 a chosen land and the land of liberty

9 and he said

10

11 "Certainly Elohiym shall not allow

12 that we who are despised

13 because we take upon us the name of Mashiach

14 shall be trampled down and destroyed

15 until we bring it upon us

16 by our own rebellion"

17

18 And when M'runi had said these words

19 he went forth among the people

20 waving the rent part of his garment in the air

21 that all might see the writing

22 which he had written upon the rent part

23 and crying with a loud voice saying

24

25 " behold whoever will maintain this title upon the land

26 let them come forth in the strength of YHVH

27 and enter into a covenant

28 that they will maintain their rights and their religion

29 that YHVH Elohiym may bless them"

30

31 And it came to pass

32 that when M'runi had proclaimed these words

33 behold the people came running together

1 with their armor bound about their waists
2 rending their garments in token
3 or as a covenant that they would not forsake YHVH their Elohiym
4 or in other words if they should transgress the mitzvot of Elohiym
5 or fall into rebellion
6 and be ashamed to take upon them the name of Mashiach
7 YHVH should rend them
8 even as they had rent their garments
9 now this was the covenant which they made
10 and they cast their garments at the feet of M'runi saying
11
12 "We covenant with our Elohiym
13 that we shall be destroyed
14 even as our brothers in the land northward
15 if we shall fall into rebellion
16 yes he may cast us at the feet of our enemies
17 even as we have cast our garments at your feet
18 to be trodden under foot
19 if we shall fall into rebellion"
20
21 M'runi said unto them
22
23 "Behold we are a remnant of the seed of Yacov
24 yes we are a remnant of the seed of Yoseph
25 whose coat was rent by his brothers into many pieces
26 yes and now behold let us remember to keep the mitzvot of Elohiym
27 or our garments shall be rent by our brothers
28 and we be cast into prison or be sold or be killed
29
30 Yes let us preserve our liberty as a remnant of Yoseph
31 yes let us remember the words of Yacov before his death
32 for behold he saw
33 that a part of the remnant of the coat of Yoseph was preserved

1 and had not decayed

2 and he said

3 'even as this remnant of garment of my son has been preserved

4 so shall a remnant of the seed of my son be preserved

5 by the hand of Elohiym

6 and be taken unto himself

7 while the remainder of the seed of Yoseph shall perish

8 even as the remnant of his garment

9 now behold this gives my soul sorrow

10 nevertheless my soul has joy in my son

11 because of that part of his seed

12 which shall be taken unto Elohiym'

13 now behold this was the language of Yacov

14 and now who knows

15 but what the remnant of the seed of Yoseph

16 which shall perish as his garment are those

17 who have dissented from us

18 Yes and even it shall be ourselves

19 if we do not stand fast in the faith of Mashiach"

20

21 And now it came to pass

22 that when M'runi had said these words he went forth

23 and also sent forth in all the parts of the land

24 where there were dissensions

25 and gathered together all the people

26 who desired to maintain their liberty

27 to stand against Amalick'yahu

28 and those who had dissented

29 who were called Amalick'yahiy

30

31 And it came to pass

32 that when Amalick'yahu saw

33 that the people of M'runi were more numerous

1 than the Amalick'yahiy
2 and he also saw that his people were doubtful
3 concerning the justice of the cause
4 in which they had undertaken
5 therefore fearing that he should not gain the point
6 he took those of his people who would
7 and departed into the land of Nephi
8 now M'runi thought it was not necessary
9 that the Lamaniy should have any more strength
10 therefore he thought to cut off the people of Amalick'yahu
11 or to take them
12 and bring them back
13 and put Amalick'yahu to death
14 yes for he knew that he would stir up the Lamaniy
15 to anger against them
16 and cause them to come to battle against them
17 and this he knew that Amalick'yahu would do
18 that he might obtain his purposes
19 therefore M'runi thought it was necessary
20 that he should take his armies
21 who had gathered themselves together
22 and armed themselves
23 and entered into a covenant to keep the peace
24
25 And it came to pass
26 that he took his army
27 and marched out with his tents into the wilderness
28 to cut off the course of Amalick'yahu in the wilderness
29 And it came to pass
30 that he did according to his desires
31 and marched forth into the wilderness
32 and headed the armies of Amalick'yahu
33

1 And it came to pass

2 that Amalick'yahu fled with a small number of his men

3 and the remainder were delivered up into the hands of M'runi

4 and were taken back into the land of Zarahemla

5 now M'runi being a man who was appointed

6 by the chief judges and the voice of the people

7 therefore he had power according to his will

8 with the armies of the Nephiy

9 to establish and to exercise authority over them

10

11 And it came to pass

12 that whoever of the Amalick'yahiy

13 that would not enter into a covenant

14 to support the cause of freedom

15 that they might maintain a free government

16 he caused to be put to death

17 and there were but few who denied the covenant of freedom

18

19 And it came to pass also

20 that he caused the title of liberty

21 to be hoisted upon every tower

22 which was in all the land

23 which was possessed by the Nephiy

24 and thus M'runi planted the standard of liberty among the Nephiy

25 and they began to have peace again in the land

26 and thus they did maintain peace in the land

27 until nearly the end of the nineteenth year

28 of the reign of the judges

29 and Helaman and the kohanim gadolim

30 did also maintain order in the assembly

31 yes even for the space of four years

32 did they have much peace and rejoicing in the assembly

33

1 And it came to pass

2 that there were many who died firmly believing

3 that their souls were redeemed by Adon Yehoshua Mashiach

4 thus they went out of the world rejoicing

5 and there were some who died with fevers

6 which at some seasons of the year

7 were very frequent in the land

8 but not so much so with fevers

9 because of the excellent qualities

10 of the many plants and roots which Elohiym had prepared

11 to remove the cause of diseases

12 to which men were subject by the nature of the climate

13 but there were many who died with old age

14 and those who died in the faith of Mashiach are happy in him

15 as we must needs suppose

16

17 Now we will return in our record to Amalick'yahu

18 and those who had fled with him into the wilderness

19 for behold he had taken those who went with him

20 and went up in the land of Nephi

21 among the Lamaniy

22 and did stir up the Lamaniy

23 to anger against the people of Nephi insomuch

24 that the king of the Lamaniy sent a proclamation

25 throughout all his land

26 among all his people

27 that they should gather themselves together again

28 to go to battle against the Nephiy

29

30 And it came to pass

31 that when the proclamation had gone forth among them

32 they were exceedingly afraid

33 yes they feared to displease the king

1 and they also feared to go to battle against the Nephiy
2 for fear that they should lose their lives
3
4 And it came to pass that they would not
5 or the more part of them would not
6 obey the mitzvot of the king
7
8 And now it came to pass
9 that the king was angry because of their disobedience
10 therefore he gave Amalick'yahu the command
11 of that part of his army which was obedient unto his commands
12 and commanded him that he should go forth
13 and compel them to arms
14 now behold this was the desire of Amalick'yahu
15 for he being a very subtle man to do evil
16 therefore he laid the plan in his heart
17 to dethrone the king of the Lamaniy
18 and now he had got the command
19 of those parts of the Lamaniy
20 who were in favor of the king
21 and he sought to gain favor of those
22 who were not obedient
23 therefore he went forward to the place
24 which was called Onidah
25 for there had all the Lamaniy fled
26 for they discovered the army coming
27 and supposing that they were coming to destroy them
28 therefore they fled to Onidah
29 to the place of arms
30 and they had appointed a man
31 to be a king and a leader over them
32 being fixed in their minds with a determined resolution
33 that they would not be subjected to go against the Nephiy

1

2 And it came to pass

3 that they had gathered themselves together

4 upon the top of the mount

5 which was called Passim in preparation to battle

6 now it was not Amalick'yahu's intention to give them battle

7 according to the mitzvot of the king

8 but behold it was his intention to gain favor

9 with the armies of the Lamaniy

10 that he might place himself at their head

11 and dethrone the king

12 and take possession of the kingdom

13

14 And behold it came to pass

15 that he caused his army

16 to pitch their tents in the valley

17 which was near the mount Paniym Pas[17]

18

19 And it came to pass

20 that when it was night he sent a secret embassy

21 into the mount Paniym Pas desiring

22 that the leader of those

23 who were upon the mount

24 whose name was Lehonti

25 that he should come down

26 to the foot of the mount

27 for he desired to speak with him

28

29 And it came to pass

30 that when Lehonti received the message

31 he did not go down

32 to the foot of the mount

---

[17] Hebrew Pas – sole of a foot/hand, also varied colors, Paniym- face, countenance

1
2 And it came to pass
3 that Amalick'yahu sent again the second time
4 desiring him to come down
5
6 And it came to pass
7 that Lehonti would not
8 and he sent again the third time
9
10 And it came to pass
11 that when Amalick'yahu found
12 that he could not get Lehonti
13 to come down off from the mount
14 he went up into the mount nearly to Lehonti's camp
15 and he sent again the fourth time his message unto Lehonti desiring
16 that he would come down
17 and that he would bring his guards with him
18
19 And it came to pass
20 that when Lehonti had come down
21 with his guards to Amalick'yahu
22 that Amalick'yahu desired him to come down
23 with his army in the night-time
24 and surround those men in their camps over
25 whom the king had given him command
26 and that he would deliver them up into Lehonti's hands
27 if he would make him Amalick'yahu
28 a second leader over the whole army
29
30 And it came to pass
31 that Lehonti came down with his men
32 and surrounded the men of Amalick'yahu
33 so that before they awoke at the dawn of day

1   they were surrounded by the armies of Lehonti

2

3   And it came to pass

4   that when they saw that they were surrounded

5   they pled with Amalick'yahu

6   that he would allow them to fall in with their brothers

7   that they might not be destroyed

8   now this was the very thing which Amalick'yahu desired

9

10   And it came to pass

11   that he delivered his men contrary

12   to the commands of the king

13   now this was the thing that Amalick'yahu desired

14   that he might accomplish his designs in dethroning the king

15   now it was the custom among the Lamaniy

16   if their chief leader was killed

17   to appoint the second leader

18   to be their chief leader

19

20   And it came to pass that Amalick'yahu caused

21   that one of his servants should administer poison by degrees

22   to Lehonti that he died

23   now when Lehonti was dead

24   the Lamaniy appointed Amalick'yahu

25   to be their leader and their chief commander

26

27   And it came to pass

28   that Amalick'yahu marched with his armies

29   for he had gained his desires

30   to the land of Nephi

31   to the city of Nephi

32   which was the chief city

33   and the king came out to meet him with his guards

1 for he supposed that Amalick'yahu had fulfilled his commands
2 and that Amalick'yahu had gathered together so great an army
3 to go against the Nephiy to battle
4 but behold as the king came out to meet him Amalick'yahu caused
5 that his servants should go forth to meet the king
6 and they went and bowed themselves before the king
7 as if to reverence him because of his greatness
8 And it came to pass
9 that the king put forth his hand to raise them
10 as was the custom with the Lamaniy
11 as a token of peace
12 which custom they had taken from the Nephiy
13
14 And it came to pass
15 that when he had raised the first from the ground
16 behold he stabbed the king to the heart
17 and he fell to the earth
18 now the servants of the king fled
19 and the servants of Amalick'yahu raised a cry saying
20
21 "Behold the servants of the king
22 have stabbed him to the heart
23 and he has fallen
24 and they have fled
25 behold come and see"
26
27 And it came to pass
28 that Amalick'yahu commanded
29 that his armies should march forth
30 and see what had happened to the king
31 and when they had come to the spot
32 and found the king lying in his gore
33 Amalick'yahu pretended to be angry and said

1

2 "Whoever loved the king let him go forth

3 and pursue his servants

4 that they may be killed"

5

6 And it came to pass

7 that all they who loved the king

8 when they heard these words came forth

9 and pursued after the servants of the king

10 now when the servants of the king saw

11 an army pursuing after them

12 they were frightened again

13 and fled into the wilderness

14 and came over into the land of Zarahemla

15 and joined the people of Ammon

16 and the army which pursued after them returned

17 having pursued after them in vain

18 and thus Amalick'yahu by his fraud

19 gained the hearts of the people

20

21 And it came to pass

22 on the next day he entered the city Nephi with his armies

23 and took possession of the city

24

25 And now it came to pass

26 that the queen

27 when she had heard that the king was killed

28 for Amalick'yahu had sent an embassy to the queen informing her

29 that the king had been killed by his servants

30 that he had pursued them with his army

31 but it was in vain

32 and they had made their escape

33 therefore when the queen had received this message

1   she sent unto Amalick'yahu desiring him

2   that he would spare the people of the city

3   and she also desired him

4   that he should come in unto her

5   and she also desired him

6   that he should bring witnesses with him

7   to testify concerning the death of the king

8

9   And it came to pass

10   that Amalick'yahu took the same servant

11   that killed the king

12   and all them who were with him

13   and went in unto the queen

14   unto the place where she sat

15   and they all testified unto her

16   that the king was killed by his own servants

17   and they said also

18

19   "They have fled does not this testify against them"

20

21   And thus they satisfied the queen

22   concerning the death of the king

23

24   And it came to pass

25   that Amalick'yahu sought the favor of the queen

26   and took her unto him to wife

27   and thus by his fraud

28   and by the assistance of his cunning servants

29   he obtained the kingdom

30   yes he was acknowledged king throughout all the land

31   among all the people of the Lamaniy

32   who were composed of the Lamanim

33   and the L'muelim

1   and the Ishmaeliim
2   and all the dissenters of the Nephiy
3   from the reign of Nephi
4   down to the present time
5   now these dissenters having the same instruction
6   and the same information of the Nephiy
7   yes having been instructed in the same knowledge of YHVH
8   nevertheless it is strange to relate
9   not long after their dissensions
10 they became more hardened and unrepentant
11 and more wild wicked and ferocious than the Lamaniy
12 drinking in with the traditions of the Lamaniy
13 giving way to indolence and all manner of lust
14 yes entirely forgetting YHVH their Elohiym
15
16 And now it came to pass
17 that as soon as Amalick'yahu had obtained the kingdom
18 he began to inspire the hearts of the Lamaniy
19 against the people of Nephi
20 yes he did appoint men to speak unto the Lamaniy
21 from their towers against the Nephiy
22 and thus he did inspire their hearts against the Nephiy insomuch
23 that in the latter end of the nineteenth year
24 of the reign of the judges
25 he having accomplished his designs thus far
26 yes having been made king over the Lamaniy
27 he sought also to reign over all the land
28 yes and all the people
29 who were in the land the Nephiy
30 as well as the Lamaniy
31 therefore he had accomplished his design
32 for he had hardened the hearts of the Lamaniy
33 and blinded their minds

1 and stirred them up to anger insomuch

2 that he had gathered together a numerous host

3 to go to battle against the Nephiy

4 for he was determined

5 because of the greatness of the number of his people

6 to overpower the Nephiy

7 and to bring them into bondage

8 and thus he did appoint sarim of the Zoramiy

9 they being the most acquainted with the strength of the Nephiy

10 and their places of resort

11 and the weakest parts of their cities

12 therefore he appointed them

13 to be sarim over his armies

14

15 And it came to pass

16 that they took their camp and moved forth

17 toward the land of Zarahemla in the wilderness

18

19 Now it came to pass

20 that while Amalick'yahu had thus been obtaining power

21 by fraud and deceit

22 M'runi on the other hand

23 had been preparing the minds of the people

24 to be faithful unto YHVH their Elohiym

25 Yes he had been strengthening the armies of the Nephiy

26 and erecting small forts or places of defense

27 throwing up banks of earth round about

28 to enclose his armies and also building walls of stone

29 to encircle them about round about

30 their cities and the borders of their lands

31 yes all round about the land

32 and in their weakest fortifications

33 he did place the greater number of men

1   and thus he did fortify and strengthen the land
2   which was possessed by the Nephiy
3   and thus he was preparing to support their liberty
4   their lands their wives and their children and their peace
5   and that they might live unto YHVH their Elohiym
6   and that they might maintain
7   that which was called by their enemies
8   the cause of Mashiach
9
10 And M'runi was a strong and a mighty man
11 he was a man of a perfect understanding
12 yes a man that did not delight in bloodshed
13 a man whose soul did joy
14 in the liberty and the freedom of his country
15 and his brothers from bondage and slavery
16 Yes a man whose heart did swell with thanksgiving to his Elohiym
17 for the many privileges and blessings
18 which he bestowed upon his people
19 a man who did labor exceedingly
20 for the welfare and safety of his people
21 Yes and he was a man who was firm in the faith of Mashiach
22 and he had sworn with an oath
23 to defend his people
24 his rights and his country and his religion
25 even to the loss of his blood
26 now the Nephiy were taught
27 to defend themselves against their enemies
28 even to the shedding of blood if it were necessary
29 yes and they were also taught never to give an offense
30 yes and never to raise the sword
31 except it were against an enemy
32 except it were to preserve their lives
33 and this was their faith

1 that by so doing Elohiym would prosper them in the land
2 or in other words
3 if they were faithful in keeping the mitzvot of Elohiym
4 that he would prosper them in the land
5 yes warn them to flee
6 or to prepare for war
7 according to their danger
8 and also that Elohiym would make it known unto them
9 where they should go to defend themselves against their enemies
10 and by so doing YHVH would deliver them
11 and this was the faith of M'runi
12 and his heart did glory in it
13 not in the shedding of blood
14 but in doing good in preserving his people
15 yes in keeping the mitzvot of Elohiym
16 yes and resisting lawlessness
17 Yes I am telling you the truth
18 I say unto you
19 if all men had been and were and ever would be like unto M'runi
20 behold the very powers of sheol would have been shaken forever
21 yes the evil one would never have power
22 over the hearts of the children of men
23 behold he was a man like unto Ammon the son of Mosheyahu
24 yes and even the other sons of Mosheyahu
25 yes and also Almah and his sons
26 for they were all men of Elohiym
27 now behold Helaman and his brothers
28 were no less serviceable unto the people than was M'runi
29 for they did preach the word of Elohiym
30 and they did immerse unto repentance all men
31 whoever would listen and obey unto their words
32
33 And thus they went forth

1. and the people did humble themselves
2. because of their words insomuch
3. that they were highly favored of YHVH
4. and thus they were free
5. from wars and contentions among themselves
6. yes even for the space of four years
7. but as I have said in the latter end of the nineteenth year
8. yes despite their peace among themselves
9. they were compelled reluctantly to contend
10. with their brothers the Lamaniy
11. Yes and in sum their wars never did cease
12. for the space of many years with the Lamaniy
13. despite their much reluctance
14. now they were sorry to take up arms against the Lamaniy
15. because they did not delight in the shedding of blood
16. yes and this was not all
17. they were sorry to be the means
18. of sending so many of their brothers out of this world
19. into an eternal world unprepared to meet their Elohiym
20. nevertheless they could not allow to lay down their lives
21. that their wives and their children should be massacred
22. by the savage cruelty
23. of those who were once their brothers
24. yes and had dissented from their assembly
25. and had left them
26. and had gone to destroy them
27. by joining the Lamaniy
28. Yes they could not bear
29. that their brothers should rejoice over the blood of the Nephiy
30. so long as there were any who should keep the mitzvot of Elohiym
31. for the promise of YHVH was
32. if they should keep his mitzvot
33. they should prosper in the land

1

2 And now it came to pass

3 in the eleventh month of the nineteenth year

4 on the tenth day of the month

5 the armies of the Lamaniy were seen approaching

6 towards the land of Ammoniyah

7 and behold the city had been rebuilt

8 and M'runi had stationed an army by the borders of the city

9 and they had cast up dirt round about

10 to shield them from the arrows and the stones of the Lamaniy

11 for behold they fought with stones and with arrows

12 behold I said that the city of Ammoniyah had been rebuilt

13 I say unto you yes that it was in part rebuilt

14 and because the Lamaniy had destroyed it once

15 because of the lawlessness of the people

16 they supposed that it would again become an easy prey for them

17 but behold how great was their disappointment

18 for behold the Nephiy had dug up a ridge of earth round about them

19 which was so high that the Lamaniy could not cast

20 their stones and their arrows at them

21 that they might take effect

22 neither could they come upon them

23 except it was by their place of entrance

24 now at this time the sarim of the Lamaniy were astonished exceedingly

25 because of the wisdom of the Nephiy

26 in preparing their places of security

27 now the leaders of the Lamaniy had supposed

28 because of the greatness of their numbers

29 yes they supposed that they should be privileged to come upon them

30 as they had previously done

31 yes and they had also prepared themselves

32 with shields and with breastplates

33 and they had also prepared themselves

1 with garments of skins
2 yes very thick garments
3 to cover their nakedness
4 and being thus prepared they supposed
5 that they should easily overpower and subject their brothers
6 to the yoke of bondage
7 or kill and massacre them
8 according to their pleasure
9 but behold to their uttermost astonishment
10 they were prepared for them
11 in a manner which never had been known among the children of Lechi
12 now they were prepared for the Lamaniy to battle
13 after the manner of the instructions of M'runi
14
15 And it came to pass
16 that the Lamaniy
17 or the Amalick'yahiy were exceedingly astonished
18 at their manner of preparation for war
19 now if king Amalick'yahu had come down
20 out of the land of Nephi at the head of his army
21 perhaps he would have caused the Lamaniy
22 to have attacked the Nephiy
23 at the city of Ammoniyah
24 for behold he did care not for the blood of his people
25 but behold Amalick'yahu did not come down himself to battle
26 and behold his sarim did not attack the Nephiy
27 at the city of Ammoniyah
28 for M'runi had altered the management of affairs
29 among the Nephiy insomuch
30 that the Lamaniy were disappointed
31 in their places of retreat
32 and they could not come upon them
33 therefore they retreated into the wilderness

1 and took their camp
2 and marched towards the land of Noach supposing
3 that to be the next best place for them
4 to come against the Nephiy
5 for they knew not that M'runi had fortified
6 or had built forts of security
7 for every city in all the land round about
8 therefore they marched forward to the land of Noach
9 with a firm determination
10 yes their sarim came forward and took an oath
11 that they would destroy the people of that city
12 but behold to their astonishment the city of Noach
13 which had previously been a weak place had now
14 by the means of M'runi become strong
15 yes even to exceed the strength of the city Ammoniyah
16 and now behold this was wisdom in M'runi
17 for he had supposed that they would be frightened at the city Ammoniyah
18 and as the city of Noach had previously been the weakest part of the land
19 therefore they would march there to battle
20 and thus it was according to his desires
21 and behold M'runi had appointed Lechi
22 to be sar over the men of that city
23 and it was that same Lechi who fought with the Lamaniy
24 in the valley on the east of the river Tzidon
25
26 And now behold it came to pass
27 that when the Lamaniy had found
28 that Lechi commanded the city
29 they were again disappointed
30 for they feared Lechi exceedingly
31 nevertheless their sarim had sworn
32 with an oath to attack the city
33 therefore they brought up their armies

1   now behold the Lamaniy could not get into their forts of security

2   by any other way

3   except by the entrance

4   because of the highness of the bank

5   which had been thrown up

6   and the depth of the ditch

7   which had been dug round about

8   except it were by the entrance

9   and thus were the Nephiy prepared

10   to destroy all such

11   as should attempt to climb up

12   to enter the fort

13   by any other way

14   by casting over stones and arrows at them

15   thus they were prepared

16   yes a body of their strongest men

17   with their swords and their slings

18   to strike down all who should attempt

19   to come into their place of security

20   by the place of entrance

21   and thus were they prepared

22   to defend themselves against the Lamaniy

23

24   And it came to pass

25   that the captains of the Lamaniy brought up their armies

26   before the place of entrance

27   and began to contend with the Nephiy

28   to get into their place of security

29   but behold they were driven back from time to time insomuch

30   that they were killed with an immense slaughter

31   now when they found

32   that they could not obtain power over the Nephiy by the pass

33   they began to dig down their banks of earth

1 that they might obtain a pass to their armies
2 that they might have an equal chance to fight
3 but behold in these attempts they were swept off
4 by the stones and arrows
5 which were thrown at them
6 and instead of filling up their ditches
7 by pulling down the banks of earth
8 they were filled up in a measure
9 with their dead and wounded bodies
10 thus the Nephiy had all power over their enemies
11 and thus the Lamaniy did attempt to destroy the Nephiy
12 until their sarim were all killed
13 yes and more than a thousand of the Lamaniy were killed
14 while on the other hand
15 there was not a single soul of the Nephiy which was killed
16 there were about fifty who were wounded
17 who had been exposed to the arrows of the Lamaniy
18 through the pass
19 but they were shielded by their shields
20 and their breastplates and their head-plates insomuch
21 that their wounds were upon their legs
22 many of which were very severe
23
24 And it came to pass
25 that when the Lamaniy saw
26 that their sarim were all killed
27 they fled into the wilderness
28
29 And it came to pass
30 that they returned to the land of Nephi
31 to inform their king Amalick'yahu
32 who was a Nephiy by birth
33 concerning their great loss

1
2 And it came to pass
3 that he was exceedingly angry with his people
4 because he had not obtained his desire over the Nephiy
5 he had not subjected them
6 to the yoke of bondage
7 Yes he was exceedingly angry
8 and he did curse Elohiym
9 and also M'runi swearing with an oath
10 that he would drink his blood
11 and this because M'runi had kept the mitzvot of Elohiym
12 in preparing for the safety of his people
13
14 And it came to pass
15 that on the other hand the people of Nephi
16 did thank YHVH their Elohiym
17 because of his matchless power
18 in delivering them from the hands of their enemies
19 and thus ended the nineteenth year
20 of the reign of the judges over the people of Nephi
21 Yes and there was continual peace among them
22 and exceedingly great prosperity in the assembly
23 because of their heed and observance
24 which they gave unto the word of Elohiym
25 which was declared unto them
26 by Helaman and Shiblon and Corianton
27 and Ammon and his brothers
28 yes and by all those who had been ordained
29 by the holy manner of Elohiym being immersed unto repentance
30 and sent forth to preach among the people
31
32 And now it came to pass
33 that M'runi did not stop making preparations for war

1   or to defend his people against the Lamaniy

2   for he caused that his armiesshould commence

3   in the commencement of the twentieth year

4   of the reign of the judges

5   that they should commence

6   in digging up heaps of earth round about

7   all the cities throughout all the land

8   which was possessed by the Nephiy

9   and upon the top of these ridges of earth he caused

10 that there should be timbers

11 yes works of timbers built up

12 to the height of a man round about the cities

13 and he caused that upon those works of timbers

14 there should be a frame of pickets built upon the timbers round about

15 and they were strong and high

16 and he caused towers to be erected

17 that overlooked those works of pickets

18 and he caused places of security

19 to be built upon those towers

20 that the stones and the arrows of the Lamaniy

21 could not hurt them

22 and they were prepared

23 that they could cast stones from the top thereof

24 according to their pleasure and their strength

25 and kill him who should attempt to approach

26 near the walls of the city

27 thus M'runi did prepare strongholds

28 against the coming of their enemies round about

29 every city in all the land

30

31 And it came to pass

32 that M'runi caused that his armies should go forth

33 into the east wilderness

1 yes and they went forth

2 and drove all the Lamaniy

3 who were in the east wilderness

4 into their own lands

5 which were south of the land of Zarahemla

6 and the land of Nephi did run in a straight course

7 from the east sea to the west

8

9 And it came to pass

10 that when M'runi had driven all the Lamaniy

11 out of the east wilderness

12 which was north of the lands of their own possessions

13 he caused that the inhabitants

14 who were in the land of Zarahemla

15 and in the land round about

16 should go forth into the east wilderness

17 even to the borders by the seashore

18 and possess the land

19 and he also placed armies on the south

20 in the borders of their possessions

21 and caused them to erect fortifications

22 that they might secure their armies and their people

23 from the hands of their enemies

24 and thus he cut off all the strongholds of the Lamaniy

25 in the east wilderness

26 yes and also on the west fortifying the line

27 between the Nephiy and the Lamaniy

28 between the land of Zarahemla

29 and the land of Nephi

30 from the west sea running by the head of the river Tzidon

31 the Nephiy possessing all the land northward

32 yes even all the land which was northward of the land Bountiful

33 according to their pleasure

1 thus M'runi with his armies
2 which did increase daily
3 because of the assurance of protection
4 which his works did bring forth unto them did seek
5 to cut off the strength and the power of the Lamaniy
6 from off the lands of their possessions
7 that they should have no power
8 upon the lands of their possession
9
10 And it came to pass
11 that the Nephiy began the foundation of a city
12 and they called the name of the city M'runi
13 and it was by the east sea
14 and it was on the south
15 by the line of the possessions of the Lamaniy
16 and they also began a foundation for a city
17 between the city of M'runi and the city of Aharon
18 joining the borders of Aharon and M'runi
19 and they called the name of the city
20 or the land Nephiyah
21 and they also began in that same year
22 to build many cities on the north
23 one in a particular manner
24 which they called Lechi
25 which was in the north
26 by the borders of the seashore
27 and thus ended the twentieth year
28
29 And in these prosperous circumstances were the people of Nephi
30 in the commencement of the twenty and first year
31 of the reign of the judges over the people of Nephi
32 and they did prosper exceedingly
33 and they became exceedingly rich

1 yes and they did multiply and wax strong in the land
2 and thus we see how merciful and just are all the dealings of YHVH
3 to the fulfilling of all his words unto the children of men
4 yes we can behold
5 that his words are verified even at this time
6 which he spoke unto Lechi saying
7 "Blessed are you and your children
8 and they shall be blessed inasmuch
9 as they shall keep my mitzvot
10 they shall prosper in the land
11 but remember inasmuch
12 as they will not keep my mitzvot
13 they shall be cut off
14 from the presence of YHVH"
15
16 And we see that these promises have been verified
17 to the people of Nephi
18 for it has been their quarrelings and their contentions
19 yes their murderings and their plunderings
20 their idolatry their whoredoms and their abominations
21 which were among themselves
22 which brought upon them
23 their wars and their destructions
24 and those who were faithful
25 in keeping the mitzvot of YHVH
26 were delivered at all times
27 while thousands of their wicked brothers
28 have been consigned to bondage
29 or to perish by the sword
30 or to fall away in unbelief
31 and mingle with the Lamaniy
32 but behold there never was a happier time
33 among the people of Nephi

1 since the days of Nephi
2 than in the days of M'runi
3 yes even at this time
4 in the twenty and first year
5 of the reign of the judges
6
7 And it came to pass
8 that the twenty and second year
9 of the reign of the judges also ended in peace
10 yes and also the twenty and third year
11
12 And it came to pass
13 that in the commencement of the twenty and fourth year
14 of the reign of the judges
15 there would also have been peace
16 among the people of Nephi
17 had it not been for a contention
18 which took place among them
19 concerning the land of Lechi
20 and the land of Morianton
21 which joined upon the borders of Lechi
22 both of which were on the borders by the seashore
23 for behold the people
24 who possessed the land of Morianton
25 did claim a part of the land of Lechi therefore
26 there began to be a warm contention between them insomuch
27 that the people of Morianton took up arms against their brothers
28 and they were determined by the sword to kill them
29 but behold the people
30 who possessed the land of Lechi fled
31 to the camp of M'runi
32 and appealed unto him for assistance
33 for behold they were not in the wrong

1
2   And it came to pass
3   that when the people of Morianton
4   who were led by a man whose name was Morianton found
5   that the people of Lechi had fled
6   to the camp of M'runi
7   they were exceedingly fearful
8   for fear that the army of M'runi
9   should come upon them and destroy them
10 therefore Morianton put it into their hearts
11 that they should flee to the land
12 which was northward
13 which was covered with large bodies of water a
14 and take possession of the land
15 which was northward
16 and behold they would have carried this plan into effect
17 which would have been a cause to have been mourned
18 but behold Morianton being a man of much passion
19 therefore he was angry with one of his maid servants
20 and he fell upon her and beat her much
21
22 And it came to pass
23 that she fled and came over to the camp of M'runi
24 and told M'runi all things concerning the matter
25 and also concerning their intentions
26 to flee into the land northward
27 now behold the people who were in the land Bountiful
28 or rather M'runi feared
29 that they would listen and obey to the words of Morianton
30 and unite with his people
31 and thus he would obtain possession of those parts of the land
32 which would lay a foundation for serious consequences
33 among the people of Nephi

1 yes which consequences would lead

2 to the overthrow of their liberty

3 therefore M'runi sent an army with their camp

4 to head the people of Morianton

5 to stop their flight into the land northward

6

7 And it came to pass

8 that they did not head them

9 until they had come to the borders of the land Desolation

10 and there they did head them by the narrow pass

11 which led by the sea into the land northward

12 yes by the sea on the west and on the east

13 And it came to pass

14 that the army which was sent by M'runi

15 which was led by a man whose name was Teancum

16 did meet the people of Morianton

17 and so stubborn were the people of Morianton

18 being inspired by his wickedness and his flattering words

19 that a battle commenced between them

20 in the which Teancum did kill Morianton

21 and defeat his army

22 and took them prisoners

23 and returned to the camp of M'runi

24 and thus ended the twenty and fourth year

25 of the reign of the judges over the people of Nephi

26 and thus were the people of Morianton brought back

27 and upon their covenanting to keep the peace

28 they were restored to the land of Morianton

29 and a union took place between them

30 and the people of Lechi

31 and they were also restored to their lands

32

33 And it came to pass

1   that in the same year

2   that the people of Nephi had peace restored unto them

3   that Nephiyahu the second chief judge died

4   having filled the judgment seat

5   with perfect uprightness before Elohiym

6   nevertheless he had refused Almah

7   to take possession of those records

8   and those things which were esteemed

9   by Almah and his fathers to be most sacred

10   therefore Almah had conferred them

11   upon his son Helaman

12

13   Behold it came to pass

14   that the son of Nephiyahu was appointed

15   to fill the judgment seat in the place of his father

16   yes he was appointed chief judge and governor over the people

17   with an oath and sacred ordinance

18   to judge righteously

19   and to keep the peace and the freedom of the people

20   and to grant unto them their sacred privileges

21   to worship YHVH their Elohiym

22   yes to support and maintain the cause of Elohiym all his days

23   and to bring the wicked to justice

24   according to their crime

25   now behold his name was Pahoran

26   and Pahoran did fill the seat of his father

27   and did commence his reign

28   in the end of the twenty and fourth year

29   over the people of Nephi

30

31   And now it came to pass

32   in the commencement of the twenty and fifth year

33   of the reign of the judges over the people of Nephi

1   they having established peace
2   between the people of Lechi
3   and the people of Morianton
4   concerning their lands
5   and having commenced the twenty and fifth year in peace
6   nevertheless they did not long maintain
7   an entire peace in the land
8   for there began to be a contention among the people
9   concerning the chief judge Pahoran
10 for behold there were a part of the people
11 who desired that a few particular points
12 of the mishpatim should be altered
13 but behold Pahoran would not alter
14 nor allow the mishpatim to be altered
15 therefore he did not listen or obey to those
16 who had sent in their voices with their petitions
17 concerning the altering of the mishpatim
18 therefore those who desired
19 that the mishpatim should be altered
20 were angry with him
21 and desired that he should no longer be chief judge over the land
22 therefore there arose a warm dispute concerning the matter
23 but not unto bloodshed
24
25 And it came to pass
26 that those who desired that Pahoran
27 should be dethroned from the judgment seat
28 were called king men
29 for they desired that the mishpatim should be altered
30 in a manner to overthrow the free government
31 and to establish a king over the land
32 and those who desired that Pahoran
33 should remain chief judge over the land

1   took upon them the name of freemen

2   and thus was the division among them

3   for the freemen had sworn or covenanted

4   to maintain their rights and the privileges of their religion

5   by a free government

6

7   And it came to pass

8   that this matter of their contention was settled

9   by the voice of the people

10

11   And it came to pass

12   that the voice of the people came in favor of the freemen

13   and Pahoran retained the judgment seat

14   which caused much rejoicing among the brothers of Pahoran

15   and also many of the people of liberty

16   who also put the king men to silence

17   that they did not oppose

18   but were obliged to maintain the cause of freedom

19   now those who were in favor of kings

20   were those of high birth

21   and they sought to be kings

22   and they were supported by those

23   who sought power and authority over the people

24   but behold this was a critical time

25   for such contentions to be among the people of Nephi

26   for behold Amalick'yahu had again stirred up the hearts

27   of the people of the Lamaniy

28   against the people of the Nephiy

29   and he was gathering together soldiers

30   from all parts of his land

31   and arming them

32   and preparing for war with all diligence

33   for he had sworn to drink the blood of M'runi

1 but behold we shall see that his promise
2 which he made was rash
3 nevertheless he did prepare himself and his armies
4 to come to battle against the Nephiy
5 now his armies were not so great
6 as they had previously been
7 because of the many thousands
8 who had been killed by the hand of the Nephiy
9 but notwithstanding their great loss Amalick'yahu
10 had gathered together a wonderfully great army insomuch
11 that he feared not to come down to the land of Zarahemla
12 Yes even Amalick'yahu did himself come down
13 at the head of the Lamaniy
14 and it was in the twenty and fifth year
15 of the reign of the judges
16 and it was at the same time that they had begun
17 to settle the affairs of their contentions
18 concerning the chief judge Pahoran
19
20 And it came to pass
21 that when the men who were called king men had heard
22 that the Lamaniy were coming down to battle against them
23 they were glad in their hearts
24 and they refused to take up arms
25 for they were so angry with the chief judge
26 and also with the people of liberty
27 that they would not take up arms
28 to defend their country
29
30 And it came to pass
31 that when M'runi saw this
32 and also saw that the Lamaniy were coming
33 into the borders of the land

1   he was exceedingly angry
2   because of the stubbornness of those people
3   whom he had labored with so much diligence to preserve
4   yes he was exceedingly angry
5   his soul was filled with anger against them
6
7   And it came to pass
8   that he sent a petition with the voice of the people
9   unto the governor of the land desiring
10   that he should read it
11   and give him M'runi power
12   to compel those dissenters
13   to defend their country
14   or to put them to death
15   for it was his first care
16   to put an end
17   to such contentions and dissensions among the people
18   for behold this had been previously a cause
19   of all their destruction
20
21   And it came to pass
22   that it was granted
23   according to the voice of the people
24
25   And it came to pass
26   that M'runi commanded
27   that his army should go against those king men
28   to pull down their pride and their nobility
29   and level them with the earth
30   or they should take up arms
31   and support the cause of liberty
32
33   And it came to pass

1   that the armies did march forth against them
2   and they did pull down
3   their pride and their nobility insomuch
4   that as they did lift their weapons of war
5   to fight against the men of M'runi
6   they were cut down
7   and leveled to the earth
8
9   And it came to pass
10 that there were four thousand of those dissenters
11 who were cut down by the sword
12 and those of their leaders
13 who were not killed in battle
14 were taken and cast into prison
15 for there was no time for their trials at this period
16 and the remainder of those dissenters
17 rather than be struck down to the earth by the sword
18 yielded to the standard of liberty
19 and were compelled to hoist the title of liberty
20 upon their towers and in their cities
21 and to take up arms in defense of their country
22 and thus M'runi put an end to those king men
23 that there were not any known
24 by the title of king men
25 and thus he put an end
26 to the stubbornness and the pride of those people
27 who professed the blood of nobility
28 but they were brought down
29 to humble themselves like unto their brothers
30 and to fight valiantly for their freedom from bondage
31
32 Behold it came to pass
33 that while M'runi was thus breaking down

1   the wars and contentions among his own people
2   and subjecting them to peace and civilization
3   and making regulations to prepare for war against the Lamaniy
4   behold the Lamaniy had come into the land of M'runi
5   which was in the borders by the seashore
6
7   And it came to pass
8   that the Nephiy were not sufficiently strong in the city of M'runi
9   therefore Amalick'yahu did drive them killing many
10
11 And it came to pass
12 that Amalick'yahu took possession of the city
13 yes possession of all their fortifications
14 and those who fled out of the city of M'runi came
15 to the city of Nephiyah
16 and also the people of the city of Lechi
17 gathered themselves together and made preparations
18 and were ready to receive the Lamaniy to battle
19
20 But it came to pass
21 that Amalick'yahu would not allow the Lamaniy
22 to go against the city of Nephiyah to battle
23 but kept them down by the seashore leaving men
24 in every city to maintain and defend it
25 and thus he went on taking possession of many cities
26 the city of Nephiyah
27 and the city of Lechi
28 and the city of Morianton
29 and the city of Omner
30 and the city of Gid
31 and the city of Mulek
32 all of which were on the east borders by the seashore
33 and thus had the Lamaniy obtained

1 by the cunning of Amalick'yahu
2 so many cities by their numberless armies
3 all of which were strongly fortified
4 after the manner of the fortifications of M'runi
5 all of which afforded strongholds for the Lamaniy
6
7 And it came to pass
8 that they marched to the borders of the land Bountiful
9 driving the Nephiy before them
10 and killing many
11
12 But it came to pass that
13 they were met by Teancum
14 who had killed Morianton
15 and had headed his people in his flight
16
17 And it came to pass
18 that he headed Amalick'yahu also
19 as he was marching forth with his numerous army
20 that he might take possession of the land Bountiful
21 and also the land northward
22 but behold he met with a disappointment
23 by being repulsed by Teancum and his men
24 for they were great warriors
25 for every man of Teancum did exceed the Lamaniy
26 in their strength and in their skill of war insomuch
27 that they did gain advantage over the Lamaniy
28
29 And it came to pass
30 that they did destroy them insomuch
31 that they did kill them
32 even until it was dark
33

1 And it came to pass
2 that Teancum and his men did pitch their tents
3 in the borders of the land Bountiful
4 and Amalick'yahu did pitch his tents
5 in the borders on the beach by the seashore
6 and after this manner were they driven
7

8 And it came to pass
9 that when the night had come
10 Teancum and his servant darted forth
11 and went out by night
12 and went into the camp of Amalick'yahu
13 and behold sleep had overpowered them
14 because of their much fatigue
15 which was caused by the labors and heat of the day
16

17 And it came to pass
18 that Teancum went secretly into the tent of the king
19 and put a javelin to his heart
20 and he did cause the death of the king immediately
21 that he did not awake his servants
22 and he returned again secretly to his own camp
23 and behold his men were asleep
24 and he awoke them and told them
25 all the things that he had done
26 and he caused that his armies should stand in readiness
27 for fear that the Lamaniy had awakened
28 and should come upon them
29 and thus ended the twenty and fifth year
30 of the reign of the judges over the people of Nephi
31 and thus ended the days of Amalick'yahu
32

33 And now it came to pass

1 in the twenty and sixth year
2 of the reign of the judges over the people of Nephi
3 behold when the Lamaniy awoke
4 on the first morning of the first month
5 behold they found Amalick'yahu was dead in his own tent
6 and they also saw that Teancum was ready
7 to give them battle on that day
8 and now when the Lamaniy saw this
9 they were afraid and they abandoned their design
10 in marching into the land northward
11 and retreated with all their army into the city of Mulek
12 and sought protection in their fortifications
13
14 And it came to pass
15 that the brother of Amalick'yahu
16 was appointed king over the people
17 and his name was Ammoron
18 thus king Ammoron the brother of king Amalick'yahu
19 was appointed to reign in his place
20
21 And it came to pass
22 that he did command
23 that his people should maintain those cities
24 which they had taken by the shedding of blood
25 for they had not taken any cities
26 except they had lost much blood
27 and now Teancum saw that the Lamaniy were determined
28 to maintain those cities which they had taken
29 and those parts of the land which they had obtained possession of
30 and also seeing the enormity of their number
31 Teancum thought it was not necessary
32 that he should attempt to attack them in their forts
33 but he kept his men round about

1   as if making preparations for war
2   yes and truly he was preparing
3   to defend himself against them
4   by casting up walls round about
5   and preparing places of defense
6
7   And it came to pass
8   that he kept thus preparing for war
9   until M'runi had sent a large number of men
10 to strengthen his army
11 and M'runi also sent orders unto him
12 that he should retain all the prisoners
13 who fell into his hands
14 for as the Lamaniy had taken many prisoners
15 that he should retain all the prisoners of the Lamaniy
16 as a ransom for those whom the Lamaniy had taken
17 and he also sent orders unto him
18 that he should fortify the land Bountiful
19 and secure the narrow pass
20 which led into the land northward
21 for fear that the Lamaniy should obtain that point
22 and should have power to destroy them on every side
23 and M'runi also sent unto him desiring him
24 that he would be faithful in maintaining that quarter of the land
25 and that he would seek every opportunity
26 to scourge the Lamaniy in that quarter
27 as much as was in his power
28 that perhaps he might take again
29 by stratagem or some other way
30 those cities which had been taken out of their hands
31 and that he also would fortify and strengthen the cities round about
32 which had not fallen into the hands of the Lamaniy
33 and he also said unto him

1
2 "I would come unto you
3 but behold the Lamaniy are upon us
4 in the borders of the land by the west sea
5 and behold I go against them
6   therefore I cannot come unto you"
7
8 now the king Ammoron had departed out
9 of the land of Zarahemla
10 and had made known unto the queen
11 concerning the death of his brother
12 and had gathered together a large number of men
13 and had marched forth against the Nephiy
14 on the borders by the west sea
15 and thus he was endeavoring to destroy the Nephiy
16 and to draw away a part of their forces
17 to that part of the land
18 while he had commanded those whom he had left
19 to possess the cities which he had taken
20 that they should also destroy the Nephiy
21 on the borders by the east sea
22 and should take possession of their lands
23 as much as it was in their power
24 according to the power of their armies
25 and thus were the Nephiy in those dangerous circumstances
26 in the ending of the twenty and sixth year
27 of the reign of the judges over the people of Nephi
28
29 But behold it came to pass
30 in the twenty and seventh year
31 of the reign of the judges
32 that Teancum by the command of M'runi
33 who had established armies

1 to protect the south and the west borders of the land
2 and had begun his march towards the land Bountiful
3 that he might assist Teancum with his men
4 in retaking the cities which they had lost
5
6 And it came to pass
7 that Teancum had received orders
8 to make an attack upon the city of Mulek
9 and retake it if it were possible
10
11 And it came to pass
12 that Teancum made preparations
13 to make an attack upon the city of Mulek
14 and march forth with his army against the Lamaniy
15 but he saw that it was impossible
16 that he could overpower them
17 while they were in their fortifications
18 therefore he abandoned his designs
19 and returned again to the city Bountiful
20 to wait for the coming of M'runi
21 that he might receive strength to his army
22
23 And it came to pass
24 that M'runi did arrive with his army at the land of Bountiful
25 in the latter end of the twenty and seventh year
26 of the reign of the judges over the people of Nephi
27 and in the commencement of the twenty and eighth year
28 M'runi and Teancum
29 and many of the sarim held a council of war
30 what they should do to cause the Lamaniy
31 to come out against them to battle
32 or that they might by some means flatter them
33 out of their strongholds

1 that they might gain advantage over them

2 and take again the city of Mulek

3

4 And it came to pass

5 they sent embassies to the army of the Lamaniy

6 which protected the city of Mulek

7 to their leader whose name was Yacov desiring him

8 that he would come out with his armies

9 to meet them upon the plains

10 between the two cities

11 but behold Yacov

12 who was a Zoramiy would not come out with his army

13 to meet them upon the plains

14

15 And it came to pass

16 that M'runi having no hopes

17 of meeting them upon fair grounds

18 therefore he resolved upon a plan

19 that he might decoy the Lamaniy

20 out of their strongholds

21 therefore he caused that Teancum

22 should take a small number of men

23 and march down near the seashore

24 and M'runi and his army by night marched

25 in the wilderness on the west of the city Mulek

26 and thus on the next day

27 when the guards of the Lamaniy had discovered Teancum

28 they ran and told it unto Yacov their leader

29

30 And it came to pass

31 that the armies of the Lamaniy

32 did march forth against Teancum

33 supposing by their numbers

1   to overpower Teancum

2   because of the smallness of his numbers

3   and as Teancum saw the armies of the Lamaniy

4   coming out against him he began to retreat down

5   by the seashore northward

6

7   And it came to pass

8   that when the Lamaniy saw that he began to flee

9   they took courage and pursued them with vigor

10 and while Teancum was thus leading away the Lamaniy

11 who were pursuing them in vain

12 behold M'runi commanded that a part of his army

13 who were with him should march forth into the city

14 and take possession of it

15 and thus they did

16 and killed all those who had been left to protect the city

17 yes all those who would not yield up their weapons of war

18 and thus M'runi had obtained possession of the city Mulek

19 with a part of his army

20 while he marched with the remainder

21 to meet the Lamaniy

22 when they should return from the pursuit of Teancum

23

24 And it came to pass that the Lamaniy did pursue Teancum

25 until they came near the city Bountiful

26 and then they were met by Lechi

27 and a small army which had been left

28 to protect the city Bountiful

29 and now behold when the sarim of the Lamaniy

30 had beheld Lechi with his army coming against them

31 they fled in much confusion

32 for fear that perhaps they should not obtain the city Mulek

33 before Lechi should overtake them

1 for they were weary because of their march

2 and the men of Lechi were fresh

3 now the Lamaniy did not know

4 that M'runi had been in their rear with his army

5 and all they feared was Lechi and his men

6 now Lechi did not desire to overtake them

7 until they should meet M'runi and his army

8

9 And it came to pass

10 that before the Lamaniy had retreated far

11 they were surrounded by the Nephiy

12 by the men of M'runi on one hand

13 and the men of Lechi on the other

14 all of whom were fresh and full of strength

15 but the Lamaniy were weary

16 because of their long march

17 and M'runi commanded his men

18 that they should fall upon them

19 until they had given up their weapons of war

20

21 And it came to pass

22 that Yacov being their leader

23 being also a Zoramim

24 and having an unconquerable ruach

25 he led the Lamaniy forth to battle

26 with exceeding fury against M'runi

27 M'runi being in their course of march

28 therefore Yacov was determined to kill them

29 and cut his way through to the city of Mulek

30 but behold M'runi and his men were more powerful

31 therefore they did not give way before the Lamaniy

32

33 And it came to pass

1   that they fought on both hands with exceeding fury

2   and there were many killed on both sides

3   yes and M'runi was wounded

4   and Yacov was killed

5   and Lechi pressed upon their rear

6   with such fury with his strong men

7   that the Lamaniy in the rear delivered up their weapons of war

8   and the remainder of them being much confused knew not

9   where to go or to strike

10   now M'runi seeing their confusion

11   he said unto them

12

13   "If you will bring forth your weapons of war

14   and deliver them up

15   behold we will forbear shedding your blood"

16

17   And it came to pass

18   that when the Lamaniy had heard these words

19   their sarim

20   all those who were not killed came forth

21   and threw down their weapons of war

22   at the feet of M'runi

23   and also commanded their men

24   that they should do the same

25   but behold there were many that would not

26   and those who would not deliver up their swords

27   were taken and bound

28   and their weapons of war were taken from them

29   and they were compelled to march with their brothers forth

30   into the land Bountiful

31   and now the number of prisoners who were taken

32   exceeded more than the number

33   of those who had been killed

1 yes more than those who had been killed

2 on both sides

3

4 And it came to pass

5 that they did set guards over the prisoners of the Lamaniy

6 and did compel them to go forth

7 and bury their dead

8 yes and also the dead of the Nephiy who were killed

9 and M'runi placed men over them to guard them

10 while they should perform their labors

11 and M'runi went to the city of Mulek with Lechi

12 and took command of the city

13 and gave it unto Lechi

14 now behold this Lechi was a man

15 who had been with M'runi in the more part of all his battles

16 and he was a man like unto M'runi

17 and they rejoiced in each other's safety

18 yes they were beloved by each other

19 and also beloved by all the people of Nephi

20

21 And it came to pass

22 that after the Lamaniy had finished burying their dead

23 and also the dead of the Nephiy

24 they were marched back into the land Bountiful

25 and Teancum by the orders of M'runi caused

26 that they should commence laboring

27 in digging a ditch round about the land

28 or the city Bountiful

29 and he caused that they should build a breastwork of timbers

30 upon the inner bank of the ditch

31 and they cast up dirt out of the ditch

32 against the breastwork of timbers

33 and thus they did cause the Lamaniy to labor

1 until they had encircled the city of Bountiful round about
2 with a strong wall of timbers and earth
3 to an exceeding height
4 and this city became an exceeding stronghold ever after
5 and in this city they did guard the prisoners of the Lamaniy
6 yes even within a wall
7 which they had caused them to build
8 with their own hands
9 now M'runi was compelled to cause the Lamaniy to labor
10 because it was easy to guard them while at their labor
11 and he desired all his forces
12 when he should make an attack upon the Lamaniy
13
14 And it came to pass
15 that M'runi had thus gained a victory
16 over one of the greatest of the armies of the Lamaniy
17 and had obtained possession of the city of Mulek
18 which was one of the strongest holds of the Lamaniy
19 in the land of Nephi
20 and thus he had also built a stronghold
21 to retain his prisoners
22
23 And it came to pass
24 that he did no more attempt a battle
25 with the Lamaniy in that year
26 but he did employ his men in preparing for war
27 yes and in making fortifications
28 to guard against the Lamaniy
29 yes and also delivering
30 their women and their children
31 from famine and affliction
32 and providing food for their armies
33

1 And now it came to pass

2 that the armies of the Lamaniy

3 on the west sea south

4 while in the absence of M'runi

5 on account of some intrigue amongst the Nephiy

6 which caused dissensions amongst them

7 had gained some ground over the Nephiy

8 yes insomuch that they had obtained possession

9 of a number of their cities in that part of the land

10 and thus because of lawlessness among themselves

11 yes because of dissensions and intrigue among themselves

12 they were placed in the most dangerous circumstances

13

14 And now behold I have somewhat to say

15 concerning the people of Ammon

16 who in the beginning were Lamaniy

17 but by Ammon and his brothers

18 or rather by the power and word of Elohiym

19 they had been converted unto YHVH

20 and they had been brought down into the land of Zarahemla

21 and had ever since been protected by the Nephiy

22 and because of their oath

23 they had been kept from taking up arms against their brothers

24 for they had taken an oath

25 that they never would shed blood more

26 and according to their oath they would have perished

27 yes they would have allowed themselves

28 to have fallen into the hands of their brothers had it not been

29 for the pity and the exceeding love

30 which Ammon and his brothers had had for them

31 and for this cause

32 they were brought down into the land of Zarahemla

33 and they ever had been protected by the Nephiy

1
2 But it came to pass
3 that when they saw the danger
4 and the many afflictions and tribulations
5 which the Nephiy bore for them
6 they were moved with compassion
7 and desired to take up arms
8 in the defense of their country
9 but behold as they were about to take their weapons of war
10 they were overpowered by the persuasions
11 of Helaman and his brothers
12 for they were about to break the oath
13 which they had made
14 and Helaman feared that by so doing
15 they should lose their souls
16 therefore all those who had entered into this covenant were compelled
17 to behold their brothers wade through their afflictions
18 in their dangerous circumstances at this time
19
20 But behold it came to pass
21 they had many sons who had not entered into a covenant
22 that they would not take their weapons of war
23 to defend themselves against their enemies
24 therefore they did assemble themselves together at this time
25 as many as were able to take up arms
26 and they called themselves Nephiy
27 and they entered into a covenant
28 to fight for the liberty of the Nephiy
29 yes to protect the land unto the laying down of their lives
30 yes even they covenanted
31 that they never would give up their liberty
32 but they would fight in all cases
33 to protect the Nephiy and themselves

1   from bondage

2

3   Now behold there were two thousand of those young men

4   who entered into this covenant

5   and took their weapons of war

6   to defend their country

7   and now behold

8   as they never had previously been a disadvantage to the Nephiy

9   they became now at this period of time also a great support

10 for they took their weapons of war

11 and they desired that Helaman should be their leader

12 and they were all young men

13 and they were exceedingly valiant for courage

14 and also for strength and activity

15 but behold this was not all

16 they were men who were true at all times

17 in whatever thing they were entrusted

18 Yes they were men of truth and soberness

19 for they had been taught to keep the mitzvot of Elohiym

20 and to walk uprightly before him

21

22 And now it came to pass

23 that Helaman did march at the head

24 of his two thousand young soldiers

25 to the support of the people

26 in the borders of the land

27 on the south by the west sea

28 and thus ended the twenty and eighth year

29 of the reign of the judges over the people of Nephi

30

31 And now it came to pass

32 in the commencement of the twenty and ninth year

33 of the judges

1   that Ammoron sent unto M'runi desiring

2   that he would exchange prisoners

3

4   And it came to pass

5   that M'runi felt to rejoice exceedingly at this request

6   for he desired the provisions

7   which were imparted for the support of the Lamaniy prisoners

8   for the support of his own people

9   and he also desired his own people

10   for the strengthening of his army

11   now the Lamaniy had taken many women and children

12   and there was not a woman nor a child among all the prisoners of M'runi

13   or the prisoners whom M'runi had taken

14   therefore M'runi resolved upon a plan

15   to obtain as many prisoners of the Nephiy

16   from the Lamaniy as it were possible

17   therefore he wrote a scroll

18   and sent it by the servant of Ammoron

19   the same who had brought a scroll to M'runi

20   now these are the words which he wrote unto Ammoron saying

21

22   "Behold Ammoron I have written unto you somewhat

23   concerning this war which you have waged against my people

24   or rather which your brother has waged against them

25   and which you are still determined to carry on after his death

26   behold I would tell you somewhat

27   concerning the justice of Elohiym

28   and the sword of his almighty wrath

29   which does hang over you

30   except you repent and withdraw your armies

31   into your own lands

32   or the land of your possessions

33   which is the land of Nephi

1

2 Yes I would tell you these things

3 if you were capable of listening unto them

4 yes I would tell you concerning that awful sheol

5 that awaits to receive such murderers

6 as you and your brother have been

7 except you repent and withdraw your murderous purposes

8 and return with your armies to your own lands

9 but as you have once rejected these things

10 and have fought against the people of YHVH

11 even so I may expect you will do it again

12

13 And now behold we are prepared to receive you

14 yes and except you withdraw your purposes

15 behold you will pull down the wrath of that Elohiym

16 whom you have rejected upon you

17 even to your utter destruction

18 but as YHVH lives

19 our armies shall come upon you

20 except you withdraw

21 and you shall soon be visited with death

22 for we will retain our cities and our lands

23 yes and we will maintain our religion

24 and the cause of our Elohiym

25

26 but behold I think that I talk to you

27 concerning these things in vain

28 or I think that you are a child of sheol

29 therefore I will close my communication by telling you

30 that I will not exchange prisoners

31 except it be on conditions

32 that you will deliver up a man and his wife and his children

33 for one prisoner

1 if this be the case that you will do it

2 I will exchange

3 and behold if you do not this

4 I will come against you with my armies

5 yes even I will arm my women and my children

6 and I will come against you

7 and I will follow you even into your own land

8 which is the land of our first inheritance

9 yes and it shall be blood for blood

10 yes life for life

11 and I will give you battle

12 even until you are destroyed

13 from off the face of the earth

14

15 Behold I am in my anger

16 and also my people

17 you have sought to murder us

18 and we have only sought to defend ourselves

19 but behold if you seek to destroy us more

20 we will seek to destroy you

21 yes and we will seek our land

22 the land of our first inheritance

23 now I close my communication

24 I am M'runi

25 I am a leader of the people of the Nephiy"

26

27 Now it came to pass

28 that Ammoron when he had received this communicatoin was angry

29 and he wrote another scroll unto M'runi

30 and these are the words which he wrote saying

31

32 " I am Ammoron the king of the Lamaniy

33 I am the brother of Amalick'yahu

1 whom you have murdered
2 behold I will avenge his blood upon you
3 yes and I will come upon you with my armies
4 for I fear not your threats
5
6 For behold your fathers did wrong their brothers insomuch
7 that they did rob them of their right to the government
8 when it rightly belonged unto them
9 and now behold if you will lay down your arms
10 and subject yourselves to be governed by those
11 to whom the government does rightly belong
12 then will I cause that my people shall lay down their weapons
13 and shall be at war no more
14
15 Behold you have breathed out
16 many threats against me and my people
17 but behold we fear not your threats
18 nevertheless I will grant to exchange prisoners
19 according to your request gladly
20 that I may preserve my food
21 for my men of war
22 and we will wage a war
23 which shall be eternal
24 either to the subjecting the Nephiy to our authority
25 or to their eternal extinction
26
27 And as concerning that Elohiym
28 whom you say we have rejected
29 behold we know not such a being
30 neither do you
31 but if it so be that there is such a being
32 we know not
33 but that he has made us as well as you

1   and if it so be that there is an evil one and sheol

2   behold will he not send you there

3   to dwell with my brother

4   whom you have murdered

5   whom you have hinted

6   that he has gone to such a place

7   but behold these things matter not

8

9   I am Ammoron

10 and a descendant of Zoram

11 whom your fathers compelled

12 and brought out of Yerushalayim

13 and behold now I am a bold Lamaniy

14 behold this war has been waged

15 to avenge their wrongs

16 and to maintain

17 and to obtain their rights to the government

18 and I close my communication to M'runi"

19

20 Now it came to pass

21 that when M'runi had received this communication

22 he was more angry

23 because he knew that Ammoron had a perfect knowledge of his fraud

24 yes he knew that Ammoron knew

25 that it was not a just cause

26 that had caused him to wage a war

27 against the people of Nephi

28 and he said

29

30 "behold I will not exchange prisoners with Ammoron

31 except he will withdraw his purpose

32 as I have stated in my communication

33 for I will not grant unto him

1 that he shall have any more power

2 than what he has got

3

4 Behold I know the place

5 where the Lamaniy do guard my people

6 whom they have taken prisoners

7 and as Ammoron would not grant unto me

8 according to my communication

9 behold I will give unto him according to my words

10 yes I will seek death among them

11 until they shall sue for peace"

12

13 And now it came to pass

14 that when M'runi had said these words he caused

15 that a search should be made among his men

16 that perhaps he might find a man

17 who was a descendant of Laman among them

18

19 And it came to pass

20 that they found one whose name was Laman

21 and he was one of the servants of the king

22 who was murdered by Amalick'yahu

23 now M'runi caused that Laman a

24 and a small number of his men

25 should go forth unto the guards

26 who were over the Nephiy

27 now the Nephiy were guarded in the city of Gid

28 therefore M'runi appointed Laman

29 and caused that a small number of men

30 should go with him

31 and when it was evening Laman went to the guards

32 who were over the Nephiy

33 and behold they saw him coming

1 and they hailed him but he said unto them
2
3 "Fear not
4 behold I am a Lamaniy
5 behold we have escaped from the Nephiy
6 and they sleep
7 and behold we have taken of their wine
8 and brought with us"
9
10 Now when the Lamaniy heard these words
11 they received him with joy
12 and they said unto him
13
14 "Give us of your wine
15 that we may drink
16 we are glad
17 that you have thus taken wine with you
18 for we are weary"
19
20 but Laman said unto them
21
22 "Let us keep of our wine
23 until we go against the Nephiy to battle"
24
25 But this saying only made them want more
26 to drink of the wine
27 for said they
28
29 "We are weary
30 therefore let us take of the wine
31 and by and by we shall receive wine for our rations
32 which will strengthen us to go against the Nephiy"
33

1   and Laman said unto them

2

3   "You may do according to your desires"

4

5   And it came to pass

6   that they did take of the wine freely

7   and it was pleasant to their taste

8   therefore they took of it more freely

9   and it was strong having been prepared in its strength

10

11   And it came to pass

12   they did drink and were merry

13   and by and by

14   they were all drunk

15   and now when Laman and his men saw

16   that they were all drunk

17   and were in a deep sleep

18   they returned to M'runi

19   and told him all the things

20   that had happened

21   and now this was according to the design of M'runi

22   and M'runi had prepared his men with weapons of war

23   and he went to the city Gid

24   while the Lamaniy were in a deep sleep and drunk

25   and cast in weapons of war unto the prisoners insomuch

26   that they were all armed

27   Yes even to their women and all those of their children

28   as many as were able to use a weapon of war

29   when M'runi had armed all those prisoners

30   and all those things were done in a profound silence

31   but had they awakened the Lamaniy

32   behold they were drunk

33   and the Nephiy could have killed them

1 but behold this was not the desire of M'runi

2 he did not delight in murder or bloodshed

3 but he delighted in the saving of his people from destruction

4 and for this cause he might not bring upon him injustice

5 he would not fall upon the Lamaniy

6 and destroy them in their drunkenness

7 but he had obtained his desires

8 for he had armed those prisoners of the Nephiy

9 who were within the wall of the city

10 and had given them power

11 to gain possession of those parts

12 which were within the walls

13 and then he caused the men who were with him

14 to withdraw a step back from them

15 and surround the armies of the Lamaniy

16 now behold this was done in the nighttime

17 so that when the Lamaniy awoke in the morning

18 they beheld that they were surrounded by the Nephiy without

19 and that their prisoners were armed within

20

21 And thus they saw that the Nephiy had power over them

22 and in these circumstances

23 they found that it was not necessary

24 that they should fight with the Nephiy

25 therefore their sarim demanded their weapons of war

26 and they brought them forth

27 and cast them at the feet of the Nephiy pleading for mercy

28 now behold this was the desire of M'runi

29 he took them prisoners of war

30 and took possession of the city

31 and caused that all the prisoners should be liberated

32 who were Nephiy

33 and they did join the army of M'runi

1 and were a great strength to his army

2

3 And it came to pass

4 that he did cause the Lamaniy

5 whom he had taken prisoners

6 that they should commence a labor

7 in strengthening the fortifications round about the city Gid

8

9 And it came to pass

10 that when he had fortified the city Gid

11 according to his desires he caused

12 that his prisoners should be taken to the city Bountiful

13 and he also guarded that city

14 with an exceedingly strong force

15

16 And it came to pass

17 that they did

18 despite all of the schemes of the Lamaniy keep and protect

19 all the prisoners whom they had taken

20 and also maintain all the ground and the advantage

21 which they had retaken

22

23 And it came to pass

24 that the Nephiy began again to be victorious

25 and to reclaim their rights and their privileges

26 many times did the Lamaniy attempt

27 to encircle them about by night

28 but in these attempts

29 they did lose many prisoners

30 and many times did they attempt

31 to administer of their wine to the Nephiy

32 that they might destroy them

33 with poison or with drunkenness

1   but behold the Nephiy were not slow

2   to remember YHVH their Elohiym

3   in this their time of affliction

4   they could not be taken in their snares

5   yes they would not partake of their wine

6   except they had first given to some of the Lamaniy prisoners

7   and they were thus cautious

8   that no poison should be administered among them

9   for if their wine would poison a Lamaniy

10 it would also poison a Nephiy

11 and thus they did try all their liquors

12

13 And now it came to pass

14 that it was necessary for M'runi to make preparations

15 to attack the city Morianton

16 for behold the Lamaniy had

17 by their labors fortified the city Morianton

18 until it had become an exceeding stronghold

19 and they were continually bringing new forces into that city

20 and also new supplies of provisions

21 and thus ended the twenty and ninth year

22 of the reign of the judges over the people of Nephi

23

24 And now it came to pass

25 in the commencement of the thirtieth year

26 of the reign of the judges

27 on the second day in the first month

28 M'runi received a communication from Helaman

29 stating the affairs of the people

30 in that quarter of the land

31 and these are the words which he wrote saying

32

33 "My dearly beloved brother M'runi

1 as well in YHVH
2 as in the tribulations of our warfare
3 behold my beloved brother
4 I have somewhat to tell you
5 concerning our warfare in this part of the land
6
7 Behold two thousand of the sons of those men
8 whom Ammon brought down out of the land of Nephi
9 now you have known that these were descendants of Laman
10 who was the eldest son of our father Lechi
11 now I need not rehearse unto you
12 concerning their traditions or their unbelief
13 for you know concerning all these things
14 therefore it satisfies me
15 that I tell you that two thousand of these young men
16 have taken their weapons of war
17 and desired that I should be their leader
18 and we have come forth to defend our country
19
20 And now you also know concerning the covenant
21 which their fathers made
22 that they would not take up their weapons of war
23 against their brothers to shed blood
24 but in the twenty and sixth year
25 when they saw our afflictions and our tribulations
26 for them they were about to break the covenant
27 which they had made
28 and take up their weapons of war in our defense
29 but I would not allow them
30 that they should break this covenant
31 which they had made supposing
32 that Elohiym would strengthen us insomuch
33 that we should not allow more

1 because of the fulfilling the oath
2 which they had taken
3
4 But behold here is one thing
5 in which we may have great joy
6 for behold in the twenty and sixth year
7 I Helaman did march at the head
8 of these two thousand young men
9 to the city of Yehudah to assist Antipus
10 whom you had appointed a leader
11 over the people of that part of the land
12 and I did join my two thousand sons
13 for they are worthy to be called sons
14 to the army of Antipus
15 in which strength Antipus did rejoice exceedingly
16 for behold his army had been reduced by the Lamaniy
17 because their forces had killed a vast number of our men
18 for which cause we have to mourn
19
20 Nevertheless we may console ourselves in this point
21 that they have died in the cause
22 of their country and of their Elohiym
23 yes and they are happy
24 and the Lamaniy had also retained many prisoners
25 all of whom are sarim
26 for none other have they spared alive
27 and we suppose
28 that they are now at this time in the land of Nephi
29 it is so
30 if they are not killed
31 and now these are the cities
32 of which the Lamaniy have obtained possession
33 by the shedding of the blood

1 of so many of our valiant men

2 the land of Manti or the city of Manti

3 and the city of Zeezrom

4 and the city of Qum'ani

5 and the city of Paniym-parah[18]

6 and these are the cities which they possessed

7 when I arrived at the city of Yehudah

8 and I found Antipus and his men toiling with their might

9 to fortify the city

10 Yes and they were depressed in body as well as in ruach

11 for they had fought valiantly by day

12 and toiled by night to maintain their cities

13 and thus they had suffered great afflictions of every kind

14 and now they were determined to conquer in this place or die

15 therefore you may well suppose

16 that this little force which I brought with me

17 yes those sons of my gave them great hopes and much joy

18

19 And now it came to pass

20 that when the Lamaniy saw

21 that Antipus had received a greater strength to his army

22 they were compelled by the orders of Ammoron

23 to not come against the city of Yehudah

24 or against us to battle

25 and thus were we favored of YHVH

26 for had they come upon us in this our weakness

27 they might have perhaps destroyed our little army

28 but thus were we preserved

29 they were commanded by Ammoron

30 to maintain those cities which they had taken

31 and thus ended the twenty and sixth year

32 and in the commencement of the twenty and seventh year

---

[18] Parah- bearing much fruit

1 we had prepared our city and ourselves for defense

2 now we desired that the Lamaniy should come upon us

3 for we did not desire to make an attack upon them in their strongholds

4

5 And it came to pass

6 that we kept spies out round about

7 to watch the movements of the Lamaniy

8 that they might not pass us

9 by night nor by day to make an attack

10 upon our other cities

11 which were on the northward

12 for we knew in those cities

13 they were not sufficiently strong to meet them

14 therefore we desired if they should pass by us

15 to fall upon them in their rear

16 and thus bring them up in the rear

17 at the same time they were met in the front

18 we supposed that we could overpower them

19 but behold we were disappointed in this our desire

20 they did not pass by us with their whole army

21 neither did they with a part

22 lest they should not be sufficiently strong

23 and they should fall

24 neither did they march down against the city of Zarahemla

25 neither did they cross the head of Tzidon

26 over to the city of Nephiyah

27 and thus with their forces

28 they were determined to maintain those cities

29 which they had taken

30

31 And now it came to pass

32 in the second month of this year

33 there was brought unto us many provisions

1 from the fathers of those

2 my two thousand sons

3 and also there were sent two thousand men unto us

4 from the land of Zarahemla

5 and thus we were prepared

6 with ten thousand men and provisions for them

7 and also for their wives and their children

8 and the Lamaniy thus seeing our forces increase daily

9 and provisions arrive for our support

10 they began to be fearful

11 and began to rush forth if it were possible

12 to put an end to our receiving provisions and strength

13 now when we saw that the Lamaniy began to grow uneasy

14 as a consequence we desired to bring a plan into effect upon them

15 therefore Antipus ordered

16 that I should march forth with my little sons

17 to a neighboring city

18 as if we were carrying provisions

19 to a neighboring city

20 and we were to march near the city of Paniym-parah

21 as if we were going to the city

22 beyond in the borders by the seashore

23

24 And it came to pass

25 that we did march forth

26 as if with our provisions

27 to go to that city

28

29 And it came to pass

30 that Antipus did march forth

31 with a part of his army

32 leaving the remainder to maintain the city

33 but he did not march forth

1   until I had gone forth with my little army

2   and came near the city Paniym-parah

3   and now in the city Paniym-parah

4   were stationed the strongest army of the Lamaniy

5   yes the most numerous

6

7   And it came to pass

8   that when they had been informed by their spies

9   they came forth with their army

10   and marched against us

11

12   And it came to pass

13   that we did flee before them northward

14   and thus we did lead away

15   the most powerful army of the Lamaniy

16   Yes even to a considerable distance insomuch

17   that when they saw the army of Antipus

18   pursuing them with their might

19   they did not turn to the right nor to the left

20   but pursued their march in a straight course after us

21   and as we suppose it was their intent to kill us

22   before Antipus should overtake them

23   and this that they might not be surrounded by our people

24   and now Antipus beholding our danger

25   did speed the march of his army

26   but behold it was night

27   therefore they did not overtake us

28   neither did Antipus overtake them

29   therefore we did camp for the night

30

31   And it came to pass

32   that before the dawn of the morning

33   behold the Lamaniy were pursuing us

1   now we were not sufficiently strong to contend with them
2   yes I would not allow that my little sons
3   should fall into their hands
4   therefore we did continue our march
5   and we took our march into the wilderness
6   now they did not turn to the right
7   nor to the left
8   for fear that they should be surrounded
9   neither would I turn to the right
10 nor to the left
11 for fear that they should overtake me
12 and we could not stand against them
13 or we would be killed
14 and they would make their escape
15 and thus we did flee all that day into the wilderness
16 even until it was dark
17
18 And it came to pass
19 that again when the light of the morning came
20 we saw the Lamaniy upon us
21 and we did flee before them
22
23 But it came to pass
24 that they did not pursue us far
25 before they stopped
26 and it was in the morning
27 of the third day of the seventh month
28 and now whether they were overtaken by Antipus
29 we knew not
30 but I said unto my men
31
32 'Behold we know not
33 but they have stopped for the purpose

1 that we should come against them
2 that they might catch us in their trap
3 therefore what say you my sons will you go
4 against them to battle'
5
6 And now I say unto you
7 my beloved brother M'runi
8 that never had I seen so great courage
9 no not among all the Nephiy
10 for as I had ever called them my sons
11 for they were all of them very young
12 even so they said unto me
13
14 'Father behold our Elohiym is with us
15 and he will not allow that we should fall
16 then let us go forth
17 we would not kill our brothers
18 if they would let us alone
19 therefore let us go
20 for fear that they should overpower the army of Antipus'
21
22 Now they never had fought
23 yet they did not fear death
24 and they did think more upon the liberty of their fathers
25 than they did upon their lives
26 yes they had been taught by their mothers
27 that if they did not doubt Elohiym would deliver them
28
29 and they rehearsed unto me the words of their mothers saying
30
31 "We do not doubt our mothers knew it"
32
33 And it came to pass

1   that I did return with my two thousand

2   against these Lamaniy who had pursued us

3   and now behold the armies of Antipus had overtaken them

4   and a terrible battle had commenced

5   the army of Antipus being weary

6   because of their long march

7   in so short a space of time

8   were about to fall

9   into the hands of the Lamaniy

10   and had I not returned with my two thousand

11   they would have obtained their purpose

12   for Antipus had fallen by the sword

13   and many of his leaders because of their weariness

14   which was occasioned by the speed of their march

15   therefore the men of Antipus being confused

16   because of the fall of their leaders began

17   to give way before the Lamaniy

18

19   And it came to pass

20   that the Lamaniy took courage

21   and began to pursue them

22   and thus were the Lamaniy pursuing them with great vigor

23   when Helaman came upon their rear

24   with his two thousand

25   and began to kill them exceedingly insomuch

26   that the whole army of the Lamaniy stopped

27   and turned upon Helaman

28   now when the people of Antipus saw

29   that the Lamaniy had turned them about

30   they gathered together their men

31   and came again upon the rear of the Lamaniy

32

33   And now it came to pass

1   that we the people of Nephi
2   the people of Antipus
3   and I with my two thousand did surround the Lamaniy
4   and did kill them
5   yes insomuch that they were compelled
6   to deliver up their weapons of war
7   and also themselves as prisoners of war
8
9   And now it came to pass
10   that when they had surrendered themselves up unto us
11   behold I numbered those young men
12   who had fought with me fearing
13   that there were many of them killed
14   but behold to my great joy
15   there had not one soul of them fallen to the earth
16   yes and they had fought as if with the strength of Elohiym
17   yes never were men known
18   to have fought with such miraculous strength
19   and with such mighty power
20   did they fall upon the Lamaniy
21   that they did frighten them
22   and for this cause did the Lamaniy deliver themselves up
23   as prisoners of war
24   and as we had no place for our prisoners
25   that we could guard them
26   to keep them from the armies of the Lamaniy
27   therefore we sent them to the land of Zarahemla
28   and a part of those men who were not killed of Antipus with them
29   and the remainder I took and joined them
30   to my young Ammoniy
31   and took our march back to the city of Yehudah
32
33   And now it came to pass

1 that I received an scroll from Ammoron the king stating

2 that if I would deliver up those prisoners of war

3 whom we had taken

4 that he would deliver up the city of Paniym-parah unto us

5 but I sent an communication unto the king

6 that we were sure our forces were sufficient

7 to take the city of Paniym-parah by our force

8 and by delivering up the prisoners for that city

9 we would find ourselves unwise

10 and that we would only deliver up our prisoners on exchange

11 and Ammoron refused my proposal

12 for he would not exchange prisoners

13 therefore we began to make preparations

14 to go against the city of Paniym-parah

15 but the people of Paniym-parah did leave the city

16 and fled to their other cities

17 which they had possession of

18 to fortify them

19 and thus the city of Paniym-parah fell into our hands

20 and thus ended the twenty and eighth year

21 of the reign of the judges

22

23 And it came to pass

24 that in the commencement of the twenty and ninth year

25 we received a supply of provisions

26 and also an addition to our army from the land of Zarahemla

27 and from the land round about

28 to the number of six thousand men

29 besides sixty of the sons of the Ammoniy

30 who had come to join their brothers

31 my little band of two thousand

32 and now behold we were strong

33 yes and we had also plenty of provisions brought unto us

1

2 And it came to pass

3 that it was our desire

4 to wage a battle with the army

5 which was placed to protect the city Qum'ani

6 and now behold I will show unto you

7 that we soon accomplished our desire

8 yes with our strong force

9 or with a part of our strong force

10 we did surround by night the city Qum'ani

11 a little before they were to receive a supply of provisions

12

13 And it came to pass

14 that we did camp round about the city for many nights

15 but we did sleep upon our swords and keep guards

16 that the Lamaniy could not come upon us by night

17 and kill us which they attempted many times

18 but as many times as they attempted this

19 their blood was spilt

20 at length their provisions did arrive

21 and they were about to enter the city by night

22 and we instead of being Lamaniy were Nephiy

23 therefore we did take them and their provisions

24 and notwithstanding the Lamaniy being cut off

25 from their support

26 after this manner they were still determined

27 to maintain the city

28 therefore it became necessary

29 that we should take those provisions

30 and send them to Yehuda

31 and our prisoners to the land of Zarahemla

32

33 And it came to pass

1   that not many days had passed away

2   before the Lamaniy began to lose all hopes of aid

3   therefore they yielded up the city unto our hands

4   and thus we had accomplished our designs

5   in obtaining the city Qum'ani

6

7   But it came to pass

8   that our prisoners were so numerous

9   that notwithstanding the enormity of our numbers

10   we were obliged to employ all our force

11   to keep them or to put them to death

12   for behold they would break out in great numbers

13   and would fight with stones and with clubs

14   or whatever thing they could get into their hands insomuch

15   that we did kill upwards of two thousand of them

16   after they had surrendered themselves prisoners of war

17   therefore it became necessary for us

18   that we should put an end to their lives

19   or guard them sword in hand down

20   to the land of Zarahemla

21   and also our provisions were not any more than sufficient

22   for our own people notwithstanding that

23   which we had taken from the Lamaniy

24   and now in those critical circumstances

25   it became a very serious matter

26   to determine concerning these prisoners of war

27   nevertheless we did resolve to send them down

28   to the land of Zarahemla

29   therefore we selected a part of our men

30   and gave them charge over our prisoners to go down

31   to the land of Zarahemla

32

33   But it came to pass

1   that on the next day they did return

2   and now behold we did not inquire of them

3   concerning the prisoners

4   for behold the Lamaniy were upon us

5   and they returned in season

6   to save us from falling into their hands

7   for behold Ammoron had sent to their support

8   a new supply of provisions

9   and also a numerous army of men

10

11   And it came to pass

12   that those men whom we sent with the prisoners

13   did arrive in season to check them

14   as they were about to overpower us

15   but behold my little band

16   of two thousand and sixty fought most desperately

17   yes they were firm before the Lamaniy

18   and did administer death

19   unto all those who opposed them

20   and as the remainder of our army

21   were about to give way before the Lamaniy

22   behold those two thousand and sixty

23   were firm and undaunted

24   yes and they did obey and observe

25   to perform every word of command with exactness

26   yes and even according to their faith it was done unto them

27   and I did remember the words which they said unto me

28   that their mothers had taught them

29

30   And now behold it was these my sons

31   and those men who had been selected

32   to convey the prisoners

33   to whom we owe this great victory

1   for it was they who did beat the Lamaniy

2   therefore they were driven back

3   to the city of Manti

4   and we retained our city Qum'ani

5   and were not all destroyed by the sword

6   nevertheless we had suffered great loss

7

8   And it came to pass

9   that after the Lamaniy had fled

10   I immediately gave orders

11   that my men who had been wounded

12   should be taken from among the dead

13   and caused that their wounds should be dressed

14

15   And it came to pass

16   that there were two hundred

17   out of my two thousand and sixty

18   who had fainted because of the loss of blood

19   nevertheless according to the goodness of Elohiym

20   and to our great astonishment

21   and also the joy of our whole army

22   there was not one soul of them

23   who did perish

24   yes and neither was there one soul among them

25   who had not received many wounds

26

27   And now their preservation was astonishing to our whole army

28   yes that they should be spared

29   while there was a thousand of our brothers who were killed

30   and we do justly ascribe it to the miraculous power of Elohiym

31   because of their exceeding faith

32   in that which they had been taught to believe—

33   that there was a just Elohiym

1   and whoever did not doubt that
2   they should be preserved by his marvelous power
3   now this was the faith of these
4   of whom I have spoken
5   they are young and their minds are firm
6   and they do put their trust in Elohiym continually
7   And now it came to pass
8   that after we had thus taken care of our wounded men
9   and had buried our dead
10 and also the dead of the Lamaniy
11 who were many
12 behold we did inquire of Gid
13 concerning the prisoners
14 whom they had started to go down
15 to the land of Zarahemla with
16 now Gid was the sar over the band
17 who was appointed to guard them down to the land
18 and now these are the words
19 which Gid said unto me
20
21 "behold we did start to go down
22 to the land of Zarahemla with our prisoners
23 And it came to pass
24 that we did meet the spies of our armies
25 who had been sent out to watch the camp of the Lamaniy
26 and they cried unto us saying
27
28 'Behold the armies of the Lamaniy are marching
29 towards the city of Qum'ani
30 and behold they will fall upon them
31 yes and will destroy our people'
32
33 And it came to pass

1   that our prisoners did hear their cries
2   which caused them to take courage
3   and they did rise up in rebellion against us
4
5   And it came to pass
6   because of their rebellion we did cause
7   that our swords should come upon them
8
9   And it came to pass
10 that they did in a body run upon our swords
11 in the which the greater number of them were killed
12 and the remainder of them broke through and fled from us
13 and behold when they had fled
14 and we could not overtake them
15 we took our march with speed
16 towards the city Qum'ani
17 and behold we did arrive in time
18 that we might assist our brothers
19 in preserving the city
20 and behold we are again delivered out
21 of the hands of our enemies
22 and blessed is the name of our Elohiym
23 for behold it is he that has delivered us
24 yes that has done this great thing for us
25
26 Now it came to pass
27 that when I Helaman had heard these words of Gid
28 I was filled with exceeding joy
29 because of the goodness of Elohiym in preserving us
30 that we might not all perish
31 yes and I trust that the souls of them
32 who have been killed have entered
33 into the rest of their Elohiym

1
2 And behold now it came to pass
3 that our next object was to obtain the city of Manti
4 but behold there was no way
5   that we could lead them out of the city
6 by our small bands
7 for behold they remembered
8 that which we had previously done
9 therefore we could not decoy them away
10 from their strongholds
11 and they were so much more numerous
12 than was our army
13 that we did not go forth and attack them
14 in their strongholds
15 Yes and it became necessary
16 that we should employ our men
17 to the maintaining those parts of the land
18 which we had regained of our possessions
19 therefore it became necessary that we should wait
20 that we might receive more strength
21 from the land of Zarahemla
22 and also a new supply of provisions
23
24 And it came to pass
25 that I thus did send an embassy
26 to the governor of our land
27 to acquaint him
28 concerning the affairs of our people
29
30 And it came to pass
31 that we did wait
32 to receive provisions and strength
33 from the land of Zarahemla

1 but behold this did profit us but little
2 for the Lamaniy were also receiving great strength
3 from day to day
4 and also many provisions
5 and thus were our circumstances
6 at this period of time
7 and the Lamaniy were rushing forth against us
8 from time to time resolving by stratagem
9 to destroy us
10 nevertheless we could not come to battle with them
11 because of their retreats and their strongholds
12
13 And it came to pass
14 that we did wait in these difficult circumstances
15 for the space of many months
16 even until we were about to perish
17 for the want of food
18
19 But it came to pass
20 that we did receive food
21 which was guarded to us
22 by an army of two thousand men to our assistance
23 and this is all the assistance which we did receive
24 to defend ourselves and our country
25 from falling into the hands of our enemies
26 yes to contend with an enemy
27 which was innumerable
28 and now the cause of these our embarrassments
29 or the cause why they did not send more strength unto us
30 we knew not
31 therefore we were grieved
32 and also filled with fear
33 thatt by any means the judgments of Elohiym

1   should come upon our land

2   to our overthrow and utter destruction

3   therefore we did pour out our souls in prayer to Elohiym

4   that he would strengthen us

5   and deliver us out of the hands of our enemies

6   yes and also give us strength

7   that we might retain our cities

8   and our lands and our possessions

9   for the support of our people

10

11   Yes and it came to pass

12   that YHVH our Elohiym did visit us with assurances

13   that he would deliver us

14   yes insomuch that he did speak peace to our souls

15   and did grant unto us great faith

16   and did cause us that we should hope

17   for our deliverance in him

18   and we did take courage with our small force

19   which we had received

20   and were fixed with a determination

21   to conquer our enemies

22   and to maintain our lands and our possessions

23   and our wives and our children

24   and the cause of our liberty

25

26   And thus we did go forth

27   with all our might against the Lamaniy

28   who were in the city of Manti

29   and we did pitch our tents by the wilderness side

30   which was near to the city

31

32   And it came to pass

33   that on the next day that when the Lamaniy saw

1 that we were in the borders by the wilderness
2 which was near the city
3 that they sent out their spies round about us
4 that they might discover the number
5 and the strength of our army
6
7 And it came to pass
8 that when they saw that we were not strong
9 according to our numbers
10 and fearing that we should cut them off from their support
11 except they should come out to battle against us and kill us
12 and also supposing that they could easily destroy us
13 with their numerous army
14 therefore they began to make preparations
15 to come out against us to battle
16 and when we saw that they were making preparations
17 to come out against us
18 behold I caused that Gid
19 with a small number of men
20 should secrete himself in the wilderness
21 and also that Teomner
22 and a small number of men
23 should secrete themselves also in the wilderness
24 now Gid and his men were on the right
25 and the others on the left
26 and when they had thus secreted themselves
27 behold I remained with the remainder of my army
28 in that same place where we had first pitched our tents
29 against the time that the Lamaniy
30 should come out to battle
31
32 And it came to pass
33 that the Lamaniy did come out

1   with their numerous army against us
2   and when they had come
3   and were about to fall upon us with the sword
4   I caused that my men
5   those who were with me
6   should retreat into the wilderness
7   And it came to pass
8   that the Lamaniy did follow after us
9   with great speed
10 for they greatly desired to overtake us
11 that they might kill us
12 therefore they did follow us into the wilderness
13 and we did pass by in the midst of Gid and Teomner insomuch
14 that they were not discovered by the Lamaniy
15
16 And it came to pass
17 that when the Lamaniy had passed by
18 or when the army had passed by
19 Gid and Teomner did rise up from their secret places
20 and did cut off the spies of the Lamaniy
21 that they should not return to the city
22
23 And it came to pass
24 that when they had cut them off
25 they ran to the city
26 and fell upon the guards
27 who were left to guard the city insomuch
28 that they did destroy them
29 and did take possession of the city
30 now this was done
31 because the Lamaniy did allow their whole army
32 except a few guards only
33 to be led away into the wilderness

1 And it came to pass

2 that Gid and Teomner

3 by this means had obtained possession

4 of their strongholds

5

6 And it came to pass

7 that we took our course

8 after having traveled much in the wilderness

9 towards the land of Zarahemla

10 and when the Lamaniy saw

11 that they were marching towards the land of Zarahemla

12 they were exceedingly afraid

13 that there was a plan laid

14 to lead them on to destruction

15 therefore they began to retreat

16 into the wilderness again

17 yes even back by the same way

18 which they had come

19 and behold it was night

20 and they did pitch their tents

21 for the sarim of the Lamaniy had supposed

22 that the Nephiy were weary

23 because of their march

24 and supposing that they had driven their whole army

25 therefore they took no thought

26 concerning the city of Manti

27

28 Now it came to pass

29 that when it was night I caused

30 that my men should not sleep

31 but that they should march forward

32 by another way

33 towards the land of Manti

1 and because of this
2 our march in the night time
3 behold on the next day
4 we were beyond the Lamaniy insomuch
5 that we did arrive before them
6 at the city of Manti
7
8 And thus it came to pass
9 that by this plan
10 we did take possession
11 of the city of Manti
12 without the shedding of blood
13
14 And it came to pass
15 that when the armies of the Lamaniy
16 did arrive near the city
17 and saw that we were prepared to meet them
18 they were astonished exceedingly
19 and struck with great fear insomuch
20 that they did flee into the wilderness
21
22 Yes And it came to pass
23 that the armies of the Lamaniy did flee out
24 of all this quarter of the land
25 but behold they have carried with them
26 many women and children out of the land
27 and those cities
28 which had been taken by the Lamaniy
29 all of them are at this period of time in our possession
30 and our fathers
31 and our women
32 and our children are returning to their homes
33 all except it be those

1   who have been taken prisoners
2   and carried off by the Lamaniy
3   but behold our armies are small
4   to maintain so great a number of cities
5   and so great possessions
6   but behold we trust in our Elohiym
7   who has given us victory over those lands insomuch
8   that we have obtained
9   those cities and those lands
10 which were our own
11
12 Now we do not know the reason
13 that the government does not grant us more strength
14 neither do those men who came up unto us know
15 why we have not received greater strength
16 behold we do not know
17 but what you are unsuccessful
18 and you have drawn away the forces
19 into that quarter of the land
20 if so we do not desire to complain
21 and if it is not so
22 behold we fear
23 that there is some faction in the government
24 that they do not send more men to our assistance
25 for we know that they are more numerous
26 than that which they have sent
27 but behold it matters not
28 we trust Elohiym will deliver us
29 notwithstanding the weakness of our armies
30 yes and deliver us out of the hands of our enemies
31 behold this is the twenty and ninth year
32 in the latter end
33 and we are in the possession of our lands

1　and the Lamaniy have fled to the land of Nephi
2　and those sons of the people of Ammon
3　of whom I have so highly spoken are with me
4　in the city of Manti
5　and YHVH has supported them
6　yes and kept them from falling by the sword insomuch
7　that even one soul has not been killed
8
9　But behold they have received many wounds
10　nevertheless they stand fast in that liberty
11　in which Elohiym has made them free
12　and they are strict to remember YHVH their Elohiym
13　from day to day
14　yes they do observe to keep his chukkim
15　and his mishpatim
16　and his mitzvot continually
17　and their faith is strong in the prophecies
18　concerning that which is to come
19
20　And now my beloved brother M'runi
21　may YHVH our Elohiym
22　who has redeemed us and made us free
23　keep you continually in his presence
24　yes and may he favor this people
25　even that you may have success
26　in obtaining the possession
27　of all that which the Lamaniy have taken from us
28　which was for our support
29　and now behold I close my communication
30　I am Helaman the son of Almah"
31
32　Now it came to pass
33　in the thirtieth year of the reign of the judges

1   over the people of Nephi
2   after M'runi had received and had read Helaman's communication
3   he was exceedingly rejoiced
4   because of the welfare
5   yes the exceeding success
6   which Helaman had had in obtaining those lands
7   which were lost
8   Yes and he did make it known unto all his people
9   in all the land round about
10   in that part where he was
11   that they might rejoice also
12
13   And it came to pass
14   that he immediately sent a communication to Pahoran desiring
15   that he should cause men to be gathered together
16   to strengthen Helaman or the armies of Helaman insomuch
17   that he might with ease maintain that part of the land
18   which he had been so miraculously prospered in regaining
19
20   And it came to pass
21   when M'runi had sent this communication
22   to the land of Zarahemla he began again
23   to lay a plan that he might obtain the remainder
24   of those possessions and cities
25   which the Lamaniy had taken from them
26
27   And it came to pass
28   that while M'runi was thus making preparations
29   to go against the Lamaniy to battle
30   behold the people of Nephiyah
31   who were gathered together
32   from the city of M'runi
33   and the city of Lechi

1 and the city of Morianton
2 were attacked by the Lamaniy
3 Yes even those who had been compelled
4 to flee from the land of Manti
5 and from the land round about had come over
6 and joined the Lamaniy in this part of the land
7 and thus being exceedingly numerous
8 yes and receiving strength from day to day
9 by the command of Ammoron
10 they came forth against the people of Nephiyah
11 and they did begin to kill them
12 with an exceedingly great slaughter
13 and their armies were so numerous
14 that the remainder of the people of Nephiyah were obliged
15 to flee before them
16 and they came even
17 and joined the army of M'runi
18 And now as M'runi had supposed
19 that there should be men sent to the city of Nephiyah
20 to the assistance of the people
21 to maintain that city
22 and knowing that it was easier
23 to keep the city from falling into the hands of the Lamaniy
24 than to retake it from them he supposed
25 that they would easily maintain that city
26 therefore he retained all his force
27 to maintain those places which he had recovered
28 and now when M'runi saw
29 that the city of Nephiyah was lost
30 he was exceedingly sorrowful
31 and began to doubt because of the wickedness of the people
32 whether they should not fall into the hands of their brothers
33 now this was the case with all his sarim

1 they doubted and marveled also
2 because of the wickedness of the people
3 and this because of the success of the Lamaniy over them
4
5 And it came to pass
6 that M'runi was angry with the government
7 because of their indifference
8 concerning the freedom of their country
9
10 And it came to pass
11 that he wrote again to the governor of the land
12 who was Pahoran
13 and these are the words which he wrote saying
14
15 "behold I direct my communication to Pahoran
16 in the city of Zarahemla
17 who is the chief judge and the governor
18 over the land
19 and also to all those
20 who have been chosen by this people
21 to govern and manage the affairs of this war
22
23 For behold I have somewhat to say unto them
24 by the way of condemnation
25 for behold you yourselves know
26 that you have been appointed
27 to gather together men and arm them
28 with swords and with cimeters
29 and all manner of weapons of war of every kind
30 and send forth against the Lamaniy in whatever parts
31 they should come into our land
32 and now behold I say unto you
33 that myself and also my men

1 and also Helaman and his men have suffered

2 exceedingly great suffering

3 yes even hunger thirst and fatigue

4 and all manner of afflictions of every kind

5 but behold were this all we had suffered

6 we would not grumble nor complain

7 but behold great has been the slaughter among our people

8 yes thousands have fallen by the sword

9 while it might have otherwise been

10 if you had rendered unto our armies

11 sufficient strength and aid for them

12 Yes great has been your neglect towards us

13

14 And now behold we desire to know the cause

15 of this exceedingly great neglect

16 yes we desire to know the cause

17 of your thoughtless state

18 can you think to sit upon your thrones

19 in a state of thoughtless stupor

20 while your enemies are spreading the work of death around you

21 Yes while they are murdering thousands of your brothers

22 Yes even they who have looked up to you for protection

23 yes have placed you in a situation

24 that you might have given them aid

25 yes you might have sent armies unto them

26 to have strengthened them

27 and have saved thousands of them

28 from falling by the sword

29

30 But behold this is not all

31 you have withheld your provisions from them insomuch

32 that many have fought and bled out their lives

33 because of their great desires

1 which they had for the welfare of this people
2 yes and this they have done
3 when they were about to perish with hunger
4 because of your exceedingly great neglect towards them
5
6 And now my beloved brothers
7 for you ought to be beloved
8 yes and you ought to have stirred yourselves more diligently
9 for the welfare and the freedom of this people
10 but behold you have neglected them insomuch
11 that the blood of thousands
12 shall come upon your heads for vengeance
13 yes for known unto Elohiym were all their cries
14 and all their sufferings
15
16 Behold do you think that you could sit upon your thrones
17 and because of the exceeding goodness of Elohiym
18 you could do nothing
19 and he would deliver you
20 behold if you have thought this
21 you have thought in vain
22
23 Do you think
24 that because so many of your brothers have been killed
25 it is because of their wickedness
26 I say unto you
27 if you have thought this you have thought in vain
28 for I say unto you there are many who have fallen by the sword
29 and behold it is to your condemnation
30 for YHVH suffers the righteous to be killed
31 that his justice and judgment
32 may come upon the wicked
33 therefore you need not think that the righteous are lost

1   because they are killed
2   but behold they do enter into the rest
3   of YHVH their Elohiym
4
5   And now behold I say unto you I fear exceedingly
6   that the judgments of Elohiym will come upon this people
7   because of their exceeding laziness
8   yes even the laziness of our government
9   and their exceedingly great neglect towards their brothers
10   yes towards those who have been killed
11   for were it not for the wickedness
12   which first commenced at our head
13   we could have withstood our enemies
14   that they could have gained no power over us
15   Yes had it not been for the war
16   which broke out among ourselves
17   yes were it not for these king men
18   who caused so much bloodshed among ourselves
19   yes at the time we were contending among ourselves
20   if we had united our strength
21   as we previously have done
22   yes had it not been
23   for the desire of power and authority
24   which those king men had over us
25   had they been true to the cause of our freedom
26   and united with us
27   and gone forth against our enemies
28   instead of taking up their swords against us
29   which was the cause of so much bloodshed among ourselves
30   yes if we had gone forth against them
31   in the strength of YHVH we should have dispersed our enemies
32   for it would have been done
33   according to the fulfilling of his word

1
2 But behold now the Lamaniy are coming upon us
3 taking possession of our lands
4 and they are murdering our people with the sword
5 yes our women and our children
6 and also carrying them away captive causing them
7 that they should suffer all manner of afflictions
8 and this because of the great wickedness
9 of those who are seeking
10 for power and authority
11 yes even those king men
12
13 But why should I say much concerning this matter
14 for we know not
15 but what you yourselves are seeking for authority
16 we know not
17 but what you are also traitors to your country
18 or is it that you have neglected us
19 because you are in the heart of our country
20 and you are surrounded by security
21 that you do not cause food to be sent unto us
22 and also men to strengthen our armies
23
24 Have you forgotten the mitzvot of YHVH your Elohiym
25 Yes have you forgotten the captivity of our fathers
26 have you forgotten the many times
27 we have been delivered out of the hands of our enemies
28 or do you think that YHVH will still deliver us
29 while we sit upon our thrones
30 and do not make use of the means
31 which YHVH has provided for us
32 Yes will you sit in idleness
33 while you are surrounded with thousands of those

1 yes and tens of thousands
2 who do also sit in idleness
3 while there are thousands round about
4 in the borders of the land
5 who are falling by the sword
6 yes wounded and bleeding
7

8 Do you suppose that Elohiym will look upon you as guiltless
9 while you sit still and behold these things
10 behold I say unto you No
11 now I would that you should remember
12 that Elohiym has said
13 that the inward vessel shall be cleansed first
14 and then shall the outer vessel be cleansed also
15

16 And now except you do repent
17 of that which you have done
18 and begin to be up and doing
19 and send forth food and men unto us
20 and also unto Helaman
21 that he may support those parts of our country
22 which he has regained
23 and that we may also recover the remainder
24 of our possessions in these parts
25 behold it will be necessary
26 that we contend no more with the Lamaniy
27 until we have first cleansed our inward vessel
28 yes even the great head of our government
29

30 And except you grant my request
31 and come out and show unto me
32 a true spirit of freedom
33 and strive to strengthen and fortify our armies

1   and grant unto them food for their support

2   behold I will leave a part of my freemen

3   to maintain this part of our land

4   and I will leave the strength and the blessings of Elohiym upon them

5   that none other power can operate against them

6   and this because of their exceeding faith

7   and their patience in their tribulations

8   and I will come unto you

9   and if there be any among you

10 that has a desire for freedom

11 yes if there be even a spark of freedom remaining

12 behold I will stir up insurrections among you

13 even until those who have desires

14 to usurp power and authority

15 shall become extinct

16

17 Yes behold

18 I do not fear your power nor your authority

19 but it is my Elohiym whom I fear

20 and it is according to his mitzvot

21 that I do take my sword

22 to defend the cause of my country

23 and it is because of your lawlessness

24 that we have suffered so much loss

25

26 Behold it is time

27 yes the time is now at hand

28 that except you do take action yourselves

29 in the defense of your country and your little ones

30 the sword of justice does hang over you

31 yes and it shall fall upon you

32 and visit you even to your utter destruction

33 Behold I wait for assistance from you

1 and except you do administer unto our relief

2 behold I come unto you even in the land of Zarahemla

3 and strike you with the sword insomuch

4 that you can have no more power

5 to impede the progress of this people

6 in the cause of our freedom

7 for behold YHVH will not allow

8 that you shall live and wax strong in your lawlessness

9 to destroy his righteous people

10

11 Behold can you suppose that YHVH will spare you

12 and come out in judgment against the Lamaniy

13 when it is the tradition of their fathers

14 that has caused their hatred

15 yes and it has been redoubled

16 by those who have dissented from us

17 while your lawlessness is the reason

18 your love of glory and the vain things of the world

19

20 You know that you do rebel against the mitzvot of Elohiym

21   and you do know that you do trample them under your feet

22 behold YHVH says unto me

23

24 'If those whom you have appointed your governors do not repent

25 of their sins and lawlessness you

26 shall go up to battle against them'

27

28 And now behold I M'runi am constrained

29 according to the covenant which I have made

30 to keep the mitzvot of my Elohiym

31 therefore I desire

32 that you should adhere to the word of Elohiym

33 and send speedily unto me

1   of your provisions and of your men
2   and also to Helaman
3   and behold if you will not do this
4   I come unto you speedily
5   for behold Elohiym will not allow
6   that we should perish with hunger
7   therefore he will give unto us of your food
8   even if it must be by the sword
9   now see that you fulfil the word of Elohiym
10
11   behold I am M'runi your sar
12   I seek not for power
13   but to pull it down
14   I seek not for honor of the world
15   but for the glory of my Elohiym
16   and the freedom and welfare of my country
17   and thus I close my communication"
18
19   Behold now it came to pass
20   that soon after M'runi had sent his scrolll unto the chief governor
21   he received an scroll from Pahoran the chief governor
22   and these are the words which he received
23
24   "I Pahoran
25   who am the chief governor of this land do send these words
26   unto M'runi the sar over the army
27   behold I say unto you M'runi
28   that I do not joy in your great afflictions
29   yes it grieves my soul
30
31   But behold there are those who do joy in your afflictions
32   yes insomuch that they have risen up in rebellion against me
33   and also those of my people who are freemen

1   yes and those who have risen up are exceedingly numerous
2   and it is those who have sought
3   to take away the judgment seat from me
4   that have been the cause of this great lawlessness
5   for they have used great flattery
6   and they have led away the hearts of many people
7   which will be the cause of sore affliction among us
8   they have withheld our provisions
9   and have intimidated our freemen
10 that they have not come unto you
11
12 And behold they have driven me out before them
13 and I have fled to the land of Gid`on
14 with as many men as it were possible
15 that I could get
16 and behold I have sent a proclamation
17 throughout this part of the land
18 and behold they are flocking to us daily to their arms
19 in the defense of their country and their freedom
20 and to avenge our wrongs
21 and they have come unto us insomuch
22 that those who have risen up
23 in rebellion against us are set at defiance
24 yes insomuch that they do fear us
25 and did not come out against us to battle
26
27 They have got possession of the land or the city of Zarahemla
28 they have appointed a king over them
29 and he has written unto the king of the Lamaniy
30 in the which he has joined an alliance with him
31 in the which alliance he has agreed to maintain the city of Zarahemla
32 which maintenance he thinks will enable the Lamaniy
33 to conquer the remainder of the land

1 and he shall be placed king over this people
2 when they shall be conquered under the Lamaniy
3
4 and now in your communication you have blamed me
5 but it matters not
6 I am not angry but do rejoice in the greatness of your heart
7 I Pahoran do not seek for power
8 except only to retain my judgment seat
9 that I may preserve the rights and the liberty of my people
10 my soul stands fast in that liberty
11 in the which Elohiym has made us free
12 and now behold we will resist wickedness
13 even unto bloodshed
14 we would not shed the blood of the Lamaniy
15 if they would stay in their own land
16 we would not shed the blood of our brothers
17 if they would not rise up in rebellion
18 and take the sword against us
19 we would subject ourselves to the yoke of bondage
20 if it were requisite with the justice of Elohiym
21 or if he should command us so to do
22
23 But behold he does not command us
24 that we shall subject ourselves to our enemies
25 but that we should put our trust in him
26 and he will deliver us
27 therefore my beloved brother M'runi
28 let us resist evil
29 and whatever evil we cannot resist with our words
30 yes such as rebellions and dissensions
31 let us resist them with our swords
32 that we may retain our freedom
33 that we may rejoice in the great privilege of our assembly

1 and in the cause of our redeemer and our Elohiym
2 therefore come unto me speedily with a few of your men
3 and leave the remainder in the charge of Lechi and Teancum
4 give unto them power to conduct the war in that part of the land
5 according to the Ruach of Elohiym
6 which is also the Ruach of freedom
7 which is in them
8
9 Behold I have sent a few provisions unto them
10 that they may not perish until you can come unto me
11 gather together whatever force you can upon your march here
12 and we will go speedily against those dissenters
13 in the strength of our Elohiym
14 according to the faith
15 which is in us
16 and we will take possession of the city of Zarahemla
17 that we may obtain more food
18 to send forth unto Lechi and Teancum
19 yes we will go forth against them in the strength of YHVH
20 and we will put an end to this great lawlessness
21 and now M'runi
22 I do joy in receiving your scroll
23 for I was somewhat worried
24 concerning what we should do
25 whether it should be just in us
26 to go against our brothers
27 but you have said
28 'except they repent YHVH has commanded you
29 that you should go against them'
30
31 See that you strengthen Lechi and Teancum in YHVH
32 tell them to fear not
33 for Elohiym will deliver them

1   yes and also all those who stand fast
2   in that liberty in which Elohiym has made them free
3   and now I close my communication
4   to my beloved brother M'runi
5
6   And now it came to pass
7   that when M'runi had received this communication
8   his heart did take courage
9   and was filled with exceedingly great joy
10 because of the faithfulness of Pahoran
11 that he was not also a traitor
12 to the freedom and cause of his country
13 but he did also mourn exceedingly
14 because of the lawlessness of those
15 who had driven Pahoran from the judgment seat
16 yes in sum because of those who had rebelled
17 against their country and also their Elohiym
18
19 And it came to pass
20 that M'runi took a small number of men
21 according to the desire of Pahoran
22 and gave Lechi and Teancum command
23 over the remainder of his army
24 and took his march towards the land of Gid`on
25 and he did raise the standard of liberty
26 in whatever place he did enter
27 and gained whatever force he could in all his march
28 towards the land of Gid`on
29
30 And it came to pass
31 that thousands did flock unto his standard
32 and did take up their swords
33 in the defence of their freedom

1   that they might not come into bondage
2   and thus when M'runi had gathered together
3   whatever men he could in all his march
4   he came to the land of Gid`on
5   and uniting his forces with those of Pahoran
6   they became exceedingly strong
7   even stronger than the men of Pachus
8   who was the king of those dissenters
9   who had driven the freemen out of the land of Zarahemla
10 and had taken possession of the land
11
12 And it came to pass
13 that M'runi and Pahoran went down with their armies
14 into the land of Zarahemla
15 and went forth against the city
16 and did meet the men of Pachus insomuch
17 that they did come to battle
18 and behold Pachus was killed
19 and his men were taken prisoners
20 and Pahoran was restored to his judgment seat
21 and the men of Pachus received their trial
22 according to the mishpatim
23 and also those king men
24 who had been taken and cast into prison
25 and they were executed according to the mishpatim
26 yes those men of Pachus and those king-men
27 whoever would not take up arms
28 in the defence of their country
29 but would fight against it were put to death
30
31 And thus it became necessary
32 that this mishpat should be strictly observed
33 for the safety of their country

1 yes and whoever was found denying their freedom
2 was speedily executed according to the mishpatim
3 and thus ended the thirtieth year of the reign
4 of the judges over the people of Nephi
5 M'runi and Pahoran having restored peace
6 to the land of Zarahemla
7 among their own people having inflicted death
8 upon all those who were not true
9 to the cause of freedom
10
11 And it came to pass
12 in the commencement of the thirty and first year
13 of the reign of the judges over the people of Nephi
14 M'runi immediately caused that provisions should be sent
15 and also an army of six thousand men should be sent unto Helaman
16 to assist him in preserving that part of the land
17 and he also caused
18 that an army of six thousand men
19 with a sufficient quantity of food
20 should be sent to the armies of Lechi and Teancum
21
22 And it came to pass
23 that this was done
24 to fortify the land
25 against the Lamaniy
26
27 And it came to pass
28 that M'runi and Pahoran leaving a large body
29 of men in the land of Zarahemla
30 took their march with a large body of men
31 towards the land of Nephiyah being determined
32 to overthrow the Lamaniy in that city
33

1 And it came to pass
2 that as they were marching towards the land
3 they took a large body of men of the Lamaniy
4 and killed many of them
5 and took their provisions
6 and their weapons of war
7
8 And it came to pass
9 after they had taken them
10 they caused them to enter into a covenant
11 that they would no more take up
12 their weapons of war against the Nephiy
13 and when they had entered into this covenant
14 they sent them to dwell with the people of Ammon
15 and they were in number about four thousand
16 who had not been killed
17
18 And it came to pass
19 that when they had sent them away
20 they pursued their march
21 towards the land of Nephiyah
22
23 And it came to pass
24 that when they had come to the city of Nephiyah
25 they did pitch their tents in the plains of Nephiyah
26 which is near the city of Nephiyah
27 now M'runi desired that the Lamaniy
28 should come out to battle against them upon the plains
29 but the Lamaniy knowing of their exceedingly great courage
30 and beholding the greatness of their numbers
31 therefore they did not come out against them
32 therefore they did not come to battle in that day
33 and when the night came

1 M'runi went forth in the darkness of the night
2 and came upon the top of the wall
3 to spy out in what part of the city the Lamaniy
4 did camp with their army
5
6 And it came to pass
7 that they were on the east by the entrance
8 and they were all asleep
9 and now M'runi returned to his army
10 and caused that they should prepare in haste
11 strong cords and ladders
12 to be let down from the top of the wall
13 into the inner part of the wall
14
15 And it came to pass
16 that M'runi caused that his men should march forth
17 and come upon the top of the wall
18 and let themselves down into that part of the city
19 yes even on the west
20 where the Lamaniy did not camp with their armies
21
22 And it came to pass
23 that they were all let down into the city by night
24 by the means of their strong cords and their ladders
25 thus when the morning came
26 they were all within the walls of the city
27 and now when the Lamaniy awoke
28 and saw that the armies of M'runi were within the walls
29 they were frightened exceedingly insomuch
30 that they did flee out by the pass
31 and now when M'runi saw
32 that they were fleeing before him he did cause
33 that his men should march forth against them

1 and killed many and surrounded many others
2 and took them prisoners
3 and the remainder of them fled into the land of M'runi
4 which was in the borders by the seashore
5 thus had M'runi and Pahoran obtained the possession
6 of the city of Nephiyah
7 without the loss of one soul
8 and there were many of the Lamaniy
9 who were killed
10
11 Now it came to pass
12 that many of the Lamaniy that were prisoners
13 desired to join the people of Ammon
14 and become a free people
15
16 And it came to pass
17 that as many as desired to join unto them
18 it was granted according to their desires
19 therefore all the prisoners of the Lamaniy
20 did join the people of Ammon
21 and did begin to labor exceedingly
22 tilling the ground
23 raising all manner of grain and flocks
24 and herds of every kind
25 and thus were the Nephiy relieved
26 from a great burden
27 yes insomuch that they were relieved
28 from all the prisoners of the Lamaniy
29 Now it came to pass
30 that M'runi
31 after he had obtained possession of the city of Nephiyah
32 having taken many prisoners
33 which did reduce the armies of the Lamaniy exceedingly

1 and having regained many of the Nephiy
2 who had been taken prisoners
3 which did strengthen the army of M'runi exceedingly
4 therefore M'runi went forth from the land of Nephiyah
5 to the land of Lechi
6
7 And it came to pass
8 that when the Lamaniy saw
9 that M'runi was coming against them
10 they were again frightened
11 and fled before the army of M'runi
12
13 And it came to pass
14 that M'runi and his army did pursue them
15 from city to city
16 until they were met by Lechi and Teancum
17 and the Lamaniy fled from Lechi and Teancum
18 even down upon the borders by the seashore
19 until they came to the land of M'runi
20 and the armies of the Lamaniy
21 were all gathered together insomuch
22 that they were all in one body
23 in the land of M'runi
24 now Ammoron the king of the Lamaniy
25 was also with them
26
27 And it came to pass
28 that M'runi and Lechi and Teancum did encamp
29 with their armies round about
30 in the borders of the land of M'runi insomuch
31 that the Lamaniy were encircled about
32 in the borders by the wilderness on the south
33 and in the borders by the wilderness on the east

1   and thus they did encamp for the night

2   for behold the Nephiy and the Lamaniy also were weary

3   because of the greatness of the march

4   therefore they did not resolve upon any plan in the night time

5   except it were Teancum

6   for he was exceedingly angry with Ammoron insomuch

7   that he considered that Ammoron

8   and Amalick'yahu his brother had been the cause

9   of this great and lasting war

10   between them and the Lamaniy

11   which had been the cause

12   of so much war and bloodshed

13   yes and so much famine

14

15   And it came to pass

16   that Teancum in his anger did go forth

17   into the camp of the Lamaniy

18   and did let himself down over the walls of the city

19   and he went forth with a cord from place to place insomuch

20   that he did find the king

21   and he did cast a javelin at him

22   which did pierce him near the heart

23   but behold the king did awaken his servants before he died insomuch

24   that they did pursue Teancum and killed him

25

26   Now it came to pass

27   that when Lechi and M'runi knew that Teancum was dead

28   they were exceedingly sorrowful

29   for behold he had been a man

30   who had fought valiantly for his country

31   yes a true friend to liberty

32   and he had allowed very many exceedingly sore afflictions

33   but behold he was dead

1 and had gone the way of all the earth

2

3 Now it came to pass

4 that M'runi marched forth on the next day

5 and came upon the Lamaniy insomuch

6 that they did kill them with a great slaughter

7 and they did drive them out of the land

8 and they did flee

9 even that they did not return at that time

10 against the Nephiy

11 and thus ended the thirty and first year

12 of the reign of the judges over the people of Nephi

13 and thus they had had wars and bloodsheds

14 and famine and affliction

15 for the space of many years

16 and there had been murders and contentions

17 and dissensions and all manner of lawlessness

18 among the people of Nephi

19 nevertheless for the righteous sake

20 yes because of the prayers of the righteous they were spared

21 but behold because of the exceedingly great length

22 of the war between the Nephiy and the Lamaniy

23 many had become hardened

24 because of the exceedingly great length of the war

25 and many were softened

26 because of their afflictions insomuch

27 that they did humble themselves before Elohiym

28 even in the depth of humility

29

30 And it came to pass

31 that after M'runi had fortified those parts of the land

32 which were most exposed to the Lamaniy

33 until they were sufficiently strong

1　he returned to the city of Zarahemla
2　and also Helaman returned to the place of his inheritance
3　and there was once more peace established
4　among the people of Nephi
5　and M'runi yielded up the command of his armies
6　into the hands of his son whose name was M'nruniyah
7　and he retired to his own house
8　that he might spend the remainder of his days in peace
9　and Pahoran did return to his judgment seat
10　and Helaman did take upon him again
11　to preach unto the people the word of Elohiym
12　for because of so many wars and contentions
13　it had become necessary that a regulation
14　should be made again in the assembly
15　therefore Helaman and his brothers went forth
16　and did declare the word of Elohiym with much power
17　unto the convincing of many people of their wickedness
18　which did cause them to repent of their sins
19　and to be immersed unto YHVH their Elohiym
20
21　And it came to pass
22　that they did establish again the assembly of Elohiym
23　throughout all the land
24　Yes and regulations were made in regard to the Torah
25　and their judges and their chief judges were chosen
26　and the people of Nephi began to prosper again in the land
27　and began to multiply
28　and to wax exceedingly strong again in the land
29　and they began to grow exceedingly rich
30　but notwithstanding their riches
31　or their strength
32　or their prosperity
33　they were not lifted up in the pride of their eyes

1 neither were they slow to remember YHVH their Elohiym
2 but they did humble themselves exceedingly before him
3 Yes they did remember how great things YHVH had done for them
4 that he had delivered them from death and from bonds
5 and from prisons and from all manner of afflictions
6 and he had delivered them out of the hands of their enemies
7 and they did pray unto YHVH their Elohiym continually insomuch
8 that YHVH did bless them according to his word
9 so that they did wax strong and prosper in the land
10
11 And it came to pass
12 that all these things were done
13 and Helaman died in the thirty and fifth year
14 of the reign of the judges over the people of Nephi
15
16 And it came to pass
17 in the commencement of the thirty and sixth year
18 of the reign of the judges over the people of Nephi
19 that Shiblon took possession of those sacred things
20 which had been delivered unto Helaman by Almah
21 and he was a just man
22 and he did walk uprightly before Elohiym
23 and he did observe to do good continually
24 to keep the mitzvot of YHVH his Elohiym
25 and also did his brother
26
27 And it came to pass that M'runi died also
28 and thus ended the thirty and sixth year
29 of the reign of the judges
30
31 And it came to pass
32 that in the thirty and seventh year of the reign of the judges
33 there was a large company of men

1 even to the amount of five thousand and four hundred men
2 with their wives and their children departed out of the land of Zarahemla
3 into the land which was northward
4
5 And it came to pass
6 that Hagoth he being an exceedingly curious man
7 therefore he went forth
8 and built him an exceedingly large ship
9 on the borders of the land Bountiful
10 by the land Desolation
11 and launched it forth into the west sea
12 by the narrow neck
13 which led into the land northward
14 and behold there were many of the Nephiy
15 who did enter therein
16 and did sail forth with much provisions
17 and also many women and children
18 and they took their course northward
19 and thus ended the thirty and seventh year
20 and in the thirty and eighth year
21 this man built other ships
22 and the first ship did also return
23 and many more people did enter into it
24 and they also took much provisions
25 and set out again to the land northward
26
27 And it came to pass
28 that they were never heard of more
29 and we suppose
30 that they were drowned
31 in the depths of the sea
32 And it came to pass
33 that one other ship also did sail forth

1   and where she did go we know not

2

3   And it came to pass

4   that in this year there were many people

5   who went forth into the land northward

6   and thus ended the thirty and eighth year

7   And it came to pass

8   in the thirty and ninth year

9   of the reign of the judges Shiblon died also

10   and Corianton had gone forth

11   to the land northward in a ship

12   to carry forth provisions unto the people

13   who had gone forth into that land

14   therefore it became necessary for Shiblon

15   to confer those sacred things before his death

16   upon the son of Helaman

17   who was called Helaman being called

18   after the name of his father

19   now behold all those engravings

20   which were in the possession of Helaman

21   were written and sent forth

22   among the children of men

23   throughout all the land

24   except it were those parts

25   which had been commanded by Almah

26   should not go forth

27   nevertheless these things were to be kept sacred

28   and handed down

29   from one generation to another

30   therefore in this year

31   they had been conferred upon Helaman

32   before the death of Shiblon

33

1 And it came to pass
2 also in this year
3 that there were some dissenters
4 who had gone forth unto the Lamaniy
5 and they were stirred up again
6 to anger against the Nephiy
7 and also in this same year
8 they came down with a numerous army
9 to war against the people of M'runiyah
10 or against the army of M'runiyah
11 in the which they were beaten
12 and driven back again
13 to their own lands suffering great loss
14 and thus ended the thirty and ninth year
15 of the reign of the judges over the people of Nephi
16 and thus ended the account
17 of Almah and Helaman his son
18 and also Shiblon who was his son
19
20
21
22
23
24
25
26
27
28
29
30
31
32
33
34
35

GLOSSARY OF TERMS

1
2 Adon - Lord
3 Adonai- My Lord
4 Besorah- tidings,
5 Chukkim- decrees, statutes
6 Chupah- canopy or covering
7 El Gibbor – ALL POWERFUL GOD
8 EL SHADDAI – GOD ALMIGHTY
9 Eloah- God
10 ELOHIYM- God
11 Etz Chaim- Tree of Life
12 Gan Eden – Garden of Eden
13 Goyim - Nations
14 Hoshia`na – plea of deliverance/ exhortation unto salvation
15 Kadosh- Holy
16 Kohanim – priest/officiator
17 L'mu'elim- Literal descendants of Lemuel
18 Lamanim – Literal descendants of Laman
19 Lamaniy - All Peoples associated collectively with the Civilization of Laman
20 Ma'asim- works
21 MASHIACH- Messiah
22 Mishpatim- Judgments
23 Mitzvot - Commandments
24 Moreh/Morim- Teacher/ Teachers
25 Nephiy – All Peoples associated collectively with the Civilization of Nephi
26 Nephiy'im – Literal descendant of Nephi
27 OY- to cry out in the sense of grief or despair
28 Paniym- Countenant of/face of
29 QEDEM ELOHIYM
30 Ruach- spirit
31 Ruach of Elohiym- spirit of God, Holy Ghost
32 Sheol- Hell
33 Talmidim- student
34 Teshuvah- Repentance
35 Torah- Literally the first five books of Moses
36 Tzedekah- Charity/Love
37 Yacovim- Literal descendants of Yacov
38 Yehudah- Judah

1 YEHUDI- a person from the Southern Kingdom of Israel
2 YEHUDIM- (plural) referring to the people of the Southern Kingdom of
3 Israel
4 YERUSHALAYIM- Jerusalem
5 YHVH- The name of God
6 YHVH Tza'vaot – YHVH of Heavens Armies
7 Yishma'elim- Literal descendants of Yishma'el
8 Yoseph'im- descendants of Yoseph son of Lechi
9 Zoramim – Literal descendants of Zoram

Made in the USA
Las Vegas, NV
17 March 2022